Common Knowledge about Chinese Culture

The Overseas Chinese Affairs Office of the State Council

China Overseas Exchanges Association

中国文化常识

国务院侨务办公室
中国海外交流协会

前言

　　《中国历史常识》、《中国地理常识》和《中国文化常识》是中华人民共和国国务院侨务办公室、中国海外交流协会委托南京师范大学、安徽师范大学和北京华文学院分别编写的一套华文教学辅助读物,供海外华裔青少年通过课堂学习或自学的方式了解中国历史、地理、文化常识,也可供家长辅导孩子学习使用。我们希望学习者通过学习,初步了解、掌握中国历史、地理和文化的知识,进而达到普及、弘扬中华文化和促进中外文化交流的目的。

　　根据海外华文教学的实际情况和需求,我们分别选编了中国历史的重大事件和重要人物,进行客观记述;选取了中国地理最主要的自然特点和人文特征,进行概略描述;筛选了中华文化和民俗风情的精华,加以介绍。突出体现科学性、思想性和实用性的编写原则,在编排设计等方面力求有所创新。

　　在上述三本书的编写过程中,苏寿桐、王宏志、臧嵘、侯明、刘淑英、李芳芹等参加了《中国历史常识》的审稿工作;王永昌、乐平兰、刘淑梅、毕超、徐玉奎、董乃灿、张桂珠、李文君等参加了《中国地理常识》的审稿工作;张英、张猛、董明、武惠华、陶卫、杨二林等参加了《中国文化常识》的审稿工作。在此,谨表示诚挚的谢意。

　　书中考虑不周或疏漏之处,祈盼使用者不吝赐正,以期再版时修订。

编　者

2001年12月

Preface

The Overseas Chinese Affairs Office of the State Council of the People's Republic of China and China Overseas Exchanges Association commissioned Nanjing Normal University, Anhui Normal University and Beijing Chinese Language College to respectively write this set of auxiliary Chinese language teaching materials, namely, *Common Knowledge about Chinese History*, *Common Knowledge about Chinese Geography* and *Common Knowledge about Chinese Culture* which acquaint overseas Chinese teenagers with basic knowledge on these subjects through class education or self-teaching. Parents can also use them to help their children with study. Moreover, we hope this set of books can offer a wider group of readers some rudimentary knowledge about Chinese history, geography and culture, thus promoting cultural exchanges between China and other countries.

According to the actual condition and needs of overseas Chinese language teaching, in this set of books, we objectively narrate important events and figures in Chinese history; briefly describe the major natural and cultural features of Chinese geography; carefully select and introduce the essence of the Chinese culture, habits and customs. We have used to introduce new ideas in typesetting, design and so on and to embody scientific, ideological and practical principles in the writing.

We are deeply grateful to Su Shoutong, Wang Hongzhi, Zang Rong, Hou Ming, Liu Shuying and Li Fangqin for revising *Common Knowledge about Chinese History*, Wang Yongchang, Yue Pinglan, Liu Shumei, Bi Chao, Xu Yukui, Dong Naican, Zhang Guizhu and Li Wenjun for revising *Common Knowledge about Chinese Geography*, and Zhang Ying, Zhang Meng, Dong Ming, Wu Huihua, Tao Wei and Yang Erlin for revising *Common Knowledge about Chinese Culture*.

Advice is welcomed if there were any mistake in the books. We will revise them when republishing the books.

Compilers

December, 2001

目录 Contents

传统美德篇
Traditional Virtues

古代科技篇
Ancient Science and Technology

目录 Contents

艺术体育篇
Artistic Work and Sport

古建筑篇
Ancient Architecture

目录 Contents

概述
Introduction

中国是一个统一的多民族国家。在漫长的历史发展过程中，勤劳、勇敢、智慧的各族人民，共同开拓了中国的疆域，创造了灿烂的文化，缔造了中华民族大家庭。

中国有56个民族，由于地理环境和生活条件的不同，每个民族都形成了自己独特的风俗习惯和优秀的文化传统。在中华民族大家庭中，各民族之间团结友爱，和睦相处，相互融合，共同奋斗，为中华民族的繁荣昌盛，贡献自己的才智和力量。

China is a unitary multi-national country where, through the long process of historical development, people from many different ethnic groups have together opened up the vast Chinese territory, created an outstanding culture, and helped shape the current form of the Chinese nation.

There are 56 ethnic groups in China. Due to a differing geographical environment and living conditions, each ethnic group has formed its own unique traditions and customs, while, at the same time, working to promote the prosperity of the Chinese nation.

中华始祖——
黄帝和炎帝

Earliest Ancestor of the Chinese Nation — Huangdi (Yellow Emperor) and Yandi (Red Emperor)

黄帝和炎帝是中华民族的共同祖先，海内外的中国人都称自己为"炎黄子孙"。

据传说和古书记载，黄帝是中国历史上第一个帝王，姓姬，号轩辕氏或有熊氏。炎帝也是传说中的一个帝王，姓姜，号烈山氏或神农氏。

黄帝和炎帝都生活在距今4,000多年前中国原始社会后期，是两个部落的首领。当时，黄帝部落和炎帝部落都居住在现在陕西省境内的黄河边上。后来，又先后沿黄河两岸向东部迁移。为了争夺一块土地，炎帝族同住在中国东部的九黎族发生了战争。九黎族的首领蚩尤 (chīyóu) 打败了炎帝族。炎帝族向黄帝求援，他们联合起来打败了蚩尤。九黎族失败后，一部分逃到了南方，另一部分加入了炎黄二族。后来，炎帝族和黄帝族也发生了冲突，炎帝族失败后，加入了黄帝部落，由此黄帝族的力量增大。后来，黄帝族、炎帝族和九黎族的一部分在黄河流域定居下来，繁衍生息，构成了华夏族的主干。他们共同开发了黄河中下游地区，使这里成为中国古代文化的摇篮。从此，这些来自不同部落的居民，都认为自己是黄帝和炎帝的后代，称自己为"炎黄子孙"。

据说，黄帝生下来就非常聪明，当了部落首领后，便教人们建筑房屋、喂养家畜、种植五谷，他还发明了车、船、乐器和文字

等。黄帝的妻子嫘祖（léizǔ）发明了养蚕、抽丝和织锦。炎帝创造了农具，指导人们进行农业生产，他还亲尝百草，发现了治病的药材。聪明能干、热心为大家办事的黄帝和炎帝，深受人们爱戴，他们一直被当作中华民族的杰出代表，成为中华民族的共同祖先。

现在，在陕西省黄陵县松柏常青的桥山上，还保留着黄帝陵和黄帝庙。湖南省炎陵县也保留着炎帝陵。黄帝和炎帝的子孙们，世世代代缅怀这两位中华民族的共同始祖。

Huangdi and Yandi were the common ancestors of the Chinese nation, and Chinese people at home and abroad all call themselves "descendents of Yandi and Huangdi".

As recorded in legends and ancient books, Huangdi was the first emperor in Chinese history. His surname was Ji, and his assumed name Xuanyuan Shi or Youxiong Shi. Yandi was also a legendary ruler whose surname was Jiang and assumed name Lieshan Shi or Shennong Shi.

Huangdi and Yandi both lived in the late period of China's primitive society about 4,000 years ago, and were the leaders of two different tribes living along the Yellow River in present-day Shaanxi Province. Later, they expanded their territories along both sides of the Yellow River to the east. The Yandi had invaded the territory of another tribe, the Jiuli, whose leader was Chiyou. The result was a defeat for the Yandi, who then sought help from the Huangdi tribe, and together they defeated Chiyou. After the defeat, some people of the Jiuli fled to the south, while others were assimilated into the Yandi or Huangdi tribes. The

1. 黄帝像
   A portrait of Huangdi
2. 位于陕西省黄陵县桥山上的黄帝陵
   The mausoleum of Huangdi, Qiao Mountain, Huangling County, Shaanxi Province

alliance did not last and eventually, fighting broke out that led to the Huangdi defeating the Yandi, whose members were forced to join and thus further strengthen the power of the Huangdi tribe. Later, segments of the three tribes (Huangdi, Yandi and Jiuli) settled down in the Yellow River valley, where they began to develop China's ancient culture and eventually formed the mainstay of what we know today as the Chinese people. It is from this time that people began to call themselves "the descendents of Yandi and Huangdi".

Huangdi was born clever. After he became the tribal leader, he taught people how to build houses, breed livestock and grow food crops, and invented the cart, boat, musical instrument and written characters. His wife, Leizu, discovered how to breed silkworms, how to reel off raw silk from cocoons, and how to brocade. Yandi, meanwhile, invented various farm implements and taught his people how to engage in agricultural production. He tasted all kinds of plants and discovered various medicinal materials for treating diseases.

At present, there are still preserved the Mausoleum and the Temple of the Yellow Emperor on Qiaoshan Mountain planted with evergreen pines and cypresses in Huangling County, Shaanxi Province. And in Yanling County, Hunan Province, the Mausoleum of the Red Emperor is also well preserved. Later generations greatly cherished their memory.

1. 黄帝像
   A statue of Huangdi
2. 炎帝陵
   The mausoleum of Yandi

中国的民族
Chinese Ethnic Groups

中国是一个统一的多民族国家，中华民族是中国各民族的总称。中国有56个民族，其中汉族人口约占全国总人口的91.59%，其余为55个少数民族。

在全国的少数民族中，壮族、回族、维吾尔族、彝 (yí) 族、苗族、满族、藏族、蒙古族、土家族、布依族、朝鲜族、侗族、瑶族、白族、哈尼族、哈萨克族、傣 (dǎi) 族和黎族的人口超过了100万；傈僳 (lìsù) 族、畲 (shē) 族、拉祜 (hù) 族、佤 (wǎ) 族、水族、东乡族、纳西族、土族、柯尔克孜 (zī) 族、羌 (qiāng) 族、达斡 (wò) 尔族、景颇 (pō) 族、仫佬 (mùlǎo) 族、锡伯族、仡 (gē) 佬族、高山族的人口超过了10万；撒拉族、布朗族、毛南族、塔吉克族、普米族、怒族、阿昌族、鄂 (è) 温克族、基诺族、德昂族、乌孜别克族、京族、裕固族、保安族、俄罗斯族的人口在1万以上；门巴族、独龙族、鄂伦春族、塔塔尔族、珞 (luò) 巴族、赫 (hè) 哲族人口不足1万。

中国的少数民族人数少，分布区域广，居住相对集中。广西、内蒙古、新疆、西藏、宁夏5个民族自治区分别是壮、蒙古、维吾尔、藏、回几个较大的少数民族集中居住的地区。云南、青海、贵州、甘肃、四川等省份也有大量少数民族聚居。其中云南省内就有20多个少数民族，是中国少数民族聚居最集中的省份。除此以外，吉林省有朝鲜族聚居区，湖南湘西有土家族和苗族聚居区，海南省有黎族和苗族聚居区，台湾省有高山族聚居区等等。很多少数民族居住在中国的边疆地区，那里多是山区、高原、森林和草原，自然资源丰富。

在长期的历史发展过程中，少数民族大都形成了自己特有的风俗习惯和宗教信仰，除了回族、满族一般使用汉语外，其他少数民族都有自己的语言，有的还有自己的文字。中国的少数民族大都能歌善舞，具有自己民族优秀的文化艺术传统、独特的民族乐器、优美的民族歌舞、丰富多彩的神话、诗歌和源远流长的历史传说。在

中国是一个由多民族组成的国家
China is a country composed of many ethnic groups.

少数民族中，还涌现了一大批科学家，他们为科学技术的进步作出了贡献。

China has 56 ethnic groups, among which the Han ethnic group accounts for 91.59% of the total population, with the remainder broken up into 55 ethnic minorities.

Among them, the population of the Zhuang, Hui, Uygur, Yi, Miao, Manchu, Tibetan, Mongolian, Tujia, Bouyei, Korean, Dong, Yao, Bai, Hani, Kazakh, Dai and Li nationalities is more than a million; that of the Lisu, She, Lahu, Wa, Shui, Dongxiang, Naxi, Tu, Kyrgyz, Qiang, Daur, Jingpo, Mulam, Xibe, Gelao, and Gaoshan nationalities exceeds 100,000; that of the Salar, Blang, Maonan, Tajik, Primi, Nu, Achang, Ewenki, Jino, De'ang, Uzbek, Jing, Yugur, Bao'an, and Russian nationalities is over 10,000; and that of the Monba, Drung, Oroqen, Tatar, Lhoba, and Hezhen nationalities is less than 10,000.

China's ethnic minorities are scattered over a vast area, but live in relatively compact communities. The five national autonomous regions of Guangxi, Inner Mongolia, Xinjiang, Tibet, Ningxia are compact communities inhabited by five comparably populous minority groups — Zhuang,

Mongolian, Uygur, Tibetan, and Hui respectively. And in Yunnan, Qinghai, Guizhou, Gansu, and Sichuan, there also live a great number of minority people. Yunnan Province is an area where minority groups are most concentrated with more than 20 represented. There is also a region in Jilin Province inhabited by the Korean people, one in the western part of Hunan Province, inhabited by the Tujia and Miao nationalities, one in Hainan Province inhabited by the Li and Miao nationalities, and one in Taiwan Province inhabited by the Gaoshan people. Many ethnic minorities live in China's frontier areas, which mostly comprise mountains, plateaus, forests and plains with rich natural resources.

In the long process of historical development, most ethnic minorities have formed their own special traditions, customs and religious beliefs. Except for the Hui and Manchu, who use the Chinese language, other minority groups have their own spoken languages, and some even have written characters. Almost all the ethnic minorities of China are good at singing and dancing, and have their own splendid cultural and artistic traditions, unique national musical instruments, beautiful national songs and dances, rich and varied fairy tales and poems and historical legends of longstanding.

汉 族
The Han

1. 汉族妇女
   A Han lady
2. 汉族民族服装
   Traditional Han clothing
3. 福、禄、寿三星，是汉族最喜爱的吉祥形象
   The gods of Happiness, Prosperity and Longevity are Han people's favorite auspicious symbols.

汉族人口约占中国人口总数的91.59%。汉族不仅是中国人口最多的民族，也是世界上人口最多的民族。汉族是中国古代华夏族同其他许多民族互相同化、融合形成的。从汉代开始，称为汉族。

汉族有近4,000年文字记录的历史，人口遍及中国各地，通用的语言是汉语。汉语历史悠久，语汇丰富，现在通行的方块汉字，是从甲骨文[1]和金文[2]演变而来的。汉族人民勤劳俭朴，积极进取，创造了举世瞩目的古代文明。早在春秋时期，汉族人就开始了大规模的农田水利建设，建于战国初期的四川都江堰水利工程至今仍在发挥作用；汉族人的养蚕、织锦、制茶、制瓷等技术，名扬海外；造纸术、印刷术、指南针和火药的发明，为世界文化与科学技术的发展作出了突出贡献。汉族人在文学艺术方面也取得了伟大的成就，楚辞、汉乐府、唐诗、宋词、元杂剧、明清小说等形成了汉文学在各个历史时期发展的高峰。系统完备的历史著作，忠实地记录了中华民族成长发展的辉煌历程。历史悠久的书法、绘画和建筑艺术，具有独特的魅力，留下了许多传世佳作。汉族人中还涌现出许多闻名中外的思想家、科学家、文学家、艺术家、政治家和军事家。

汉族人的宗族观念较深，祭祀祖先、传宗接代被认为是大事、大孝。汉族人最重视的节日是春节，此外还有元宵节、端午节、中秋节等。

在长期的历史发展过程中，汉族和各兄弟民族之间有着广泛的政治、经济联系和文化交流。因为历史和人口的原因，汉族在国家生活中起主导作用。汉族人性格宽厚，珍视友谊，重视品德修养。现在，汉族与各兄弟民族之间和睦相处，团结互助，共同为建设自己的国家贡献着力量。

The Han is the most populous ethnic group not only in China, but also throughout the world. It was formed after the ancient Chinese nation assimilated and merged with many other ethnic groups. Since the Han Dynasty, it was called the Han.

The Han ethnic group has a recorded history of about 4,000 years, the people are scattered throughout China, and the commonly used language is Chinese. The Chinese language has a long history with a rich vocabulary. The current Chinese characters are square ones, which evolved from ancient Chinese characters[①] carved on tortoise shells or animal bones and an ancient language[②] used in inscriptions on bronze objects. As early as the Spring and Autumn Period (770-476 BC), the Han had begun large-scale irrigation and water conservancy projects; the Dujiang Weirs in Sichuan Province built in early Warring States Period (475-221 BC) still function today. The techniques they invented for sericulture, weaving brocade, producing tea and making porcelain continue to thrive; the invention of papermaking, printing, the compass and gun powder made outstanding contributions to the development of world culture and scientific technology. The Han have also made great achievements in literature and arts: *The Songs of Chu, Yuefu* (folk songs or ballads in the Han style) of the Han Dynasty, *ci* poetry of the Song Dynasty, *zaju* (poetic drama set to music, usually consisting of four acts called *zhe*, with one character having the singing role throughout) of the Yuan Dynasty, and the novels of the Ming and Qing dynasties are the cultural high points of each era. Systematically complete historical works faithfully recorded the course of the Chinese nation. Calligraphy, painting, and architectural arts of a great antiquity have their unique charm, and many excellent works remain to be appreciated by today's generations. Many Han ideologists, scientists, men of letters, artists, statesmen and strategists, with prestige beyond national border, also emerged.

The Han people have a deep sense of patriarchal clan. It is considered an important event and also a critical act of filial piety to offer sacrifices to the ancestors and to produce a male heir to continue the family line. The Han people attach most importance to the Spring Festival; besides, they have the Lantern Festival, the Dragon Boat Festival and the Mid-autumn Festival, etc.

Through their long historical development, the Han people have forged extensive political, economic links and cultural exchanges with other fraternal nationalities. Because of their preponderance and long history, they have tended to always play a leading role in state affairs.

2

🔍 **小注解 Footnotes**

① 甲骨文：殷商时代刻在龟甲、兽骨上的文字。
② 金文：刻或铸在西周青铜器上的文字。

① These ancient Chinese characters are referred as *Jiaguwen*.
② Also known as *Jinwen*. *Jinwen* can be found on many bronze vessels of the Western Zhou Dynasty.

3

满 族
The Manchu

2,000多年前，在中国东北的长白山以北、黑龙江中下游一带被称为"白山黑水"的地方，居住着满族人的祖先——女真①人。明朝末年，努尔哈赤②经过30年的努力，统一了中国东北的女真部落。1635年，皇太极命改女真为满洲，以后简称满族。努尔哈赤用一种军事建制来管理满族，他把满族人分别组织在正黄、正白、正红、正蓝、镶黄、镶白、镶红、镶蓝八旗之中，实行全民皆兵，所以，人们也称满族人为"八旗人"或"旗人"。1644年，八旗兵从东北打入北京，建立了大清帝国，从此，满族贵族统治了中国近300年之久。

过去，满族男子都要留发辫，穿马蹄袖长袍和"马褂"（套在长袍外面的短褂）。女子的发式也很独特，一般都把头发梳上头顶，盘成发髻，然后再戴上漂亮的头饰。妇女穿的是直筒宽袖的旗袍，后来这种旗袍逐渐演变出了各种样式，成为中华民族富有特色的服装。

满族的传统食品中有一种非常好吃的点心，叫"萨其玛"。"萨其玛"是用面粉、鸡蛋、糖、芝麻、瓜子仁等原料做成的。很多人都非常喜欢吃。

满族人注重礼节，平时见了面都要行请安礼。如果见到长辈，要请安以后才能讲话。

满族人曾经创制了满文，由于后来与汉族人共同生活，使用了汉字、汉语，懂得满文、满语的人就很少了。满族人勤奋好学，涌现了许多文化名人。如《红楼梦》的作者曹雪芹、语言学家罗常培、作家老舍、书法家启功、京剧表演艺术家程砚秋等。

More than 2,000 years ago, ancestors of the Manchu people — Nuzhen① — lived in the area to the north of the Changbai Mountains and in the

1. 沈阳故宫。满族入主中原前，定都于此。
   Shenyang Imperial Palace (Before the Manchu people took over China, they chose Shenyang as the capital.)
2. 满族人注重礼节，不论皇室和平民，见面都要行请安礼
   Manchu nobles and commoners alike stressed etiquette. When they met each other, they saluted by bending the left knee and dropping the right hand.

downstream region of the Heilongjiang River in northeast China, which was called an area of "white mountains and black river". At the end of the Ming Dynasty, Nurhachi[2] succeeded over a 30-year period in unifying the Nuzhen tribes in northeast China. In 1635, Huangtaiji ordered that Nuzhen be renamed as Manchuria, which was simply called Manchu later. Nurhachi used a military system to administer the Manchu people by organizing them into Eight Banners: Pure Yellow, Pure White, Pure Red, Pure Blue, Bordered Yellow, Bordered White, Bordered Red, and Bordered Blue. Thus, people also call the Manchu the

"Eight Banner people" or "Banner people". In 1644, soldiers of the Eight Banners entered Beijing from northeast China, and set up the Great Qing Empire. From then on, Manchu aristocrats ruled China for nearly 300 years.

Manchu men were supposed to wear their hair in a single plait, and dress in a gown with horse-hoof-shaped cuffs and a mandarin jacket. The women's hairstyle was also quite unique; they usually coiled their hair on the top of the head in a bun, and then wore beautiful headdress. Manchu women wore a cheongsam with a straight skirt and broad sleeves. Later, this kind of cheongsam gradually evolved into various styles, and became a feature of Chinese fashion.

Among the traditional foods of the Manchu ethnic group, there is a very delicious snack called saqima (a kind of Manchu candied fritter). It is made of flour, eggs, sugar, sesame and kernels of melon seeds.

The Manchu people stressed etiquette. When they met each other, they saluted by bending the left knee and dropping the right hand. If one met a superior, he should salute before talking.

They had their own Manchu language. Since they later lived with the Han people and used the Han characters and spoken language, few people know the Manchu characters and spoken language today.

The Manchu people are diligent and fond of learning, and among them were many famous men of letters, such as the author of *A Dream of Red Mansions* Cao Xueqin, linguist Luo Changpei, writer Lao She, calligraphist Qi Gong and performance artists of Beijing opera such as Cheng Yanqiu.

小注解 Footnotes

① 女真：中国古代民族，满族的祖先，居住在今天的吉林、黑龙江一带。

② 努尔哈赤（公元1559－1626年）：满族，爱新觉罗氏。他经营40多年，统一了女真各部，在满族的初期发展中，起了重要作用。清朝建立后，被追尊为太祖。

① Nuzhen, an ancient Chinese ethnic group, was the ancestor of the Manchu ethnic group, living in present-day Jilin and Heilongjiang areas.

② Nurhachi (1559-1626 AD) had the family name Aisin Gioro with a Manchu origin. He played an important role in the early development of the Manchu ethnic group. After the Qing Dynasty was established, he was honored with a posthumous title "Taizu".

蒙古族
The Mongolian

蒙古族主要居住在中国北部边疆的内蒙古自治区。那里土地辽阔，物产丰富。广阔的草原成为天然的牧场。河套平原和东部农业区出产小麦、玉米、高粱、甜菜、大豆等农产品。北部大兴安岭林区有很多珍禽异兽，并出产名贵的木材、毛皮和药材。

蒙古族牧民的生活方式很有特色。他们冬季穿用丝绸或棉布做衣面的皮袍，夏季穿布袍，喜欢用红绿绸缎做腰带，常常佩挂荷包和蒙古刀。男子习惯戴帽子，妇女则用红、蓝色的布包头。牧民们喜欢吃牛羊肉和奶制品，喜欢喝红茶和砖茶。他们大多住在圆形的蒙古包里。蒙古包顶上开有天窗，用来通风和采光。

蒙古族是一个能骑善射、能歌善舞的民族。蒙古族民歌高亢悠扬，蒙古族舞蹈节奏欢快，蒙古族人最喜欢的乐器马头琴，琴声悦耳动听。他们以自己的智慧创造了丰富的歌舞音乐和诗歌作品，被称为"音乐民族"和"诗歌民族"。

每年七八月举行的"那达慕"①大会，是蒙古族人民一年一度的盛大节日。大会上有赛马、摔跤、射箭比赛和精彩的歌舞表演。每逢盛会，人们都从四面八方赶来参加比赛、观看表演，宁静的大草原顿时变成了欢乐的海洋。

小注解 Footnotes

1

① 那达慕：蒙古语，是"娱乐"或"欢聚"的意思。

① Nadam is a Mongolian word, meaning "entertainment" or "happy get-together".

2

The Mongolian people mainly live in the Mongolian Autonomous Region in the frontier areas in northern China, which has a far-flung territory and abundant produce. The vast grassland is a natural pasture. The Hetao Plain and eastern agricultural area produce wheat, maize, Chinese sorghum, beet, soybean, etc. To the north, the Greater Xing'an Mountains is home to many rare birds and animals, and the area produces timber, pelts and medicinal herbs.

Mongolian herdsmen have long lived a unique lifestyle. They wear a fur gown with a silk or cotton-cloth surface in winter and wear a cloth gown in summer; they love to wear red or green silks and satins as a waistband, and often carry with them a pouch and a Mongolian knife. Mongolian men are used to wearing a hat and women are used to wearing a red or blue headpiece. The herdsmen like to eat beef, mutton and dairy products, and drink black tea and brick tea. Most of them live in round Mongolian tents known as a yurt, which has a skylight ceiling for ventilation and lighting.

The Mongolian people excel in horsemanship and archery, singing and dancing. Mongolian folk songs are sonorous and melodious, Mongolian dances have cheerful rhythm. And the *morin hort* (a bowed stringed instrument with a scroll carved like a horse's head), which the Mongolians like most, sounds sweet and beautiful. Mongolians have created many songs, dances, music and poems, earning them the title of a "musical ethnic group" and a "poetic ethnic group".

The Nadam[①] Fair held from July to August is an annual grand festival for the Mongolian people. It features horse racing, wrestling, archery competition and exciting song and dance performances. Every time this magnificent fair is held, people come from all directions to participate in competitions and watch performances, and the tranquil grasslands are then turned into a land of fun and games.

1. 那达慕大会上赛马
   Horse racing at the Nadam Fair
2. 蒙古族婚礼
   A Mongolian wedding
3. 蒙古族人传统居所——蒙古包
   The traditional home of the Mongolian —— yurt

回　族
The Hui

回族是中国少数民族中人口较多的一个民族，他们散居在中国各地，主要聚居在宁夏回族自治区。

回族人大多信仰伊斯兰教，习惯在聚居的地方修建清真寺。主要的节日有开斋节、圣纪节和古尔邦节。

伊斯兰教对回族人的生活习惯有很深的影响：回族小孩出生后，要请阿訇①(hòng) 起一个回族名字；回族人结婚时，要请阿訇证婚；去世后，要请阿訇主持葬礼；回族人不吃猪肉，也不吃一切动物的血和自死的动物。回族在穿戴上基本和汉族相同，但男人习惯戴白帽和黑帽。

回族最初使用阿拉伯语、波斯语和汉语。由于长期和汉族杂居，逐渐通用汉语，并吸收了汉族文化。现在，回族在衣饰、姓名和习惯等方面，已基本与汉族相同。

"花儿"是流传在甘肃、青海一带深受回族人民喜爱的民歌形式。每年农历②六月初一到初六，在甘肃康乐县景色秀丽的莲花山，都要举行"花儿盛会"。每逢盛会，莲花山上歌如潮，花如海，通宵达旦的歌声唱出了回族人民对幸福生活的追求和向往。

回族是勤劳、勇敢、智慧的民族，在历史上出过不少杰出人物。回族人民为中国的繁荣和发展，作出了积极的贡献。

The Hui ethnic group is relatively populous among China's ethnic minority groups. They are scattered all over China, but mainly live in Ningxia Hui Autonomous Region. Most of the Hui people are Muslims, and are accustomed to build a mosque where they live in a community. Major festivals are the Lesser Bairam, Mawlid al-Nabi (*Shengji* Festival or the Birthday of the

Prophet Mohammed), and the Corban Festival.

Islam has a deep influence on the life and customs of the Hui people: When a baby is born, he will be given a Hui name by an imam[1]; when people get married, they invite an imam as the chief witness; when one dies, an imam will be invited to preside over the funeral; the Hui people never eat pork, and nor do they eat the blood of any animal or corpse of animals that die naturally.

At first, the Hui people used the Arabic, Persian and Chinese languages. Since they have lived for a long time alongside the Han people, they have gradually adopted use of Chinese, and absorbed much from Chinese culture. Now, the Hui people are almost the same as the Han in terms of clothes, ornaments, names and customs, only that men normally wear white or black caps.

Hua'er is a kind of folk song popular in Gansu and Qinghai provinces and with the Hui people. Every year, from the first to the sixth day in June in the lunar calendar[2], a "hua'er meeting" is held in the Lotus Mountain in Kangle County, Gansu Province, where beautiful songs flow all night.

There are outstanding figures in the history of the Hui ethnic group and the Hui people have made positive contributions to the prosperity and development of China.

1. 回族老人
   The Hui elder
2. 回族学生
   The Hui students
3. 宁夏银川南关清真寺
   The mosque in Nanguan, Yinchuan, Ningxia
4. 清真寺内穆斯林在做礼拜
   Muslims worshipping in a mosque

小注解 Footnotes

① 阿訇：伊斯兰教主持教仪、讲授经典的人。

② 农历：中国传统的历法。

① An imam presides over Islamic religious activities.

② The lunar calendar is a traditional Chinese one.

壮族
The Zhuang

壮族在中国少数民族中是人口最多的一个少数民族，主要居住在广西壮族自治区，少数分布在云南、广东、湖南、贵州等省份。

壮族居住的地区，草木常青，百花盛开，风景美丽如画。名扬天下的桂林山水，更是山峰秀丽，河水清澈。那迷人的美景，吸引了来自世界各地的游客。

壮族在历史发展的过程中，创造了瑰丽多彩的文化艺术。分布在左江两岸峭壁上的花山崖壁画，长100多米，高40多米，反映了2,000多年前壮族先民的生活情况。早在战国时期，壮族人就能制造铜鼓，铜鼓既是乐器，也是权力和财富的象征。久负盛名的壮锦，是壮族妇女独创的手工艺品，壮锦用色彩鲜艳的棉、丝、绒线织成，图案非常美丽、别致。壮族人家里的被面、台布、门帘、坐垫、手提袋等用品，都是用壮锦做成的。

壮族人特别喜欢唱山歌。传说唐代有个被称为歌仙的女歌手刘三姐，创造了壮族歌谣，至今仍在各族人民中传唱。"歌圩"(xū)是壮族人传统的歌节。每到节日，青年男女都要穿上节日盛装，聚集到山坡上，对唱山歌。人们用唱歌来表达爱情，结交朋友，祈求风调雨顺，五谷丰登。

壮族人崇拜巨石、老树、高山、土地、龙蛇和祖先等。中元节、牛魂节是壮族特有的节日。中元节又称鬼节，在每年的农历七月十四日举行，是祭祀祖先和野鬼的节日。牛魂节在春耕以后举行，人们给牛吃五色糯米饭和鲜草，为耕牛招魂。

1. 壮族姑娘表演麒麟凤凰白鹭舞
   The Zhuang ladies are performing the traditional Kylin and Phoenix Dance.
2. 绣球是壮族男女的传情之物
   These embroidered balls are the perfect romantic gifts for the Zhuang lovers.
3. 龙胜山区的壮族
   The Zhuang people who live in Longsheng mountain area
4. 壮族姑娘
   A Zhuang lady

The Zhuang, the most populous among the minority groups, mainly live in Guangxi Zhuang Autonomous Region, with a small number distributed in Yunnan, Guangdong, Hunan and Guizhou provinces.

The area where the Zhuang people live has evergreen grass and trees, blossoming flowers and a picturesque landscape, especially that in Guilin, which attracts tourists from all over the world.

Among the man-made attractions are the Huashan Cliff Murals along the Zuojiang River,

2

3

which are more than 100 m long and over 40 m high, reflecting the life of the inhabitants over 2,000 years ago. As early as the Warring States Period (475-221 BC), the Zhuang people could make a bronze drum, which was not only a musical instrument but also a symbol of power and wealth. Zhuang brocade, which has long enjoyed a great reputation, is woven with cotton, silk and floss threads of bright color in exquisite patterns. Quilt covers, tablecloths, door curtains, cushions, handbags and the like in this region are all made of Zhuang brocade.

The Zhuang people like to sing folk songs. According to legend, a female singer Liu Sanjie, who was called the Immortal Singer in the Tang Dynasty, invented Zhuang ballads that still circulate and are sung by various ethnic groups. The Antiphonal Song Day is a traditional Zhuang singing festival, when young men and women dressed in their most splendid attire gather on the hills to sing in antiphonal style. Through these songs, people express love, make friends and pray for good weather and a good harvest.

The Zhuang people worship big stones, old trees, lofty mountains, land, dragons, snakes, and their ancestors. The Festival of the Dead Spirits and the Festival of the Ox Souls are peculiar to them. The Festival of the Dead Spirits, also called the Ghosts' Festival, is held on the 14th day of the seventh lunar month, when sacrifices are offered to the ancestors and to wild ghosts. The Festival of the Ox Souls is held after the spring plowing when people feed their ox with cooked glutinous rice in five colors and fresh grass to recall the spirit of the dead plowing ox.

4

维吾尔族
The Uygur

在新疆维吾尔自治区，居住着维吾尔、塔吉克、柯尔克孜、乌孜别克等十多个少数民族，维吾尔族是其中人口最多的一个民族。

"维吾尔"是维吾尔族的自称，有"联合"、"团结"的意思。维吾尔族人大多居住在新疆维吾尔自治区天山以南，但在新疆其他地区也有分布。

维吾尔族人的服装鲜艳美丽，无论男女老少都喜欢戴一种叫"尕巴"(gǎbā)的四楞小帽，男子穿的对襟长袍叫"袷袢"(qiàpàn)，女子喜欢穿宽袖连衣裙，外套黑色对襟背心。姑娘出嫁以前，要把头发梳成很多根辫子披在肩上，她们认为，头发越长越漂亮。维吾尔族人喜欢喝奶茶，吃羊肉和用面粉烤制的馕(náng)。别具民族风味的"抓饭"，是过节和待客时不可缺少的食品。"抓饭"是用大米、羊肉、羊油、胡萝卜、葡萄干、洋葱做成的，因为用手抓着吃，所以被称为"抓饭"。

维吾尔族大多信仰伊斯兰教，有自己的语言和文字。历史悠久的维吾尔族文学艺术具有独特的民族风格，其中"阿凡提的故事"是中国各族人民非常熟悉和喜欢的。

维吾尔族是个能歌善舞的民族，每逢节日和喜庆的日子，男女老少都要载歌载舞，尽情欢乐。维吾尔族舞蹈和维吾尔族民歌深受各族人民的喜爱。

维吾尔族人很早就开始从事农业生产。他们在盆地的边缘和戈壁上开发出片片绿洲，利用地下水修建"坎儿井"①，灌溉良田。主要的粮食作物是小麦、玉米、水稻。无核白葡萄、哈密瓜、长绒棉、和田玉是新疆的特产。维吾尔族人的手工业历史也很悠久，工艺精湛的地毯、丝绸、小刀和绣花帽驰名中外，受到了各国朋友的喜爱。

1. 维吾尔族刺绣
   The Uygur embroidery
2. 美丽的维吾尔族少女
   A charming Uygur lady
3. 别具民族风味的"抓饭"
   The Uygur ethnic food, *zhuafan*
4. 维吾尔人的主食——馕
   Uygur people's main diet —— *nang*

Xinjiang Uygur Autonomous Region contains more than 10 ethnic minorities, including the Uygur, Tajik, Kyrgyz and Uzbek, among which the Uygur (which means "rally" or "unity") is the most populous. They live mainly in the area to the south of Tianshan Mountains in Xinjiang Uygur Autonomous Region.

The clothes of the Uygur people are brightly colored and beautiful, and all men or women like to wear a diamond-shaped skullcap named *gaba*. Uygur men traditionally wear *qiapan*, a robe buttoning down the front, and women like to wear a one-piece dress that has loose sleeves with a black front-buttoned waistcoat over it. Young women wear many plaits over the shoulders before marriage, believing the longer the hair, the more beautiful a woman is. Uygurs like to drink milk tea, eat mutton and *nang* (a kind of crusty pancake) baked with flour. A favorite dish is *zhuafan*, which is made of rice, mutton, goat oil, carrots, raisins and onions, and eaten with the hands.

Most Uygurs are Muslims. They have their own spoken and written languages. Uygur literature and arts have a long history and a special ethnic style; *The Story of Afanti* is familiar to, and liked by, all ethnic groups in China.

The Uygur people are good at singing and dancing, and their dances and folk songs are quite popular among all ethnic groups.

Uygurs took up farming long ago. They have opened up oases at the edge of basins or in the Gobi Desert, and built the karez[1] using underground water to irrigate fertile farmland. The main grain crops are wheat, corn and rice. Coreless grape, long staple cotton, Hami melon, and Hotan jade are special local products of Xinjiang.

The Uygur ethnic group has a long history of handicrafts; their carpets, silk cloth, knives and embroidered skullcaps of exquisite craftsmanship are famous at home and abroad.

小注解 Footnotes

① 坎儿井：新疆干旱地区流行的一种灌溉工程，从山坡上直到田里挖成一连串的井，再把井底挖通，连成暗沟，把天山上融化的雪水和地下水引来浇灌田地。

① Karez is an irrigation system in dry areas of Xinjiang, which is a series of wells from the hills down to the fields connected at the bottom by underground channels, so as to draw newly-melt snow in the Tianshan Mountains and underground water to irrigate the fields.

朝鲜族
The Koreans

朝鲜族主要居住在中国的东北三省和内地的一些大城市，其中居住最集中的地方，是吉林省长白山麓的延边朝鲜族自治州和长白朝鲜族自治县。

朝鲜族聚居的地区山川秀丽，物产丰富，特别是被称为"长白林海"的长白山地区，不但出产红松、白松等珍贵木材，还有闻名全国的"东北三宝"：人参、貂皮和鹿茸。延边地区是中国北方著名的"水稻之乡"，那里出产的大米洁白如玉，营养丰富。

朝鲜族人住房的屋顶是由四个斜面构成的。屋内用砖或石板铺成炕①，客人来访时，要脱鞋进屋，坐在炕上。朝鲜族人喜欢穿素白色的衣服。男子一般穿白色上衣，黑色坎肩和肥大的白色裤子。妇女喜欢穿素白色的短衣和长裙。儿童喜欢穿颜色鲜艳的七彩上衣。朝鲜族的食品独具风味，泡菜、冷面、打糕和酱汤都是他们喜欢吃的食品。

朝鲜族是一个能歌善舞的民族，伽耶②(jiāyē)琴、弹唱、顶水舞、扇子舞、长鼓舞等是他们的传统歌舞。朝鲜族男子喜欢摔跤、踢足球等体育活动，妇女喜欢荡秋千和跳跳板。

朝鲜族是个尊老爱幼的民族。老年人在家庭中和社会上处处受到尊敬。每年的老人节，朝鲜族都要举行庆祝活动，为60岁以上的老年人祝福。

Ethnic Koreans live mainly in Heilongjiang, Liaoning and Jilin provinces in northeast China and some inland big cities, and the most concentrated areas are the Korean Autonomous Prefecture of Yanbian and the Korean Autonomous County of Changbai near the Changbai Mountains in Jilin Province.

These areas have beautiful mountains and abundant produce. In particular the Changbai Mountains area, which is called "Changbai Forest

Sea", produces not only valuable timber such as Korean pine and kahikatea, but also "Three Treasures in Northeast China" famous around the country — ginseng, marten and pilose antler. The Yanbian area is a well-known "land of rice" in northern China, its rice being as white as jade and very nutritious.

Korean homes have a roof with four inclined planes. In the house, there is a *kang*① built of bricks or slates. When a guest visits, he should take off his shoes before entering the room and sitting on the *kang*.

The Korean people like to dress in white. Men usually wear a white jacket, black waistcoat and loose white trousers, while women like to wear plain and white clothes. Children like to wear a bright-colored jacket. Korean food has special tastes, including *kimchi* (hot pickled vegetables), cold noodles, sticky rice cakes and soy sauce soup.

The Korean people are good at singing and dancing. They sing while playing a plucked stringed instrument called the *kayago*②. Also traditional are the water-carrying dance (carrying water in a pitcher on the head), fan dance and

drum dance. Korean men like sports such as wrestling and playing football; while women like to play on the swing and do seesaw jumping (with one girl jumping up and down on her end of the seesaw to bounce up the girl standing on the other end, who will then return the favor).

Koreans respect the old and cherish the young. Each year, on the day of the Festival of the Aged, they hold celebratory activities to extend their wishes to anyone aged over 60.

1. 跳跷跷板
   Seesaw jumping
2. 朝鲜族家庭
   A Korean family
3. 朝鲜族婚礼
   A Korean wedding

🔍 小注解 Footnotes

① 炕：中国北方用土坯或砖砌成的睡觉的长方台，上面铺席，下面有烟道，可以烧火取暖。

② 伽耶琴：朝鲜族使用的一种拨弦乐器，形似古筝。

① Made of adobe or bricks in northern China, *kang* is a rectangular sleeping platform, which is covered with a mat above and the flues underneath for heating.

② The shape of the *kayago* resembles the *zheng* (Chinese zither with 21 or 25 strings).

高山族
The Gaoshan

　　高山族世代居住在中国的台湾省，是台湾省最早的居民，主要分布在台湾岛的山区和东部纵谷平原等地，也有少数散居在中国的福建省，以及北京、上海、武汉等地。

　　高山族人主要从事农业生产，种植水稻、小米、芋头和红薯，有的也以捕鱼为生。

　　高山族人的服装大多是用麻布和棉布做成的，手工非常精细。男子穿披肩、背心、短褂、短裤。妇女会染织各种彩色麻布，穿短上衣和斜披在肩上的偏衫，系围裙，喜欢在衣襟、衣袖、头巾、围裙上刺绣花纹，佩带用贝壳、兽骨磨制的装饰品。

　　高山族有优美的民歌、古谣、神话和传说。嘴琴、竹笛、鼻箫和弓琴是他们常用的乐器。每逢节日，高山族人都要聚集在一起唱歌、跳舞。高山族人还非常喜欢雕刻和绘画，在他们的住房、乐器和生活用品上，都雕有各种美丽的图案，其中最多的是蛇身人首的图像。

1. 盛装的高山族男子
   A Gaoshan man in traditional clothing
2. 兰屿雅美人(高山族的一种)用的木船
   The wooden boats of Yamei people (Gaoshan clan), Lanyu Island
3. 在民族大集会上，高山族人齐起舞
   Performing the ritual dance at the traditional Gaoshan festival
4. 高山族女子
   A Gaoshan lady

The Gaoshan people have lived for generations in Taiwan Province, and were the earliest residents of the island, mainly distributed in mountainous areas and the Zonggu Plain in eastern Taiwan, with a few scattered around the mainland in Fujian Province, Beijing, Shanghai, Wuhan, etc.

The Gaoshan people mainly engage in farming, planting rice, millet, taro and sweet potato, but some live on fishing.

Their clothes are mostly made of linen and cotton, with exquisite craftsmanship. Men wear a shawl, waistcoat, short gown and short pants. Women can dye and weave various pieces of colorful linen cloth. They wear a short jacket, a gown draped over one shoulder, and an apron. Also, they like to embroider the two pieces making up the front of a Chinese jacket or gown, sleeves, scarf, apron, and wear ornaments made of shells and animal bones.

The Gaoshan ethnic group has beautiful folk songs, ancient ballads, myths and legends. The mouth *qin* (a kind of wind musical instrument made of bamboo slices with threaded covers at both ends, played by blowing across holes), bamboo flute, nose *xiao* (a vertical bamboo flute) and bow *qin* are commonly used. On festive occasions, people gather to sing and dance. The Gaoshan people also like carving and painting; their houses, musical instruments, and daily necessities are all carved with beautiful patterns, most of which are images with a snake's head and human's body.

苗　族
The Miao

　　苗族是中国西南地区人口较多的一个民族。苗族分布很广，主要在贵州、湖南、云南、四川、广西、湖北、广东、海南等省区，大多数苗族人居住在贵州省。

　　苗族是个爱美的民族。勤劳的苗族人用他们创造的刺绣、挑花、织花、蜡染、银饰装扮自己的衣着，美化自己的生活。苗族姑娘一般从五六岁就开始学绣花，能绣一手好花的姑娘，在苗族地区是最受称赞的。如果有贵客来到苗家，姑娘们会在敬酒的时候，把自己特意刺绣的一根花带送给客人。

　　由于苗族分布很广，各地苗族人过的节日也不太一样。苗族人的节日很多，主要有龙舟节、花山节、吃新节、清明节、赶秋节等。每到节日，穿得最漂亮的是妇女。她们身穿有银器装饰的绣花

衣，头上、脖子上戴着各种银饰，走起路来，银饰叮当作响，闪闪发光。在节日里，苗族人要举行各种各样的庆祝活动，其中吹芦笙、对歌、斗牛是最有特色的活动。芦笙是苗族人喜欢的一种乐器，据说已经有2,000多年的历史。

1. 盛装的贵州黔东南苗族
   The distinctive traditional attires of Miao people, southeast of Guizhou Province
2. 苗族芦笙会
   Miao's Sheng Festival
3. 一身银饰的苗族姑娘
   A Miao lady is fully dressed up with silver ornaments.
4. 苗族腊染
   The batik print of Miao

The Miao form a relatively populous ethnic group in southwest China, and are widely distributed in Guizhou, Hunan, Yunnan, Sichuan, Guangxi, Hubei, Guangdong, and Hainan provinces, although most live in Guizhou Province.

The Miao like to be well groomed. They dress themselves up and beautify their lives with embroidery, cross-stitch work, woven patterns, wax printing, and silver ornaments made by themselves. Miao girls usually start to learn embroidery at the age of five or six, and those who become good at it are widely praised. If any distinguished guest visits, girls will present a patterned band specially made by themselves when proposing a toast.

Since the Miao are widely distributed, their festivals differ from place to place. The Miao people have many festivals, such as the Dragon-Boat Festival, the Flower-Mountain Festival, the New Crop Tasting Festival, the Pure Brightness Day and the Autumn Harvest Festival. On festive days, women dress most beautifully, wearing embroidered clothes with silver articles and varied silver ornaments on the head and around the neck; when they walk, these silver ornaments jingle and glitter. There are various kinds of celebratory activities, among which, playing the *sheng* (a reed pipe wind instrument), antiphonal singing and bullfighting are the most characteristic. The *sheng* is a musical instrument that has a history of more than 2,000 years as it is said.

彝 族
The Yi

彝族是中国西南地区人口最多的一个少数民族。远在2,000多年前，彝族的祖先就在那里生活。他们主要居住在云南、四川、贵州、广西等省区，四川凉山彝族自治州是最大的彝族聚居区。

彝族的传统服装样式很多。妇女常穿镶边或绣花的大襟上衣和多褶长裙，裙边镶着各种颜色的布。云南红河地区的彝族姑娘还喜欢戴一种鸡冠式的绣花帽，据说这是吉祥、幸福的象征。彝族男子一般都穿黑色窄袖、右开襟的短上衣和多褶、宽裤脚的长裤，喜欢用长长的青布或蓝布包头，并且在前面扎一个长锥形的"英雄结"。男女外出时都要披一件用羊毛线织成的斗篷，白天用它挡风寒，晚上用它当被子。

火把节是彝族最隆重的传统节日，一般在农历的六月二十四日前后举行。每逢节日，各地的彝族人都要身穿节日盛装，举行各种活动。火把节上，人们举着火把边唱边跳，形成一条长长的火龙，把村村寨寨映得通红。据说，人们点燃火把，是为了驱赶害虫，保护庄稼。节日期间，彝族人还要杀鸡宰羊，祈求丰年。

在漫长的历史发展过程中，彝族人民创造了灿烂的文化。"阿细跳月"是著名的彝族舞蹈；流传全国的叙事长诗《阿诗玛》，讲述了彝族姑娘阿诗玛的动人故事。除此之外，彝族在天文、历法、气象、医药等方面也有独特的创造。相传，"云南白药"就是根据彝族民间医生的祖传秘方配制而成的。

1

1. 彝族姑娘
   A Yi lady
2. 彝族火把节
   Yi's Torchlight Festival
3. 彝族人个个都是饮酒高手
   The Yi people are alcohol lovers.

The Yi is the most populous ethnic group in southwest China, where their ancestors lived more than 2,000 years ago. They are predominant in Yunnan, Sichuan, Guizhou and Guangxi provinces. The Yi Autonomous Prefecture of Liangshan in Sichuan Province is the largest Yi community.

Traditional Yi clothes have many styles. Women often wear an edged or embroidered jacket with buttons on the right side of the front and a pleated long skirt edged with cotton of various colors. Yi girls in Honghe area of Yunnan Province like to wear a kind of cockscomb-shaped embroidered hat, regarded as a symbol of good luck and happiness. Yi men generally wear a short black jacket with tight sleeves, buttons on the right, and long trousers with many pleats and loose bottoms; they like to use a long black or blue cloth for a head covering, tying it in an awl-like "hero knot" in the front. When the Yi people go out, they wear a sleeveless cloak woven with wool, which they can use as a quilt at night.

The Torchlight Festival is the grandest traditional festival of the Yi people, usually held around the 24th day of June in the lunar calendar. The people hold torches while singing and dancing in their festive attire, forming a long fiery dragon that bathes villages in a crimson glow. Traditionally, people lit torches to drive away pests and protect crops, and during this festival, the Yi also kill chickens and goats to pray for a good harvest.

During the long process of historical development, the Yi people have created a diversified culture. "Axi Dancing Under the Moon" is a famous Yi dance; a long narrative poem *Ashima* which circulates throughout the country tells a touching story of a Yi girl Ashima. The Yi have also made unique contributions in the fields of astronomy, calendar, meteorology, and medicine. Legend has it that the White Medicinal Powder of Yunnan is compounded according to a secret recipe of a folk Yi doctor handed down in the family from generation to generation.

傣　族
The Dai

傣族主要聚居在云南省西双版纳地区。那里山川秀丽，气候温和，雨量充足，到处有竹林、椰树和香蕉林，是个四季常青的地方。在大片的原始森林中，有很多珍禽异兽。美丽的孔雀常常在丛林中、溪水边翩翩起舞。人们便把傣族人生活的地方称为"孔雀之乡"。

竹楼，是傣族人居住的房屋。竹楼分为上下两层，上层住人，下层堆放杂物和关牲畜。在傣族居住的乡村里，还建有许多佛寺，一般男孩子长到八九岁时，都要到佛寺里当一段时间的小和尚。

傣族人的服装一般都是用妇女自己织的布做成的。男子穿无领短衫、长裤，大多用白布或蓝布包头。妇女们喜欢穿窄袖短上衣和长到脚面的筒裙，一般都把长发盘在头顶，再插上一把漂亮的月牙梳。

泼水节是傣族一年一度的盛大节日。泼水节的清晨，男女老少沐浴后，都要换上节日盛装，到佛寺里为佛洗尘，然后互相泼洒象征吉祥如意的清水。据说，身上被泼的清水越多，在新的一年里就会越幸福。

傣族人的节日非常多，每到过节的时候，能歌善舞的傣族人都要敲起芒锣和象脚鼓，跳起优美的孔雀舞，庆祝节日。

1. 傣族姑娘
   The Dai ladies
2. 傣族人居住的竹楼
   The residences of Dai people are built with bamboo.
3. 泼水节
   The Water-Sprinkling Festival
4. 傣族婚礼
   A Dai wedding

1

The Dai people mainly live in the Xishuangbanna area in Yunnan Province. It has beautiful mountains, a mild climate, abundant rainfall, and there are bamboo forests, coconut trees and banana trees everywhere. In the vast primeval forest, there are many rare birds and unusual animals. Pretty peacocks often dance gracefully along jungle trails or beside a brook. Thus, people call the place which the Dai people inhabit "the Land of Peacocks".

Dai people have traditionally lived in two-storied bamboo stilt house, the upper story for living and the lower for storage and feeding livestock. Their villages contain many temples. Generally when a Dai boy is eight or nine years old, he will be sent to a temple as a monk for a period.

Dai clothes are generally made of cloth woven by the local women. Men wear a collarless short Chinese jacket, long trousers and white or blue headpiece. Women like to wear a short jacket with tight sleeves and straight skirt covering the instep; they usually coil their hair on top of the head with a beautiful crescent comb.

The Water-Sprinkling Festival is an annual grand festival for the Dai ethnic group. In the morning, they take a bath and then dress carefully before going to the temples to wash away the dust for the Buddha, and then sprinkle water on each other as a symbol of auspiciousness. Supposedly, the more water one is sprinkled with, the happier one will be in the forthcoming year.

The Dai people are good singers and dancers. During their numerous festivals, they play the *mangluo* gong and the *xiangjiaogu* (drum on a pedestal shaped like an elephant's leg) and dance the graceful Peacock Dance to celebrate the festival.

藏　族
The Tibetan

藏族是个古老的民族。藏族的古代政权称为"吐蕃"(tǔbō)。早在公元641年，吐蕃"赞普"(王)松赞干布就派使者到当时唐朝的都城长安，代他求婚，娶回了聪明美丽的文成公主。从那时开始，汉藏两族在政治、经济、文化等方面的交往就有了很大的发展。

藏族主要分布在中国的西藏自治区和青海、甘肃、四川、云南等省份，大多居住在高原地带。青藏高原平均海拔4,000米以上，世界第一高峰珠穆朗玛峰就耸立在高原的群山之中。藏族地区草原辽阔，江河纵横。体肥毛长的牦牛，不仅耐寒，还能驮很重的东西远行，是高原上重要的运输"工具"，被称为"高原之舟"。

藏族人的服饰很有民族特色。他们一般上身穿绸、布做的长袖短褂，外面穿宽肥的长袍，脚穿牛皮长靴。为了便于活动，常常将右肩或双臂露在外面，把两只袖子系在腰间。藏族男女都留发辫，男子将发辫盘在头顶，女子将头发梳成双辫或许多条小辫，披在肩上，并在发梢上佩戴漂亮的饰物。妇女们还喜欢在腰间系一条图案

2

美丽的围裙。藏族人爱喝酥油茶和奶茶，喜欢吃用青稞粉制成的糌粑（zānbā）和牛羊肉。

藏族人有一个独特的礼仪——献哈达。哈达是一种特制的白色长巾。在拜访或接待尊贵的客人时，藏族人要用双手献上洁白的哈达，以表敬意。

藏族具有悠久的文化传统。藏文始创于公元7世纪；藏医、藏药、藏画、藏戏、藏族歌舞、藏族文学等都具有独特的风格；拉萨的布达拉宫宏伟壮观，是建筑史上的杰作，已被联合国列入世界文化遗产名录。藏族人民创造的灿烂文化，丰富了中华民族的文化宝库。

藏族人信奉藏传佛教，最隆重的节日是藏历元旦。每到这一天，人们都要身着盛装，相互拜年，并到寺庙里朝拜祈福。四月十五日，相传是释迦牟尼成佛和文成公主进藏的日子，各地的藏族人也要举行宗教活动，纪念这个特殊的日子。

1. 华丽的藏族服装
   The extraordinary Tibetan traditional clothing
2. 藏族人爱在发梢上佩戴漂亮的饰物
   The Tibetan people love to dress up their hair with beautiful adornments.
3. 藏戏
   Tibetan drama

The Tibetan ethnic group is an age-old one, where there was an ancient regime called the Tubo Kingdom. In 641 AD, after its king Songtsan Gambo united the warring tribes on the Tibetan plateau, he sent messengers to the capital of the Tang Dynasty, Chang'an (Xi'an), to seek a bride. The Tang Emperor agreed and Princess Wencheng was sent to Tibet. From this beginning, the Tibetan and Han nationalities have gone on to make great progress in political, economic and cultural exchanges.

The Tibetan people are mainly distributed in the Tibetan Autonomous Region, Qinghai, Gansu, Sichuan, and Yunnan provinces, and most of them live on plateaus at high altitude. The Qinghai-Tibet Plateau is over 4,000 m above sea level on average and the world's highest peak, Mount Qomolongma, towers above many massive peaks there. The area where the Tibetans live has vast grasslands and is crossed by many rivers. Yaks, with a fat body and long hair, can resist cold and are capable of carrying a heavy load long distances, so they have long been an important transportation "tool" on the plateau.

The clothes of the Tibetan people have unique national features. Usually they wear a short jacket with long sleeves made of silk or cotton with a

3

雪顿节晒大佛
Unveiling the huge picture of Buddha during the
Shoton Festival

loose gown over it, and a pair of high leather boots. For convenience when working, they often bare the right shoulder or even both arms, tying the two sleeves around the waist. Tibetan men and women all wear plaits; men coil the plait on top of the head while women wear two plaits, or sometimes many, over the shoulders, with beautiful ornaments woven into the ends. Women also like to tie an apron with beautiful patterns around their waist. The Tibetan people love to drink butter tea, and eat tsampa made of highland barley flour, beef and mutton.

The Tibetan people have a unique ceremony — presenting a *hada*. The *hada* is a piece of specially made white long cloth. When visiting or entertaining distinguished guests, Tibetan people present it draped over both their hands to express their respect.

The Tibetan ethnic group has a long cultural tradition. A unified written Tibetan language was established in the early years of the Tubo kingdom in the 7th century; traditional Tibetan medicine, Tibetan drugs, Tibetan pictures, Tibetan operas, Tibetan songs and dances, and Tibetan literature all have their unique style. The magnificent Potala Palace in Lhasa is a masterpiece in architectural history listed in the World Cultural Heritage List.

In religion, Tibetans follow a form of Buddhism known as Lamaism or Tibetan Buddhism, and the grandest festival is New Year's Day in the Tibetan calendar, when people greet each other and go to temples to worship and pray for good fortune. On April 15th, religious ceremonies are held to commemorate the day when Sakyamuni became Buddha and Princess Wencheng reportedly reached Tibet.

概述
Introduction

中国是一个历史悠久、地域广阔、人口众多的国家。在长期的发展过程中，各民族形成了自己丰富多彩的风俗习惯：有衣、食、住、行方面的；有节庆、礼仪、祭祀方面的；有宗教信仰、民间崇拜方面的；也有婚姻、生育、丧葬方面的。这些风俗已经延续了千百年，成为不同民族各自保留的传统，其中有一些逐渐演化成为中华民族共同的风俗。

这里我们主要介绍汉族的一些风俗习惯。

China is a country with a long history, vast territory and a large population. In the long process of development, each ethnic group has formed various customs and habits of their own, covering clothing, food, living and transport; festive occasions, etiquette and offering sacrifices; religious beliefs and folk worship; and also marriage, giving birth and funerals. These customs have lasted for many centuries and become the traditions preserved by each ethnic group; some have gradually evolved into the common customs of the Chinese nation.

Here we mainly introduce some customs and habits of the Han ethnic group.

春节
The Spring Festival

农历的正 (zhēng) 月①初一，是中国的农历新年。在中国的传统节日中，这是一个最重要、最热闹的节日。因为过农历新年的时候，正是冬末春初，所以人们也把这个节日叫"春节"。

中国人过春节有很多传统习俗。从腊月二十三②起，人们就开始准备过年了。在这段时间里，家家户户要大扫除，买年货，贴窗花，挂年画③，写春联④，蒸年糕⑤，做好各种食品，准备辞旧迎新。

春节的前夜叫"除夕"。除夕之夜，是家人团聚的时候。一家人围坐在一起，吃一顿丰盛的年夜饭，说说笑笑，直到天亮，这叫守岁。除夕零点的钟声一响，人们还要吃饺子。古时候叫零点为"子时"，除夕的子时正是新旧年交替的时候，人们在这时吃饺子，是取"更岁交子"的意思。这也是"饺子"名称的由来。

过了除夕就是大年初一。从初一开始，人们要走亲戚、看朋友，互相拜年。拜年，是春节的重要习俗。拜年时，大家都要说一些祝愿幸福、健康的吉祥话。

放爆竹是春节期间孩子们最喜欢的活动。传说燃放爆竹可以驱妖除魔，所以每年从除夕之夜起，到处就响起了接连不断的爆竹声。阵阵烟花，声声爆竹，给节日增添了喜庆的气氛。

春节期间，很多地方还要举办庙会。庙会上精彩的舞龙舞狮表演，各式各样的工艺品和地方小吃，吸引着千千万万欢度佳节的人们。

随着时代的发展，过春节的习俗也有了

1. 中国人习惯贴窗花迎春节
   One of the traditional customs of Spring Festival is to decorate windows with paper-cuts.
2. 桃花是中国人最喜爱的年花
   Peach Blossom is a must-have during the Spring Festival.

2

一些变化。比如，为防止环境污染，很多城市已禁止燃放烟花爆竹。但这并不影响节日的热闹气氛。除夕之夜，家家户户仍然要团聚在一起，一边吃年夜饭，一边看精彩的电视节目，直到大年初一的清晨。

在中国和世界各地华夏子孙的心中，春节永远是最重要的节日。

The first day of the first lunar month is the New Year in the Chinese lunar calendar. Among the traditional Chinese festivals, this is the most important and the most bustling. Since it occurs at the end of winter and the beginning of spring, people also call it the Spring Festival.

Chinese have many traditional customs relating to the Spring Festival. Since the 23rd day of the 12th lunar month[1], people start to prepare for the event. Every family will undertake thorough cleaning, do their Spring Festival

🔍 小注解 Footnotes

① 正月：农历新年的第一个月。

② 腊月二十三：腊月是农历的十二月。腊月二十三是旧时祭灶王爷的日子。

③ 年画：中国民间过春节时，贴在房间里表现欢乐喜庆气氛的图画。

④ 春联：春节时，门上贴的写在红纸上的对联。

⑤ 年糕：用糯米粉蒸成的糕，是春节时吃的食品，取"年年高"之意。

shopping, create paper-cuts for window decoration, put up New Year pictures[2], write Spring Festival couplets[3], make New Year cakes[4], and also prepare all kinds of food to bid farewell to the old and usher in the new.

New Year's Eve is the time for a happy reunion of all family members, when they sit around the table to have a sumptuous New Year's Eve dinner, talking and laughing, until daybreak, which is called "staying up to see the year out". When the bell tolls midnight on New Year's Eve, people eat dumplings. In ancient times, midnight was called *zishi* (a period of the day from 11 p.m. to 1 a.m.). Dumplings (*jiaozi*) are eaten because it sounds the same as "change of the year and the day" in Chinese.

1

From the first day of the lunar year, people pay New Year calls on relatives and friends, which is an important custom for the Spring Festival.

Setting off firecrackers is the favorite activity of children in the

Spring Festival. According to legend, this could drive off evil spirits. The continuous sound of firecrackers can be heard everywhere, adding to the atmosphere of rejoicing and festivity.

Many places hold temple fairs. The wonderful dragon lantern dance and the lion dance performances, along with various handicraft articles and

local snacks attract thousands of people.

With the development of the times, some changes have taken place in the customs of spending the Spring Festival. For example, to prevent environmental pollution, many cities have banned firecrackers. But this does not have an impact on the happy atmosphere of the festival. On New Year's Eve, family members get together to have dinner while watching TV programs.

For Chinese at home and abroad, the Spring Festival is always the most important festival.

1. 苏州桃花坞年画：一团和气
   Suzhou's Taohuawu woodblock print depicting New Year
2. 陕北过年喜打腰鼓
   Spring Festival's Drum Dance, Northern Shaanxi
3. 木板雕刻年画
   Wood carving of the scene at Spring Festival
4. 反映民间风俗的年画
   The New Year picture depicting local customs

小注解 Footnotes

① According to the Chinese lunar calendar, one lunar month is the period of time (about 29.5 days) which the moon takes to go round the Earth.

② The 23rd day in the 12th lunar month was the day to offer sacrifices to the kitchen god in olden times.

③ The New Year pictures are those put up in the room for a happy and festive atmosphere when Chinese people spend the Spring Festival.

④ The Spring couplets are written on red paper and stuck on the door in the Spring Festival.

⑤ The New Year cake, made of glutinous rice flour, is a kind of food for the Spring Festival, meaning "higher year after year".

元宵节
The Lantern Festival

1

　　农历正月十五，是中国民间传统的元宵节。因为正月又叫元月，正月十五的晚上是一年里的第一个月圆之夜，"宵"是"夜晚"的意思，所以，正月十五的这个节日就叫元宵节。

　　元宵节，中国人有赏灯和吃元宵的习俗。俗话说"正月十五闹花灯"，因此，元宵节也叫灯节。

　　元宵节赏灯的习俗是从汉朝开始的，到现在已经有2,000多年的历史。元宵节这天，到处张灯结彩，热闹非常。夜晚一到，人们就成群结队地去观赏花灯。五光十色的宫灯、壁灯、人物灯、花卉灯、走马灯、动物灯、玩具灯……汇成一片灯海。有的花灯上还写有谜语，引得观灯人争先恐后地去竞猜。

元宵节吃元宵是中国人的传统习俗。早在1,000多年前的宋朝，就有这种食品了。元宵是一种用糯米粉做成的小圆球，里面包着用糖和各种果仁做成的馅，煮熟后，吃起来香甜可口。因为这种食品是在元宵节这天吃，后来人们就把它叫做元宵了。中国人希望诸事圆满，在一年开始的第一个月圆之夜吃元宵，就是希望家人团圆、和睦、幸福、圆圆满满。

The 15th day of the first lunar month is the traditional Lantern Festival (*Yuanxiao* in Chinese). The name comes from the fact that the first lunar month is also called *Yuanyue* and *xiao* means night. The night of the 15th day of the first lunar month marks the appearance of the first full moon.

It's a tradition to admire lanterns at the festival. The custom started from the Han Dynasty, and has a history of more than 2,000 years. On the night, every place is decorated with lanterns and colorful streamers and there is a bustling atmosphere. As night falls, people go in crowds to admire the colorful lanterns: Palace lanterns, wall lamps, figure lanterns, flower lanterns, revolving horse lanterns, animal lanterns, and toy lanterns, of all hues and colors, forming a sea of flickering light and color. Some lanterns have riddles on them, which encourage people to compete to find the answer.

It is also a traditional custom to eat rice dumplings at this time. As early as the Song Dynasty over 1,000 years ago, there was such kind of food. The rice dumpling is a round ball of glutinous rice flour filled with a stuffing made of sugar and different kernels. After it is boiled, it is very fragrant, sweet and tasty. Since it is eaten on the Lantern Festival, people call it "*Yuanxiao*". The Chinese people hope that everything is satisfactory ("*yuanman*" in Chinese), and to eat rice dumplings on the first night with a full moon in a year is to wish that family members will remain united, harmonious, happy and satisfied.

3

1. 北海灯会
   Lantern Festival in Beihai Park, Beijing
2. 元宵节吃元宵（南方人称汤圆）
   It is a Chinese traditional custom to eat rice dumplings at the Lantern Festival.
3. 元宵灯饰
   The Lanterns

2

清明节
The Pure Brightness Day

1

清明，是中国的二十四节气之一，也是中国一个古老的传统节日。清明节在农历三月（公历4月5日左右），此时正是春光明媚，空气洁净的季节，因此，这个节日叫做"清明节"。

清明节人们有扫墓祭祖和踏青插柳的习俗。

中国人有敬老的传统，对去世的先人更是缅怀和崇敬。因此，每到清明节这天，家家户户都要到郊外去祭扫祖先的坟墓。人们为坟墓除去杂草，添加新土，在坟前点上香，摆上食物和纸钱，表示对祖先的思念和敬意。这叫上坟，也叫扫墓。

清明时节，山野小草发芽，河边柳树长叶，到处一片新绿，正是户外游玩的好时候。古人有到郊外散步的习俗，这叫"踏青"；还要折根柳枝戴在头上，叫"插柳"。据说插柳可以驱除鬼怪和灾难，所以，人们纷纷插戴柳枝，祈求平安幸福。

现在，殡葬方式有了很大改变。实行火葬，废止土葬后，田野里的坟墓越来越少了。但是，清明节祭祖、踏青是中国人的传统习俗，每到这一天，人们还是会用各种各样的方式来怀念自己的祖先，也会到郊外呼吸新鲜空气，观赏蓝天、绿树、小草和鲜花。

清明时节雨纷纷，
路上行人欲断魂。
借问酒家何处有，
牧童遥指杏花村。

—— 唐 杜牧《清明》

44

Pure Brightness Day, one of the 24 Seasonal Division Points, is also an ancient traditional festival in China. It falls in the third lunar month or around April 5th in the solar calendar, when the spring scene is radiant and enchanting and the air is clean — hence, its name.

> *As the rain falls thick and fast on Pure Brightness Day,*
> *Men and women sadly move along the way.*
> *May I ask where I can find a pub?*
> *The shepherd boy pointed to the distant Apricot Village.*
> — Tang Dynasty Du Mu's *Pure Brightness*

1. 江苏兴化县居民在清明节举行划船竞渡，以纪念先人
   To show remembrance and respect to their ancestors, the residents of Xinghua County, Jiangsu Province, hold an annual boat race on the Pure Brightness Day.
2. 扫墓祭祖
   Paying respect to the ancestors on the Pure Brightness Day

On this day, people have the custom to sweep a grave, offer sacrifices to ancestors, take an outing in the countryside and wear a willow twig on the head.

The Chinese have the tradition to respect the aged, and cherish the memory of their forefathers and respect them. Thus, when the day comes, every family will go to the countryside to hold a memorial ceremony at their ancestors' tombs. People get rid of any weeds growing around the tomb, add new earth, burn incense and offer food and paper coins to show their remembrance and respect for their ancestors. This is called "visiting a grave", or "sweeping a grave".

At this time, the grasses in the countryside are burgeoning, willows along rivers have put forth new buds; it is fresh green everywhere, a good time for an outing. In ancient times, people used to wear a willow twig in their hair at this time because it was supposed to be able to drive away ghosts and disasters. Thus, people wear willow twigs to pray for safety and happiness.

Nowadays, great changes have taken place in regard to funerals and interment. Since cremation began to be carried out and burial was abolished, there are less and less graves in the fields. But it remains a custom for the Chinese to offer sacrifices to their ancestors and go for a walk in the countryside, remembering their forefathers, breathing fresh air and appreciating the blue sky, green trees, grass and flowers.

端午节
The Dragon Boat Festival

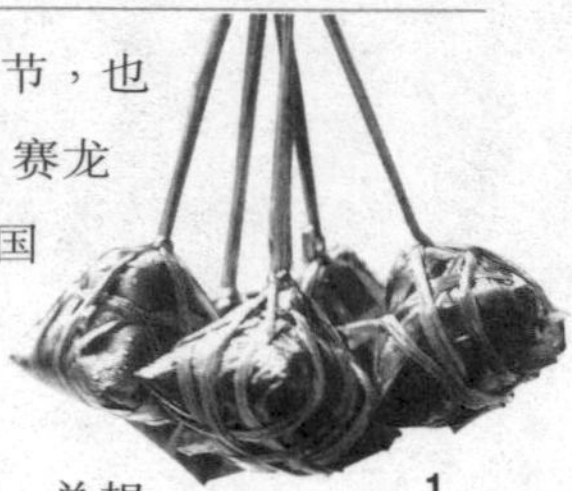

农历五月初五，是中国民间传统的端午节，也叫"五月节"。过端午节时，人们要吃粽子，赛龙舟。据说，举行这些活动，是为了纪念中国古代伟大的爱国诗人屈原①。

屈原是战国时期楚国人。战国时的齐、楚、燕、韩、赵、魏、秦七国中，秦国最强，总想吞并其他六国，称霸天下。屈原是楚国的大夫②(dàfū)，很有才能。他主张改革楚国政治，联合各国，共同抵抗秦国。但是，屈原的主张却遭到了奸佞的反对。楚王听信了谗言，不但不采纳屈原的主张，还把他赶出了楚国的国都。屈原离开国都后，仍然关心国家的命运。后来，他听到楚国被秦国打败的消息，非常悲痛，感到自己已经没有力量拯救祖国，就跳进汨(mì)罗江③自杀了。这一天正是公元前278年农历的五月初五。

人们听到屈原跳江的消息后，都划着船赶来打捞他的尸体，但始终没有找到。为了不让鱼虾吃掉屈原的身体，百姓们就把食

1

2

物扔进江中喂鱼。以后，每年五月初五人们都要这样做。后来，人们又改为用芦苇的叶子把糯米包成粽子扔进江里。于是，就形成了端午节吃粽子、赛龙舟的习俗。

The fifth day of the fifth lunar month is a traditional Chinese folk festival — the Dragon Boat Festival, also called the "Festival of the Fifth Month". On that day, people eat *zongzi* (pyramid-shaped dumpling made of glutinous rice wrapped in bamboo or reed leaves) and hold dragon-boat races. It is said, these activities commemorate the great patriotic poet Qu Yuan[1] in ancient China.

Qu Yuan lived in the State of Chu in the Warring States Period (475-221 BC). Among the states of Qi, Chu, Yan, Han, Zhao, Wei and Qin, the State of Qin was the strongest, and it wished to annex the others to become even more powerful. Qu Yuan was a *Dafu*[2]. He maintained that Chu's politics should be reformed and that it should unite with other states to resist Qin. But his stand was opposed by crafty sycophants, who used malicious accusations to persuade the king of Chu not to adopt the idea and to drive Qu Yuan from the capital. Despite being exiled, Qu Yuan was still concerned about the fate of the state. Later, when he heard the news that Qin had defeated the State of Chu, he was very grieved and felt that he had no power to save his motherland, and drowned himself in the Miluo River[3]. It was the fifth day of the fifth lunar month in 278 BC.

When people heard the news, they rowed their boats to try and find his corpse, but failed. In order not to let the fish and shrimps eat the corpse, people threw food into the river to feed them. Thereafter, on each fifth day of the fifth lunar month, people would throw food into the river. And later, people used reed leaves to wrap glutinous rice into pyramid-shaped dumplings (*zongzi*) for this purpose. Thus the custom of eating *zongzi* and staging dragon-boat race was formed.

🔍 小注解 Footnotes

① 屈原（约公元前340－公元前278年）：名平，是中国历史上第一个有名的大诗人。
② 大夫：古代官职。
③ 泊罗江：江名，发源于江西，流入湖南。

① Qu Yuan (about 340 - 278 BC), with a given name Ping, was the first famous poet in Chinese history.
② *Dafu* was an ancient official title.
③ The Miluo River originates in Jiangxi Province and ends in Hunan Province.

1. 粽子
   Zongzi
2. 龙舟比赛
   Dragon Boat Race
3. 湖北秭归屈原祠
   The Memorial Temple of Qu Yuan in Hubei Province

中秋节
The Mid-Autumn Festival

农历八月十五，是中国的传统节日中秋节。

按照中国的历法，农历七八九三个月是秋季。八月是秋季中间的一个月，八月十五又是八月中间的一天，所以这个节日叫"中秋节"。中秋节这天，中国人有赏月和吃月饼的习俗。

秋季，天气晴朗、凉爽，天上很少出现浮云，夜空中的月亮也显得特别明亮。八月十五的晚上，是月圆之夜，成了人们赏月的最好时光。人们把圆月看作团圆美满的象征，所以中秋节又叫"团圆节"。

按照传统习惯，中国人在赏月时，还要摆出瓜果和月饼等食品，一边赏月一边品尝。因为月饼是圆的，象征着团圆，所以有的地方也叫它"团圆饼"。中国月饼的品种很多，各地的制法也不相同。月饼馅有甜的、咸的、荤的、素的，月饼上面还印着各种花纹和字样，真是又好看、又好吃。

秋天，人们一年的劳动有了收获。中秋节的晚上，全家人坐在一起赏月、吃月饼，心里充满了丰收的喜悦和团聚的欢乐。这时，远离家乡的人，也会仰望明月，思念故乡和亲人。

自古以来，中国就有很多关于月亮的神话传说，其中最有名的是"嫦娥奔月"。嫦娥是中国古代神话传说中后羿 (yì) 的妻子。据说她偷吃了从西王母那里得到的长生不老之药，成了仙，飞上了月宫。

The 15th day of the eighth lunar month is China's traditional Mid-Autumn Festival.

According to the Chinese lunar calendar, the lunar eighth, ninth and 10th months make up autumn. The eighth month falls in mid-autumn, and the 15th day is in the middle of the month, hence the name "Mid-Autumn Festival". On that day, the Chinese have the custom to admire the moon and eat moon cakes.

1. 中秋放灯笼
   People showing off their lanterns on the Mid-Autumn Festival
2. 中秋舞火龙，祈求驱瘟，保佑民众
   It is believed that performing the Fire Dragon Dance on the Mid-Autumn Festival can bring blessings and drive away plagues.
3. 嫦娥奔月
   Chang'e flying to the moon

In autumn, it is fine and cool, there are few floating clouds in the sky and the moon at night seems particularly bright. This is especially true on the 15th day of the eighth lunar month. Since people consider the full moon as the symbol of reunion and satisfaction, the festival is also called "the Festival for Reunion".

According to traditional custom, Chinese people enjoy fruits and moon cakes while admiring the moon. As the moon cake is round, symbolizing reunion, it is sometimes called "Reunion Cake". The Chinese moon cake has many varieties and production methods differ from place to place. There are sweet, salty, meat and vegetable fillings. It is carved with various patterns and words.

In autumn, people reap the results of their year's labor. On the night of the Mid-Autumn Festival, the whole family will sit together to admire the moon and eat moon cakes, filled with happiness for the bumper harvest and a family reunion. At that time, people far away from hometown will also look up at the moon and miss their hometown and family members.

Since ancient times, China has had many fairy tales and legends about the moon, among which the most famous is "Chang'e Flying to the Moon". Chang'e was the wife of Houyi in ancient Chinese myths. Legend has it that she swallowed an elixir stolen from the Grand Old Lady of the West, became an immortal and flew to the moon palace.

重阳节
The Double-Ninth Festival

农历九月初九是重阳 (chóngyáng) 节。这是一个很古老的节日，距今已有1,700多年的历史。

在中国数字中，一、三、五、七、九为阳数，二、四、六、八为阴数。因此，九月初九被称作重阳或重九。中国古代，重阳节是一个重要的节日，这一天要举行各种活动，如：登高、赏菊、插茱萸 (zhūyú)、吃重阳糕等。

登高是重阳节的主要习俗。

> 独在异乡为异客，
> 每逢佳节倍思亲。
> 遥知兄弟登高处，
> 遍插茱萸少一人。
> ——唐 王维
> 《九月九日忆山东兄弟》

古人认为，九九重阳，登高可以避祸免灾。后来，重阳节登高爬山，逐渐演变成了人们放松心情、锻炼身体的体育和旅游活动。

插茱萸和赏菊也是重阳节的传统习俗。茱萸是一种植物，果实可以吃，茎、叶都是药材。菊花在九月盛开，有"长寿花"的美称。为了避免瘟疫，驱除恶气，重阳节这天，人们就把茱萸和菊花插戴在身上，还要观赏菊花，饮菊花茶和菊花酒。

重阳糕是一种用面粉做的食品，可以加枣、银杏、松子、杏仁做成甜的，也可以加肉做成咸的，讲究的还要做成九层，再在上面做两只小羊，以谐"重阳(羊)"之音。

现在过重阳节，已经见不到插茱萸等风俗了，但是很多人仍然会在这一天登高赏菊，观赏秋天的美景。近年来，这个古老的节日又增加了新的内容，成为一年一度的"敬老节"。每当佳节来临，人们都要举办各种敬老活动，祝愿老年人步步登高，健康长寿。

The Double-Ninth Festival falls on the ninth day of the ninth lunar month and has a history of more than 1,700 years.

Among Chinese numbers, one, three, five, seven and nine are positive numbers and two, four, six and eight are negative ones. Thus, the ninth day of the ninth lunar month is called Double-Positive or Double-Nine. The Double-Ninth Festival sees various activities such as climbing a mountain, admiring chrysanthemums, wearing cornel (*Cornus officinalis*) and eating Double-Ninth cake, etc.

Ancient people thought climbing a mountain on this day could help them avoid misfortune and prevent disasters, and this gradually evolved into a relaxation and exercise.

It is also the traditional custom to wear cornel and admire chrysanthemums. Cornel is a kind of plant with edible fruit, while its stem and leaves have medicinal value. Chrysanthemum blooms in September, and enjoys the reputation of a "Flower of Longevity". To prevent plague and drive off foul smells,

> *As an alien visitor in a strange land all by myself,*
> *I think all the more of my loved ones on every festive occasion.*
> *I know in the far away that when my brothers climb the mountain,*
> *All wear cornel but one person is absent.*
>
> — Tang Dynasty Wang Wei's
> *Missing Brothers in Shandong on the Double-Ninth Day*

people wear cornel and chrysanthemum on the Double-Ninth Festival, and drink tea and wine made from the flowers.

Made of flour, the Double-Ninth cake can be sweet if jujube, ginkgo, pine nuts and apricot kernel are added, or salty if meat is added. Some exquisite cakes are made into nine layers with a pattern of two sheep above, which is homophonic of "Double Ninth".

There is no longer any custom of wearing cornel on the Double-Ninth Festival, but many people will climb a mountain, admire chrysanthemums and appreciate the beautiful scenery of autumn. In recent years, new contents have been added into this ancient festival, which has become a time to show respect for the elderly. People hold various activities in honor of senior citizens, wishing them good health and a long life.

1. 传说重阳节登高可避祸免火
   Ancient people thought that climbing a mountain on the Double-Ninth Festival could help them avoid misfortune.
2. 赏菊是重阳节的传统习俗
   It is a traditional custom to admire chrysanthemums on Double-Ninth Festival.

二十四节气
The 24 Seasonal Division Points

按照中国农历的纪年法，每个月都有两个节气，一年共有24个节气。

节气是中国农历特有的，是中国劳动人民的创造。古人在长期的生产劳动中，逐渐认识了气候变化的规律，他们根据太阳和地球的相互关系，把一年的天数分成24等分，用来表示季节和气候的变化。这样，差不多每15天就有一个节气，每个月就有两个节气了。二十四节气在公历中的日期几乎是固定的，上半年（1～6月）的节气都在每个月的6日和21日前后；下半年（7～12月）的节气都在每个月的8日和23日前后。

二十四节气的名称分别是：立春、雨水、惊蛰(zhé)、春分、清明、谷雨、立夏、小满、芒种(zhòng)、夏至、小暑、大暑、立秋、处暑、白露(lù)、秋分、寒露、霜降、立冬、小雪、大雪、冬至、小寒、大寒。

立春、立夏、立秋、立冬　表示四季的开始。

春分、秋分　是一年中昼夜一样长的两天。

夏至　是一年中白天最长、黑夜最短的一天。

冬至　是一年中白天最短、黑夜最长的一天。

雨水　是开始下雨的意思。

惊蛰　表示春雷响过以后，冬眠的昆虫被惊醒了。

清明　是说春天到了以后，明净的春色代替了冬季寒冷枯黄的景色。

谷雨　表示从此雨水增多，对五谷的生长很有好处。

小满　表示在夏季成熟的农作物籽粒开始饱满了。

芒种　告诉人们小麦已经成熟了。

小暑、大暑　表示天气炎热的程度，大暑是一年中最热的时候。

处暑　表示炎热的天气快要过去了。

白露　告诉人们开始下露水，天气就要冷了。

寒露　表明露水已重，天寒加剧。

霜降 是开始下霜的意思。

小雪、大雪 表示到了下雪的时节和雪量大小的差别。

小寒、大寒 表示冬天寒冷的程度，大寒是一年中最冷的时候。

二十四节气对中国的农业生产起着很大的作用，人们为了方便记忆，还编出了《二十四节气歌》：

春雨惊春清谷天，夏满芒夏暑相连，

秋处露秋寒霜降，冬雪雪冬小大寒。

上半年是六、二一，下半年是八、二三。

According to the way of numbering the years in Chinese lunar calendar, there are two seasonal division points in each month, making 24 in a year.

The seasonal division points are peculiar to China. In the long period of productive labor, ancient men gradually realized the rule of climate change. According to the relationship between the sun and the earth, they divided all

1. 春
   Spring
2. 夏
   Summer

the days in a year into 24 parts to indicate the change of seasons and climate. Thus, there is a seasonal divisional point about every 15 days; those in the first half of the year (from January to June) all fall around the sixth or 21st day of the month, and those in the latter half of the year (from July to December), on about the eighth or 23rd day of the month.

The names for the 24 seasonal division points are: Beginning of Spring, Rain Water, Waking of Insects, Vernal Equinox, Pure Brightness, Grain Rain, Beginning of Summer, Grain Budding, Grain in Ear, Summer Solstice, Slight Heat, Great Heat, Beginning of Autumn, Limit of Heat, White Dew, Autumnal Equinox, Cold Dew, Frost's Descent, Beginning of Winter, Slight Snow, Great Snow, Winter Solstice, Slight Cold, and Great Cold, respectively.

The **Beginning of Spring, Beginning of Summer, Beginning of Autumn** and **Beginning of Winter** mark the start of four seasons. The **Vernal Equinox** and the **Autumnal Equinox** are the two points where the day and night are equal;

The **Summer Solstice** has the longest day and shortest night in a year, while the opposite is true for the **Winter Solstice**.

The **Rain Water** means the start of the spring rains. The **Waking of Insects** indicates that the spring thunder awakens hibernating insects.

The **Pure Brightness** means the onset of spring when a bright and clean spring scene replaces the cold, withered and yellow scene in winter.

The **Grain Rain** indicates that from that day, there will be more rainfall, which is beneficial to the growth of crops.

The **Grain Budding** shows that crops that will ripen in summer start to show plump seeds.

The **Grain in Ear** tells people that the wheat has ripened.

The **Slight Heat** and **Great Heat** indicate the full onset of summer, with the Great Heat being the hottest day of the year.

The **Limit of Heat** shows that scorching summer days will soon be gone.

1. 秋
   Autumn
2. 冬
   Winter

The **White Dew** tells people that dew appears in the morning to show that the weather is turning cold, and, as this intensifies, we move on to the **Cold Dew**.

The **Frost's Descent** means the appearance of the first frost of the season.

The **Slight Snow** and **Great Snow** mean the arrival of the snowy season.

The **Slight Cold** and **Great Cold** indicate the degree of coldness in winter, with the Great Cold being the coldest day of the season.

The 24 seasonal division points have great influence on China's farming. For the convenience of memory, people compiled the *Song for the 24 Seasonal Division Points*:

Following the Beginning of Spring and Rain Water, the Waking of Insects awakens the Vernal Equinox, and then comes the Pure Brightness and Grain Rain,

2

Beginning of Summer, Grain Budding, Grain in Ear, Summer Solstice, Slight Heat, Great Heat, Beginning of Autumn, Limit of Heat, White Dew, Autumnal Equinox, Cold Dew, Frost's Descent, Beginning of Winter, Slight Snow, Great Snow, Winter Solstice, Slight Cold, and Great Cold, respectively.

After the Beginning of Summer, Grain Budding, Grain in Ear, and Summer Solstice, the Slight Heat is connected with Great Heat.

The Beginning of Autumn and Limit of Heat is followed by the White Dew, Autumnal Equinox, Cold Dew and then the Frost's Descent,

And the Beginning of Winter leads to the Slight Snow, Great Snow, Winter Solstice, Slight Cold and Great Cold.

In the first half of the year, the seasonal division points fall on the sixth or 21st day of the month,

And those in the latter half year occur on the eighth or 23rd day of the month.

十二属相
Twelve Symbolic Animals

中国民间有一个传统习俗，人一出生，就有一种动物作他的属相。属相，也叫"生肖"（shēngxiào），是中国民间传统的纪年和计算年龄的方法。

按照世界通用的公历纪年，只要说出公历某某年就可以了，如：公元2002年。但中国农历的纪年法与此不同。中国古人发明了用"干支"纪年的方法。"干"是"天干"，由10个字组成，这10个字是：甲、乙、丙、丁、戊（wù）、己、庚（gēng）、辛、壬（rén）、癸（guǐ）。"支"是"地支"，由12个字组成，这12个字是：子、丑、寅（yín）、卯（mǎo）、辰（chén）、巳（sì）、午、未、申、酉（yǒu）、戌（xù）、亥（hài）。把天干的10个字和地支的12个字按顺序配合起来，可以组成60对纪年的符号，如：甲子、乙丑、丙寅……这60对符号周而复始，循环使用，每一年就有了一个纪年符号。如公历的2001年，是农历的辛巳年。公历的2002年，就是农历的壬午年。后来，人们又用鼠、牛、虎、兔、龙、蛇、马、羊、猴、鸡、狗、猪12种动物来配十二地支，组成了十二生肖，也叫十二属相。这就是：子鼠、丑牛、寅虎、卯兔、辰龙、巳蛇、午马、未羊、申猴、酉鸡、戌狗、亥猪。这样，子年就是鼠年，丑年就是牛年，寅年就是虎年……于是，每个人一出生，就有一种动物作他的属相。子年出生的属鼠，丑年出生的属牛，寅年出生的属虎……2002年是农历壬午年，就是马年，这一年出生的孩子应该属马。

现在，中国人在用公历纪年和计算年龄的同时，仍然习惯用属相纪年和推算年龄。人们只要知道一个人大概的年龄和他的属相，就能推算出他的准确年龄和出生年份了。

It is traditional in China, when a person is born, that one animal (*shuxiang*) is used to symbolize this year. *Shuxiang*, also called *shengxiao* (any of the 12 animals representing the Earthly Branches), is a traditional way in China to number the years and to record a person's age.

Under the Gregorian calendar commonly used in the world, the year can be expressed by the progression since the start of the Christian era (e.g. 2002 AD). But the Chinese lunar calendar numbers the years in a different way. Ancient Chinese people invented the method to designate the years by the Heavenly Stems and Earthly Branches. The Heavenly Stems consist of ten words: *jia* (Heavenly Stem One), *yi* (Heavenly Stem Two), *bing* (Heavenly Stem Three), *ding* (Heavenly Stem Four), *wu* (Heavenly Stem Five), *ji* (Heavenly Stem Six), *geng* (Heavenly Stem Seven), *xin* (Heavenly Stem Eight), *ren* (Heavenly Stem Nine), and *gui* (Heavenly Stem Ten). And the Earthly Branches are composed of 12 words: *zi* (Earthly Branch One), *chou* (Earthly Branch Two), *yin* (Earthly Branch Three), *mao* (Earthly Branch Four), *chen* (Earthly Branch Five), *si* (Earthly Branch Six), *wu* (Earthly Branch Seven), *wei* (Earthly Branch Eight), *shen* (Earthly Branch Nine), *you* (Earthly Branch Ten), *xu* (Earthly Branch Eleven), and *hai* (Earthly Branch Twelve). Combining each of the 10 Heavenly Stems with one of the 12 Earthly Branches in sequence creates 60 chronological symbols. For example, *jiazi* (Heavenly Stem One Earthly Branch One), *yichou* (Heavenly Stem Two Earthly Branch Two), *bingyin* (Heavenly Stem Three Earthly Branch Three), etc. These 60 symbols are used in circles and thus each year has a chronological symbol. For example, 2001 corresponds to *xinsi*, 2002 to *renwu* in the lunar calendar. Later, people used 12 animals (rat, ox, tiger, rabbit, dragon, snake, horse, sheep, monkey, rooster, dog and pig) to correspond to the 12 Earthly Branches, forming the 12 Symbolic Animals, namely, Earthly Branch One — Rat, Earthly Branch Two — Ox, Earthly Branch Three — Tiger, Earthly Branch Four — Rabbit, Earthly Branch Five — Dragon, Earthly Branch Six — Snake, Earthly Branch Seven — Horse, Earthly Branch Eight — Sheep, Earthly Branch Nine — Monkey, Earthly Branch Ten — Rooster, Earthly Branch Eleven — Dog, and Earthly Branch Twelve — Pig. Thus the *zi* Year is the Year of the Rat, and the *chou* Year is the Year of the Ox, and the *yin* Year is the Year of the Tiger, etc. Therefore, when a person is born, he has an animal as his symbolic animal. The year 2002 was a *renwu* year under lunar calendar, also the Year of Horse, and so children born in this year are all Horse babies.

Even though Chinese people now number the years and their age under the Gregorian calendar, they still continue to use the symbolic animals. As long as people know a person's probable age and his symbolic animal, people can infer his exact age and year of birth.

鼠
Rat

马
Horse

牛
Ox

羊
Sheep

虎
Tiger

猴
Monkey

兔
Rabbit

鸡
Rooster

龙
Dragon

狗
Dog

蛇
Snake

猪
Pig

四灵——
古代吉祥的象征
Four Deities — Symbol of
Auspice in Ancient Times

1

中国古代认为麒麟（qílín）、凤凰、龟和龙是有灵性的动物，因此，把它们称为"四灵"，作为祥瑞的标志。其实，除了龟以外，其他三种都是传说中的动物，是人们自己想像和创造出来的。

传说中的麒麟，身体像鹿，遍体披着鳞甲，头上长独角，角上生有肉球，脚像马蹄，尾像牛尾。麒麟被认为是有德性的仁兽，历代帝王都把它看作是太平盛世的象征。在北京的故宫和颐和园等皇帝的住处和花园里，都能见到麒麟，有铜铸的，也有石雕的。在民间，麒麟也很受重视。春节期间，中国江南各地的人们常常抬着纸扎的麒麟，到各家门前表演，表达美好的祝愿。另外，在中国还有"麒麟送子"的传说，人们一方面用麒麟象征有出息的子孙；另一方面也表示了祈望早生贵子、家道繁荣的意思。

凤凰头顶美丽的羽冠，身披五彩翎毛，它是综合了许多鸟兽的特点想像出来的瑞鸟形象。凤凰是中国传说中的"百鸟之王"，标志着吉祥、太平和政治的清明。凤和龙一样，被历代帝王当作是权力和尊严的象征。凤冠、凤车等与凤有关的东西，只有皇家和仙人才能使用。不过，后来凤凰也成了民间百姓的吉祥物。尤其在中国传统的婚礼上，凤成了新娘礼服和头饰上的装饰，代表着吉祥和喜庆。在民间的传统图案纹样中，凤凰也被广泛应用，寓意着吉祥和太平。凤凰还常和其他吉祥物配合成纹图，如"龙凤呈祥"、"凤麒呈祥"等，也是吉祥如意的象征。

龟在四灵中是惟一存在的动物，也是动物中寿命最长的。人们不仅把龟当成健康长寿的象征，还认为它具有预知未来的灵性。在古代，每当举行重大活动之前，巫师都要烧烤龟甲，然后根据龟甲上爆裂的纹路来占卜吉凶。所以，人们称龟为"神龟"、"灵龟"。神龟在中国曾经受到过极大的尊敬，在古代帝王的皇宫、宅院里，都有石雕或铜铸的神龟，用来象征国运的久远。

龙被人们认为是中国最大的神物，也是最大的吉祥物。人们都很熟悉龙的形象，但是谁也没见过真的龙。龙和凤、麒麟一样，是人们想像出来的动物，它长着牛头、鹿角、虾眼、鹰爪、蛇身、狮尾，通身还长满了鳞甲，是由多种动物复合而成的。在人们的想像中，龙能在地上行走，能在水中游弋，能在云中飞翔，充满了无穷的神力。几千年来，封建帝王把它当作权力和尊严的象征，普通老百姓也认为它是美德和力量的化身，是吉祥之物。因此，在中国到处都可以见到龙的形象。宫殿、寺庙的屋脊上，皇家的用具上，处处刻着龙、画着龙；老百姓在喜庆的日子里，也要张贴龙的图案，还要舞龙灯、划龙船；给孩子起名字也愿意用上"龙"字。龙作为"四灵"中最大的吉祥物，已成为中华民族的象征。全世界各地的中国人都认为自己是"龙的传人"。

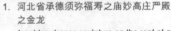

1. 河北省承德须弥福寿之庙妙高庄严殿之金龙
   A golden dragon sculpture on the roof of a temple in Hebei Province
2. 皇帝大典时穿的龙袍
   This silk dragon embroidered robe is worn by the emperor on the day of enthronement.
3. 被称为"百鸟之王"的凤凰
   The phoenix is known as the "King of Birds".

1. 明十三陵的墓道两旁分列着麒麟等石兽
   The stone sculptures of kylins and sagacious animals flank both sides of the pathway which leads to the Thirteen Tombs of the Ming Dynasty.
2. 龟象征长寿
   The tortoise symbolizes health and longevity.
3. 龙
   The Dragon
4. 明世宗嘉靖皇帝的陵墓前的龙凤石雕
   The mausoleum of Emperor Jiajing of Ming Dynasty (1368-1644 AD) is decorated with stone sculpture of phoenix and dragon.

In ancient China, people considered the kylin, the phoenix, the tortoise and the dragon as sagacious animals, calling them the "Four Deities" as the symbol of propitious omen. In fact, besides the tortoise, the other three are legendary animals created by ancient Chinese.

The legendary kylin has a deer's body covered all over with scales, one horn on the head, horse's feet and an ox's tail. It is considered as an animal of morals and benevolence and all previous monarchs considered it symbolic of times of peace and prosperity. The kylin can be found in the emperor's dwellings and gardens in the Imperial Palace and the Summer Palace in Beijing, either made of copper or stone. The Chinese people also think highly of the kylin. In the Spring Festival, people living south of the Yangtze River often carry a paper kylin to express their best wishes to others. There is also a legend of "Kylin Sending a Son" in China: On one side, people use the kylin to symbolize promising descendents; and on the other, they wish to have a son soon and see the family flourish.

The phoenix wears a beautiful crest and multi-colored plumage; it is an imagined auspicious bird combining features of many birds and animals. The phoenix is the "King of Birds" in Chinese legends, indicating auspiciousness, peace and good government. Just like the dragon, the phoenix was considered a symbol of power and dignity by ancient monarchs. The phoenix coronet, phoenix cart and anything related to the phoenix could only be

2

used by the royal family and immortals. However, later the phoenix also became the mascot of ordinary people. Particularly in traditional Chinese weddings, the phoenix becomes an ornament on the bride's wedding dress and headdress, representing auspiciousness and festive rejoicing. The phoenix is also widely used on traditional decorative patterns among Chinese people, implying auspiciousness and peace. The phoenix is often used with other mascots to form new patterns, such as "Prosperity Brought by the Dragon and the Phoenix" and "Prosperity Brought by the Phoenix and the Kylin", also symbolizing that everything is as lucky as one would wish.

The tortoise is the only existing animal among the four deities, and also the animal enjoying the longest life. People not only see the tortoise as a symbol of health and longevity, but also believe that it has the sagacity to foresee the future. In ancient times, before important activities were held, a wizard would roast a tortoise shell and then practice divination according to the way the lines split on it. Therefore, people call the tortoise the "divine tortoise" or "sagacious tortoise". The divine tortoise was highly respected in ancient China. In the imperial palace and residences of ancient monarchs, there were stone or copper tortoises to symbolize the longevity of the national destiny.

The dragon is considered the largest divine animal in China, and its most popular mascot. In this case, the dragon has an ox head, deer's horn, shrimp's eyes, eagle's claws, snake's body and lion's tail; its body is covered with scales, and it is really a combination of many animals. As people imagine, the dragon can walk on land, swim in water, and fly in the clouds, with inexhaustible magical power. For thousands of years, feudal monarchs held it as the symbol of power and dignity, and ordinary people believed that it was embodiment of virtue and strength. Thus, the dragon can be found everywhere in China. The roofs of palaces and temples, and the furniture of the royal family were all carved or drawn with a dragon. On festive occasions, ordinary people put up pictures of the dragon, dance with a dragon lantern and row a dragon boat. People like to name their children with the Chinese character of the dragon. The dragon has become the symbol of the Chinese nation. And all the Chinese throughout the world think themselves as the "offspring of the dragon".

吉祥图案
Auspicious Patterns

在中国民间，流传着许多含有吉祥意义的图案。每到年节或喜庆的日子，人们都喜欢用这些吉祥图案装饰自己的房间和物品，以表示对幸福生活的向往，对良辰佳节的庆贺。

中国的吉祥图案始于距今3,000多年前的周代，后来在民间流传开来。今天，吉祥图案仍然是中国人生活中不可缺少的内容。

中国的吉祥图案内容极其广泛，这里介绍最常见的几种：

"**双喜**"字，是双喜临门、大吉大利的意思，民间常在办喜事时采用。

"**寿**"字，字头经过加工美化，变成对称的图案，是长寿的意思。

"**福寿双全**"，是由蝙蝠和寿字组成的图案。"蝠"与"福"同音，表示幸福长寿。

两个"**有**"字组成的对称图案，意思是顺也有，倒也有。在中国农村常用来贴在收藏谷物的器具上，表示丰收富裕。

"**如意头**"，象征顺遂如意。

"**百吉**"，也叫"**盘长**"。它无头无尾，无始无终，可以想像为许多个"结"，谐"百吉"之音，作为百事吉祥如意的象征，也有福寿延绵、永无休止的意思。

"**五福捧寿**"，图案中五个蝙蝠环绕着一个寿字。五福是长寿、富贵、康宁、道德、善终。

"**四合如意**"，四个如意从四面围拢勾连起来，象征诸事如意。

1. 中国人在办喜事时多贴上 "囍" 字
   Chinese people like to decorate celebration events with the pattern of double happiness.
2. "福" 字图
   The pattern of good fortune
3. "寿" 字图
   The pattern of longevity

In China, many auspicious patterns are popular. On the occasion of the New Year, festivals or festive days, people like to decorate their rooms and articles with such auspicious patterns, expressing their desire for a happy life and celebrations on a propitious time and festive day.

These patterns emerged in the Zhou Dynasty more than 3,000 years ago, and then became popular among the Chinese people. Nowadays, they are still an indispensable part of Chinese life.

These auspicious patterns cover a wide range, and here are several commonly seen:

The pattern of **double happiness** means that two happy events occur at the same time, representing extreme auspiciousness. People often use this pattern when celebrating their weddings.

After being embellished, the Chinese character of **longevity** (寿) became a symmetrical pattern.

The pattern of **good fortune** (福) and **longevity** (寿) is composed of the character of bats (蝠) and longevity (寿). Since the pronunciation of the bat is homophonic to that of good fortune (福), this pattern indicates good fortune and longevity.

The symmetrical pattern consisting of two 有 (**possession**) means that there is 有 when the pattern is upright or viewed upside down. In China's rural areas, the pattern is often pasted on utensils for storing corns, meaning a bumper harvest and prosperity.

The pattern of the **head of ruyi** (an S-shaped wand or scepter, usually made of jade) symbolizes smoothness and good fortune.

The pattern of **baiji** (one hundred luck) is also called **panchang**. It has no beginning and no end, and thus can be conceived as many knots (结), whose pronunciation of the Chinese character is homophonic to that of 吉 (luck), symbolizing one hundred events are lucky and auspicious and also indicating happiness and longevity are continuous without end.

In the pattern of "**five good-fortunes holding longevity in the center**", five bats encircle a Chinese character 寿. The five sectors of good fortune are longevity, wealth and rank, health, morality, and a natural death.

In the pattern of "**four ruyi enclosing each other**", four *ruyi* are enclosed and connected with each other on four sides, symbolizing everything goes as one wishes.

3

中国人的姓名
Names of Chinese People

　　中国人的姓产生在母系氏族社会，那时候，人们以母亲为中心组成一个个的氏族，为了相互区别，就把姓作为氏族的称号。

　　姓的来源，大概有以下几种情况：一、母系氏族社会，以母亲的名为姓，所以，很多古姓都有"女"字旁，如姜（jiāng）、姚（yáo）、姬（ji）等，就连"姓"字本身也是由"女"、"生"二字合成的。二、以远古时代人们崇拜的生物为姓，如马、牛、羊、龙等。三、以祖先的国家为姓，如赵、宋、秦、吴等。四、以祖先的官职为姓，如司马、司徒等古代官职，就成了后代子孙的姓。五、以祖先的爵（jué）位①为姓，如王、侯（hóu）等。六、以住地的方位和景物为姓，如东郭②、西门、池、柳等。七、以职业为姓，如做陶器的人姓陶。八、以祖先的名号为姓，如中国人的祖先黄帝名叫轩辕，后来，轩辕就成了一个姓。

　　中国人的姓有一个字的，也有两个字和两个字以上的。一个字的是单姓，两个字或两个字以上的是复姓。中国到底有多少个姓，

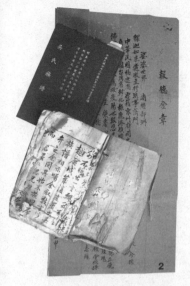

到现在也没有准确的统计数字。宋朝时，有个读书人写了一本《百家姓》，里面收有500多个姓，其中60个是复姓。近日，中国科学院遗传与发育生物学研究所研究人员经过多年的收集和研究，结果发现中国人古今姓氏已超过22,000个，这是至今有关中国人姓氏最多的统计记录。当代中国人正在使用的汉姓约有3,500个左右。在其中100个常见姓氏中，全国最大的三个姓氏是李、王、张，诸葛、欧阳、司徒、司马等是中国最常见的复姓。

1. 广州陈家祠，是陈姓望族的家祠
   Chen's ancestral temple, Guangzhou
2. 台湾吴氏的族谱
   The genealogical table of the Wu clan of Taiwan
3. 姓氏源牌
   The list of Chinese surnames

中国人的名也具有自己的传统和特点。中国人的姓名都是姓在前，名在后。名有一个字的，也有两个字的。同一家族中的人，名字要按辈份排列，同辈人的名字里，往往要有一个相同的字。古人的姓名比现代人的复杂，有文化、有地位的人除了姓、名以外，还有字和号。如：宋代文学家苏轼(shì)，姓苏，名轼，字子瞻(zhān)，号东坡。唐代诗人李白幼年时居住在四川的青莲乡，他就给自己取号"青莲居士"。

中国人的名字往往有一定的含义，表示某种愿望。有的名字中包含着出生时的地点，时间或自然现象，如"京"、"晨"、"冬"、"雪"等。有的名字表示希望具有某种美德，如"忠"、"义"、"礼"、"信"等。有的名字中有表示希望健康、长寿、幸福的意思，如"健"、"寿"、"松"、"福"等。男人的名字和女人的名字也不一样，男人的名字多用表示威武勇猛的字，如"虎"、"龙"、"雄"、"伟"、"刚"、"强"等。女人的名字常用表示温柔美丽的字，如"凤"、"花"、"玉"、"彩"、"娟"、"静"等。

现在，中国人起名已经没有古人那么多的讲究了。一般只有小名③、大名④，名字也不一定按辈份排列了。

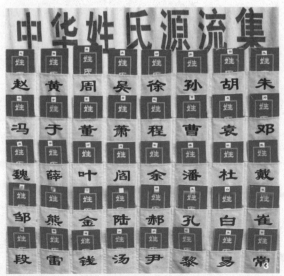

The surnames of Chinese people appeared during the matriarchal society, when clans were constituted with mothers at the center. And clans distinguished themselves from each other by using the name.

The surname has roughly several origins as follows: 1. With the first name of the mother as the surname of the clan in matriarchal society. Thus, many ancient surnames have a basic structural part of 女 (meaning "female"), such as 姜, 姚, and 姬, and the Chinese character for surname 姓 is also composed of 女 and 生 (meaning "giving birth to)". 2. With the creatures worshipped in remote antiquity as the surname, such as 马 (horse), 牛 (cattle), 羊 (sheep), 龙 (dragon), etc. 3. With ancient states' names as the surname, such as 赵 (Zhao), 宋 (Song), 秦 (Qin), 吴 (Wu), etc. 4. With ancient official titles eventually adopted as the surname, such as 司马 (Sima) and 司徒 (Situ). 5. With the rank or title of nobility[①] as the surname, such as 王 (prince) and 侯 (marquis). 6. With the location and scene in residential places as the surname. For example, 东郭[②], 西门 (western gate), 池 (pond), 柳 (willow), etc. 7. With the profession as the surname. For instance the person who makes pottery has the surname of 陶 (pottery). 8. With ancestors' official and courtesy names as the surname. For example, the Chinese nation's ancestor was named 轩辕 (Xuanyuan), which later became a surname.

Up to now, there is no exact statistic on how many surnames there are in China. In the Song Dynasty, an intellectual wrote the *Book of China's Family Names*, covering more than 500 surnames among which over 60 are compound ones. Having collected material and researched for many years, research personnel in the Research Institute of Genetics and Development Biology in the Academy of Sciences recently found that the surnames of the Chinese from ancient times to the present exceeded 22,000. Contemporary Chinese use about 3,500 Chinese surnames. Among the 100 commonly used surnames, the commonest are Li, Wang and Zhang, and Zhuge, Ouyang,

小注解 Footnotes

① 爵位：君主国家封贵族的等级。
② 东郭：中国姓氏之一。郭：古代在城的周边加筑的一道城墙。古人以住的地方为姓，于是就有了郭，东郭、南郭等姓。
③ 小名：小时候起的非正式的名字，也叫乳名。
④ 大名：正式的名字。

① Rank or title of nobility is used to rank nobles in monarchical states.
② 东郭 is one of Chinese surnames. 郭 (Guo) was the outer wall of a city in ancient times. Ancient people had their residence as the surname, thus came 郭, 东郭 (East outer wall), and 南郭 (South outer wall).
③ The infant name is an informal name for a child, also called pet name.
④ The official name is a formal personal name.

Situ and Sima are the commonest compound surnames.

In China, the surname comes first followed by the given name, and the latter has its own traditions and features. It can have one or two characters. In the same clan, the given name is arranged in the order of seniority in the family hierarchy. And the given names of peers usually have one Chinese character in common if there are more than one characters in their given names. The names of ancient men were more complicated than those of modern people. People of literacy and status have both a style name and alternative name, along with the surname and given name. For example, a man of letters Su Shi in the Song Dynasty had the style name Zizhan and the alternative name Dongpo. The poet Li Bai in the Tang Dynasty lived in the Qinglian Village in Sichuan Province in his childhood, and thus he styled himself "Qinglian *Jushi* (retired scholar)".

Chinese names usually have a certain meaning, expressing some kind of wish. Some names embody the location, time or natural phenomenon when the person was born, such as "Jing (Beijing)", "Chen (morning)", "Dong (winter)", and "Xue (snow)". Some names indicate the expectation of possessing some virtues, such as "Zhong (loyalty)", "Yi (justice)", "Li (etiquette)", and "Xin (faith)". Some names have the meaning of health, longevity and happiness, such as "Jian (health)", "Shou (longevity)", "Song (pine, representing longevity)", and "Fu (happiness)". Male names are different from female ones: men's names usually have the character meaning power and vigor, such as "Hu (tiger)", "Long (dragon)", "Xiong (grandeur)", "Wei (magnificence)", "Gang (hardness)", and "Qiang (strength)". And the names of females usually use characters representing gentleness and beauty, such as "Feng (phoenix)", "Hua (flower)", "Yu (jade)", "Cai (colors)", "Juan (graceful)", and "Jing (calmness)".

Nowadays, the Chinese do not pay as much attention to naming, as did ancient folk. Generally a person has an infant name[3] and an official name[4], and the given names are not necessarily arranged in the order of the seniority in the family hierarchy.

1. 郭是古代的城墙，也成为中国一个姓
郭 (Guo) refers to the outer wall of the ancient city, and it becomes a surname.
2. 中国同姓族人多聚居一处。浙江金华兰溪诸葛村，传说村里人是诸葛亮的后裔
In China, people with common surname live together in a clan. Legend has it that the descendants of Zhuge Liang live here in the Zhuge Village, Lanxi, Jinhua, Zhejiang Province.
3. 诸葛是最常见的复姓，三国蜀相诸葛亮即为一例
诸葛 (Zhuge) is a common compound surname (i.e. Zhuge Liang — the genius military strategist of the Three Kingdoms).

民间庙会
Folk Temple Fair

庙会是中国民间的一种社会活动，据说起源于古代的祭祀土地神，以后逐渐变成了一种民间物品交流的集市和文化表演的场所。

庙会一般设在寺庙里和寺庙附近的空场上，在节日或规定的日子举办。有的只在每年春节期间举办。虽然各地举办庙会的时间不同，但基本内容都差不多。庙会期间，农户、商贩带着自己生产的农产品、土特产和从各处收集来的古玩玉器、花鸟鱼虫，到庙会上进行交易；各路手艺人设摊展卖民间工艺品和特色小吃；民间艺人搭台表演歌舞曲艺……逛庙会的老百姓喜气洋洋地赶来买卖物品，观看表演，品尝小吃，真是热闹非常。

现在，北京市每年春节都举办庙会。比较有名的有白云观庙会、地坛庙会、龙潭湖庙会、隆福寺庙会等。北京的庙会保留了许多传统习俗，像白云观庙会的骑驴逛庙会、打金钱眼①等。庙会上出售的物品也很有北方特色，像空竹②、风车③、刀枪剑戟等玩具；冰糖葫芦、茶汤等小吃，都深受老百姓欢迎。

1. 京郊农村的春节庙会别具乡土风情
   Temple fairs in villages outside of Beijing have preserved many traditional customs.
2. 冰糖葫芦是庙会上最受欢迎的传统小吃
   Candied haw is the most popular snack in the temple fair.
3. 庙会上的高跷表演
   Stilts-walking at the temple fair
4. 北京天桥庙会上，民众多购买风车，祈求转运
   Most people would buy pinwheels in temple fair to pray for blessings.

The temple fair is a kind of social activity in China. Legend has it that it originated in ancient times when people offered sacrifices to the village god, which later gradually evolved into a marketplace for people to exchange products and a place for cultural performance.

The temple fair, usually on the open ground in or near a temple, is held on festive or specified days. Some are held only during the Spring Festival.

Although different places hold their temple fair at various dates, the contents are similar. Farmers and merchants sell their farm produce, local specialties, and antiques, jade articles, flowers, birds and fish; craftsmen set up their stalls to show and sell their handicrafts and specialty snacks; folk artists establish a stage for singing, dance, and *quyi* (Chinese folk art forms, including ballad singing, story telling, comic dialogues, clapper talk, cross talk, etc.) performance. Ordinary people come to the temple fair to buy and sell goods, watch the performances, and sample snacks, giving the temple fair a bustling atmosphere.

Now, Beijing holds temple fair every Spring Festival. Relatively famous temple fairs are those of the White Cloud Temple, the Altar of Earth, Dragon Pool and the Temple of Intense Happiness. Temple fairs in Beijing have preserved many traditional customs, such as riding a monkey to stroll around the temple fair and throwing coins through the hole in the center of a copper coin[1] in the White Cloud Temple. Many goods sold in the temple fair have typical northern features, such as toys like diabolo[2], pinwheel[3], knife, spear, sword and halberd; big sugarcoated haws on a stick and gruel of millet flour and sugar are widely popular among common people.

小注解 Footnotes

① 打金钱眼：白云观里挂着一个大铜钱，传说如果能把硬币投入铜钱中间的方孔，就会得到好运。
② 空竹：一种用竹子和木头制成的玩具。
③ 风车：一种用竹棍和纸做的玩具，形状像扇页，风吹过，扇页就会转动。

① In the White Cloud Temple, there hangs a large copper coin. It is said that anyone who can throw a coin through the hole in its center will enjoy good fortune.
② Diabolo is a kind of toy made of bamboo and wood.
③ Pinwheel is a kind of toy made of wooden stick and paper, like a fan; when a wind blows, it will turn.

中国茶
Chinese Tea

中国人喜欢喝茶，也常常用茶来招待朋友和客人。茶叶是中国人生活中的必需品。

茶树原产于中国。中国古人发现茶树后，起初是把茶叶作为药用，后来才当作饮料。早在2,000多年前，中国人就有了饮茶的习惯，以后又逐渐学会了培育茶树和制作茶叶的技术。

中国茶叶按照制作方法分为绿茶、红茶、乌龙茶、花茶、沱(tuó)茶、砖茶等几大类，各类茶中又包括许多品种。

绿茶嫩绿鲜艳，是不经过发酵的茶。著名的绿茶品种有杭州西湖龙井茶[1]、江苏碧螺春茶[2]、安徽黄山的毛峰茶[3]和产于安徽六安县一带的六安瓜片茶[4]。

红茶是经过发酵的茶，沏出的茶水颜色红艳。中国著名的红茶有安徽的祁(qí)红茶[5]和云南的滇(diān)红茶[6]。

乌龙茶是一种半发酵的茶，茶叶松散粗大，茶水颜色金黄。最好的乌龙茶是产在福建武夷(yí)山的武夷岩茶[7]。

花茶是中国独有的一个茶类，是在茶叶中加入香花熏制而成的。最有名的花茶是福建产的茉莉花茶[8]。

沱茶是产于云南、四川的一种茶，经过压制，像个圆圆的馒头。

🔍 小注解 Footnotes

① 西湖龙井茶：产于浙江省杭州西湖周边，是著名的绿茶品种之一。

② 碧螺春茶：产于江苏省吴县太湖洞庭山，具有色香味形俱美的独特风格。

③ 毛峰茶：产于安徽省黄山，是著名的绿茶品种之一。

④ 六安瓜片茶：产于安徽省大别山区，是著名的绿茶品种之一。

⑤ 祁红茶：产于安徽省祁门县，是著名的红茶品种之一。

⑥ 滇红茶：云南省出产红茶。因"滇"是云南省的别称，故称滇红。

⑦ 武夷岩茶：产于福建省武夷山，是乌龙茶中的上品。

⑧ 茉莉花茶：用茉莉花熏制而成的茶叶。

砖茶，形状像砖头，是蒙古族、藏族等少数民族喜欢喝的茶。

喝茶不但可以止渴，还能消除疲劳，帮助消化，预防一些疾病。长期饮茶，对人的身体健康很有益。

1. 中国人精于茶道
   Chinese people are the masters of tea ceremony.
2. 清明前是浙江龙井的采茶季节
   The season of picking Zhejiang's *Longjing* tea is the period before Pure Brightness Day.
3. 炒茶必须用人手，才能控制火候
   In order to obtain the perfect flavor, tea must be stir-fried by hand.

Chinese people like to drink tea, and often entertain friends and guests with it. The tealeaf is a necessity in the life of Chinese people.

Tea plants originated in China, although the ancient Chinese first used them for medicinal purposes before developing tea as a drink some 2,000 years ago, Later, they gradually learnt to grow tea plants and use the leaves to make various types of tea.

As regards the method of making tea, the Chinese variety can be classified into green tea, black tea, oolong tea, scented tea, tuo tea (bowl-shaped compressed mass of tea leaves), and brick tea, each consisting of many types.

Green tea is not fermented. Famous green tea includes *Longjing* tea[①] from the region of West Lake in Hangzhou, *Biluochun* tea[②] from Jiangsu, *Maofeng* tea[③] from the Huangshan Mountains of Anhui Province, and *Liu'an Guapian* tea[④] from Liu'an County of Anhui Province.

Black tea is fermented, and is brilliant red. Famous Chinese black tea is *keemun* tea[⑤] of Anhui Province, and *Dian* black tea[⑥] (Yunnan black tea) of Yunnan Province.

Oolong tea is half fermented, its tealeaves being loose and thick, and the tea is golden yellow. The best oolong tea is bohea[⑦] produced in the Wuyi Mountains of Fujian Province.

Scented tea is peculiar to China, which is made by smoking tea leaves with fragrant flowers. The most famous one is jasmine tea[⑧] produced in Fujian Province.

Tuo tea (bowl-shaped compressed mass of tea leaves), produced in Yunnan and Sichuan, is compressed like a round steamed bun.

Brick tea is shaped like a brick, and is a favorite of the Mongolian and Tibetan ethnic groups.

Drinking tea can quench one's thirst, dispel fatigue, help digestion and prevent some diseases. Drinking tea for a long period is quite beneficial to people's health.

小注解 Footnotes

① *Longjing* tea is produced near the West Lake in Zhejiang Province.

② *Biluochun* tea, produced in the Dongting Mountain of Taihu Lake in Wuxian County in Jiangsu Province, has special features, with good color, fragrance, taste and shape.

③ *Maofeng* tea, produced in the Huangshan Mountains in Anhui Province, is a famous brand of green tea.

④ *Liu'an Guapian* tea, produced in the mountainous area of the Dabie Mountains, is a renowned brand of green tea.

⑤ *Keemun* tea, produced at Qimen County in Anhui Province, is a famous brand of black tea.

⑥ *Dian* black tea is produced in Yunnan Province; Dian is another name for Yunnan.

⑦ Bohea, produced in the Wuyi Mountains of Fujian Province, is a top-grade oolong tea.

⑧ Jasmine tea is made by smoking with jasmine.

中国酒
Chinese Wine

在中国，酒的历史比茶还长。1986年，在河南出土的一壶酒，就是3,000多年前的古酒。

中国的名酒很多，如：茅台、五粮液、汾酒、竹叶青、泸州老窖、古井贡酒、加饭酒、张裕葡萄酒、长城葡萄酒等，都是享誉世界的名酒。

中国历史上有关酒的故事更多：晋代诗人陶渊明不能一日无酒；唐代大诗人李白"斗酒诗百篇"，喝得越多诗写得越好；宋代梁山好汉武松一口气喝了18碗酒，赤手空拳打死了一只猛虎……

1915年在巴拿马万国博览会上，中国把茅台酒送去展览、参评。据说主持博览会的美国人觉得装酒的黄瓷瓶不好看，不准茅台酒参展。中国代表团非常气愤。在激烈的争执中，一位中国酒师急中生智，故意把一瓶茅台酒摔到地上，顿时瓶碎酒洒，满屋奇香。各国代表大为惊异。最后，茅台酒被评为"世界名酒"，获得金质大奖。

In China, the history of wine is longer than that of tea. In 1986, a pot of wine excavated in Henan Province was found to have been made more than 3,000 years ago.

China has many famous brands of wine—*Maotai*, Five-Grain Liquor, Fen Liquor, Bamboo-Leaf-Green Liqueur, Luzhou Liquor, Gujing Tribute Wine, Rice Wine, Zhangyu Grape Wine, and Grape Wine of the Great Wall— that enjoy a worldwide reputation.

There are more stories about wine in Chinese history. Tao Yuanming, a poet in the Jin Dynasty, could not live without wine for a day. The great poet Li Bai in the Tang Dynasty could "write 100 poems after drinking wine"; the more wine he drank, the better the poem would be. Wu Song, a brave man from Liangshan in the Song Dynasty, drank 18 bowls of wine without a break, and then, barehanded, fought a fierce tiger to the death.

At the 1915 Panama World Exposition, China wanted to display *Maotai*, but the American organizers did not think the yellow porcelain bottle was very attractive and refused to allow the spirit to be displayed. The Chinese delegation was very angry. As they were quarreling strongly, a Chinese delegate, having a sudden flash of inspiration, deliberately dropped a bottle of *Maotai* on the ground. Immediately the bottle was broken, the spirit was sprayed, and the whole room was filled with an exceptional fragrance. Delegates of all countries were amazed. Finally, *Maotai* was appraised as a "World Famous Brand", winning a golden medal.

1. 刚蒸出来的饭，用来酿制绍兴黄酒
   Once the rice is cooked, it is ready for fermentation — a vital step of making Shaoxing wine.
2. 山东烟台的张裕酒厂历史悠久，设有酒文化博物馆
   Zhangyu wine factory is steeped in history and it has its own wine museum.
3. 古代行酒令劝饮酒浮雕
   Sculptures depicting a wine feast
4. 贵州窖藏茅台酒的库房
   The basement for *Maotai* storage, Guizhou Province

中国菜
Chinese Cuisine

中国菜在世界上和法国菜、意大利菜齐名，深受各国人民的喜爱。

中国菜不但花样多，而且具有色、香、味、形[①]俱佳的特点。

由于中国地域辽阔，各地的物产、气候和生活习惯不同，因此人们的口味也各不相同：南方人口味清淡，北方人口味较重，四川人喜欢吃辣，山西人喜欢吃酸……这样，在中国就形成了各具地方风味特色的菜系。其中山东、四川、江苏、广东、浙江、福建、湖南、安徽等地的菜就极具代表性。

山东菜在中国北方很有名。由于山东靠近黄海、渤海，所以山东菜中海鲜类较多。山东名菜有"烤大虾"、"红烧海螺"、"糖醋黄河鲤鱼"等。

四川菜的特点是麻、辣、酸。四川名菜有"怪味鸡"、"鱼香肉丝"、"麻婆豆腐"等。

江苏菜咸甜适中，吃起来很可口。江苏名菜有"清蒸鲥(shí)鱼"、"南京板鸭"、"西瓜鸡"等。

广东菜的特点是用料精细博杂；菜肴新颖奇异；口味讲究清、鲜、嫩、爽；调味品包含酸、甜、苦、辣、咸，它以色、香、味、形俱全而饮誉四海。广东名菜有"清蒸桂花鱼"、"白切鸡"、"香芋扣肉煲"、"冬瓜盅"等。

浙江菜是由杭州、宁波、绍兴等地方菜发展起来的。浙江名菜有"西湖醋鱼"、"龙井虾仁"、"叫化(huā)童鸡"等。

福建菜多用海产品作原料，味道清鲜，颜色美观。福建名菜有"太极明虾"、"清汤鱼丸"、"烧片糟鸡"和"佛跳墙"[②]等。

湖南菜喜用辣椒。酸辣、鲜香是湖南菜的特点。湖南名菜有"麻辣子鸡"、"腊味合蒸"、"红煨鱼翅"和"冰糖湘莲"等。

安徽菜中最有名的，是用山珍野味[③]做的。"雪冬烧山鸡"、"火腿炖鞭笋"、"符离集烧鸡"等都是安徽的名菜。

1. 北京填鸭店的师傅
   A chef of the Beijing Roast Duck Restaurant

2. 世界名厨甄文达推介北京宫廷菜
   The Palace Cuisine is recommended by the well recongnized chef Martin Yan.

3. 中国人认为"民以食为天"，馆子经常挤满食客
   Chinese restaurants are always full of food lovers.

4. 广东菜款式多样化
   Guangdong cuisine is varied and exquisite.

5. 中国菜花样多，厨师要费尽心思才能炮制各款佳肴
   The wide varieties of Chinese delicacies reflect an impressive knowledge of the chefs.

除此以外，北京的烤鸭、涮羊肉；湖北的豆皮；东北的酸菜白肉等也都是色鲜味美的名菜。

Chinese cuisine enjoys the same international reputation to that of France and Italy for its scent, taste, and design①.

Since China has a vast territory, and the produce, climate and living habits are quite different in each place, the flavor of food is quite different: southerners like light food, northerners prefer a heavily seasoned taste, Sichuan people like hot food, Shanxi people like sour food and so on. China has all kinds of cuisine of special local flavor, among which that of Shandong, Sichuan, Jiangsu, Guangdong, Zhejiang, Fujian, Hunan and Anhui are all quite representative.

Shandong cuisine is quite famous in northern China. Since Shandong is close to the Yellow Sea and the Bohai Sea, it includes much seafood. Famous dishes are "roast prawns", "conch braised with soy sauce" and "fried carp of the Yellow River with sweet and sour sauce".

Sichuan cuisine is hot, spicy and sour. Famous dishes are "chicken with special hot sauce", "shredded pork with chilli sauce" and "peppery hot bean curd".

Jiangsu cuisine is moderately salty and sweet, and is quite delicious. Famous dishes are "steamed shad", "Nanjing pressed duck" and "chicken in watermelon".

① 色、香、味、形：中国菜的特点。"色"指菜的颜色；"香"指肉、鱼、菜、果的香气；"味"指咸、甜、酸、辣的味道；"形"指装在盘子里的菜肴的形状。

② "佛跳墙"：福建名菜。意思是这种菜奇香，连佛闻到了也要跳过墙来吃。

③ 山珍野味：山珍，是指山野里出产的各种贵重的食品；野味，是指猎取得来的做肉食的鸟兽。现在国家提倡保护野生动植物，很多原来用野味做的菜都已改用其他原料。

① Color, scent, taste and design are features of Chinese cuisine. Color refers to that of the dish; scent refers to that of the meat, fish, vegetable and fruit; taste refers to salty, sweet, sour and hot tastes; and design refers to the way the food is placed on the plate.

② It is a famous Fujian dish, which means that the dish is so delicious that when the Buddha smells the scent, he will jump over the wall to eat it.

③ Mountain delicacies refer to every kind of precious food produced in the mountains, and delicacies of the wilderness refer to birds or beasts hunted for food. Since the government advocates protecting wild plants and animals, many dishes originally made from game now adopt other raw materials.

1. 冷盘
   Cold dishes
2. 西安饺子宴
   Xi'an Dumpling Feast

1

Guangdong cuisine features exquisite, plentiful and varied raw materials, novel and strangely cooked foods, light, delicious, tender and refreshing taste, sour, sweet, bitter, hot and salty flavoring. Famous dishes are

2

"steamed mandarin fish", "white cut chicken", "steamed fragrant potato and pork" and "white gourd soup".

Zhejiang cuisine is developed from the local dishes of Hangzhou, Ningbo and Shaoxing. Famous dishes are "fish of the West Lake in vinegar gravy", "shrimp meat in *Longjing*" and "beggar's young chicken (mud-baked young chicken)".

Fujian cuisine often takes marine products as its raw material. It tastes light and delicious and the color is beautiful. Famous dishes are "fried prawns in the shape of a pair of fish", "fish balls in clear soup", "chicken slices in wine sauce" and "Buddha jumps over the wall[②]".

Hunan cuisine is mostly seasoned with chili, and features sour, hot, delicious and fragrant tastes. Famous dishes are "chicken with chili and pepper," "steamed dish of cured meat and fish", "stewed shark's fin with soy sauce" and "lotus seeds in crystal sugar".

The most famous dishes in Anhui cuisine are made of the choicest delicacies of mountain and wilderness[③]: "pheasant stewed with potherb mustard and winter bamboo shoots", "stewed ham and subterranean stem of bamboo", and "braised chicken of *Fuliji* (a county in Anhui)" are all famous local dishes.

Besides, roast duck and dip-boiled mutton slices of Beijing, *doupi* (a kind of fried pancake made of glutinous rice, minced meat, cubes of bamboo shoots, etc. wrapped in sheets of rice and mung bean flour mixed with eggs) of Hubei Province, and "white meat with pickled Chinese cabbage" of the Northeast, are all famous dishes in terms of their bright color and good taste.

概述
Introduction

千百年来，中华民族创造了光辉灿烂的历史和文化，同时也形成了自己的道德观念。其中的精华部分，对社会的发展和进步起到了积极的促进作用，这就是我们所说的传统美德。

这些传统美德是中华民族宝贵的精神财富，直到今天，仍然具有积极的意义。它的价值已被全世界越来越多的人所认同，并在人类文明进程中发挥着重大的作用。

Over thousands of years of history, the Chinese have formed their own moral code that has played an important role in social development and progress. This is what we call traditional virtues, which still have great significance today and whose value to the development of human civilization is now widely recognized.

爱国情怀
Patriotic Sentiments

爱国情怀是指对祖国的深厚感情和信念，是中华民族评价一个人的行为和道德水准的重要尺度。

中国人的爱国情怀虽然在不同的历史时期有着不同的具体内容和特点，但也具有共同的内容。它包括：热爱国土和家乡；热爱祖国的人民；尊重民族的传统习惯和共同语言；珍视祖国的光荣历史；具有民族自尊心和自豪感；自觉维护民族团结和国家统一；保卫祖国，维护祖国尊严，敢于同一切外来敌人作斗争；关心祖国的前途和命运，并为祖国的繁荣富强而努力奋斗。"天下兴亡，匹夫有责"是千百年来中国人共同的信念。

中华民族的爱国精神代代相传。宋代抗金英雄岳飞，一生精忠报国；明代爱国志士郑成功亲率战舰，一举收复了被荷兰殖民者侵占了38年的台湾；清代的政治家林则徐，为维护国家和民族的尊严，下令收缴英、美商人输入中国的鸦片，并当众销毁；日本帝国主义侵占中国后，全中国人民奋起抗战，终于取得了抗日战争的全面胜利；许多著名的科学家如钱学森、李四光等，在祖国需要的时候，放弃国外种种优厚待遇，毅然回国效力；侨居海外的广大华侨，为祖国的发展强大贡献力量，表现了一片赤诚的爱国、爱乡之情……

1. 红军长征石雕像
   A stone wall carving depicting the Red Army campaign
2. 岳飞精忠报国的精神是高尚情操的表现
   Yue Fei's fierce patriotism has inspired many.
3. 郑成功驱逐荷兰殖民者，收复台湾，堪称爱国志士
   Zheng Chenggong was a patriotic leader who recovered Taiwan after it had been occupied by dutch colonists.

爱国精神是一种伟大的凝聚力和向心力。当出现民族纷争和国家分裂的局面时，人们总能在爱国精神影响下，从国家和民族大义出发，维护团结和统一；在遭受外敌入侵的危难时刻，各族人民总能在爱国大旗的感召下，团结对外，奋起反抗，保卫国家的独立和尊严；在发展经济建设的年代里，海内外的炎黄子孙总能在爱国热情的激励下，为中华的腾飞群策群力，共同奋斗……

爱国情怀也是催人奋进的强大精神力量，它把个人和祖国的命运紧紧地联系在一起，鼓舞着人们为祖国和人民建功立业。

Patriotic sentiments, referring to the profound feelings for and belief in the motherland, are an important criterion for the Chinese nation to evaluate a person's conduct and moral level.

Although Chinese people's patriotic sentiments have different contents and features in different historical periods, they have always included a love for the homeland and hometown, love for the people, respect for the traditional customs and common languages of ethnic groups, cherishing China's glorious history, national self-esteem and pride, safeguarding national unity and unification, defending the motherland and national dignity and fighting against all external enemies, caring for the future and fate of the motherland, and working hard for the prosperity and strength of the country. "Everyone being responsible for the fate of his country" has been a common belief for thousands of years.

The patriotic spirit of the Chinese nation has been passed on from generation to generation. Yue Fei of the Song Dynasty served his motherland with selfless loyalty all through his life. Zheng Chenggong, a patriotic person of resolve in the Ming Dynasty, led warships to recover Taiwan at the first attempt after it had been occupied by Dutch colonists for 38 years. Lin Zexu, a statesman of the Qing Dynasty, in order to defend national dignity, gave orders to confiscate and burn the opium

imported into China by English and American businessmen. After Japanese imperialists invaded China, the Chinese people rose up against them and ultimately obtained victory in the War of Resistance Against Japanese Aggression. Many famous scholars, such as Qian Xuesen and Li Siguang, gave up an easy life in foreign countries to return home to resolutely serve China when the motherland needed them. Many overseas Chinese contribute their efforts for the development and strength of the motherland, showing their sincere love for their homeland and hometown.

Patriotic spirit is a strong cohesive force. When the country has disputes between ethnic groups or is split, people can always defend national unity and unification from the overall interests of the state and the righteous cause of the Chinese nation under the influence of a patriotic spirit. At a dangerous and adverse moment of external threat, all ethnic groups, under the flag of patriotism, can always rise up in unity to resist the aggressor and safeguard the independence and dignity of the country. In time of economic development, all Chinese at home and abroad can always make joint efforts for the take-off of the Chinese nation under the inspiration of patriotic enthusiasm....

Patriotic sentiments, also a strong spiritual power to impel the advancement of individuals, links closely the fate of individual with that of the country and inspires people to render meritorious service and carve out a distinguished career for the people and the country.

1. 林则徐销毁英、美商人输入的鸦片，
维护了国家和民族的尊严
Lin Zexu defended national dignity by confiscating and burning opium imported into China by English and American businessmen.
2. 人民英雄纪念碑纪念为国捐躯的英雄
The Monument to the People's Heroes was built to remember the heros who fought and sacrified for the country.

崇尚操守
Advocate Integrity

孟子学说的精神被视为做人的最高道德标准
Mencius's ethical teaching is viewed as the highest moral standard.

"操守"指的是坚持真理、坚贞不屈、廉洁正直等优秀品质。中华民族自古以来就非常看重人的品德，把人格的尊严和独立看得比生命更重要。古代著名思想家孟子曾把富贵时不放纵自我、贫贱时不改变志向、在权势的威逼压迫下不屈服，视为做人的最高道德标准。古往今来，无数优秀的中华儿女，以自己的崇高人格，谱写了民族精神的灿烂诗篇。

东汉时，汉光武帝刘秀姐姐的家奴杀了人，洛阳县令董宣依法处死了凶手。刘秀偏信姐姐的一面之词，下令把董宣处死。董宣据理申辩，毫不屈服。刘秀自知理亏，就让董宣给他姐姐叩头赔礼了事。董宣坚决不肯。刘秀让人按下他的头，董宣就用手撑着地，宁死不低头。

南宋民族英雄文天祥，在抗击元军时不幸被俘。在敌人的威胁利诱和残酷折磨面前，宁死不屈，从容就义。他被俘后写下的诗句"人生自古谁无死，留取丹心照汗青"，激励了一代又一代的爱国志士。

在抗日战争中，中华民族千千万万的优秀儿女，面对强敌，奋起抗争，谱写了一曲曲惊天动地的英雄壮歌：八位抗日女战士，在身负重伤·打完最后一颗子弹后，毫无惧色地跳进了滔滔江水。五名八路军士兵，英勇抵抗日本侵略军，在无路可退时，宁可跳下峭壁悬崖，也绝不投降……

在中华民族的历史长河中，为了真理和正义，为了国家和民族，坚贞不屈、英勇抗敌的事例举不胜举。也正因为如此，中华民族才能延续千年万载，屹立于世界民族之林。

Integrity refers to some good virtues such as upholding the truth, faithfulness and never yielding, honesty and uprightness. Since ancient times, the Chinese nation has valued a person's moral integrity, and considers personal dignity and independence more important than life. The great ideologist

Mencius in ancient times considered it the highest moral standard not to be corrupted by riches or honors, not to depart from principle despite poverty or humble origin, and not to submit to force or threat. Through the ages, numerous outstanding Chinese have shown their noble personal integrity.

In the Eastern Han Dynasty (25-220 AD), Emperor Wudi Liu Xiu once ordered Dong Xuan, a county magistrate of Luoyang, to kowtow to his sister and apologize for some alleged wrong he had committed. The magistrate, knowing he was in the right, refused. Even when imperial guards tried to force Dong's head down to the ground, he used his arms to resist and refused to obey even in the face of death.

Wen Tianxiang, national hero in the Southern Song Dynasty (1127-1279 AD), was unfortunately captured when fighting against Yuan Dynasty (1271-1368 AD) soldiers. Despite alternate use of cajolery and cruel torture to force him to submit, Wen Tianxiang refused and eventually went to his death unflinchingly. The lines he wrote after being captured — "No one can live forever; let me die with a loyal heart shining in the pages of history" — has inspired patriotic people of ideals and integrity.

In the War of Resistance Against Japanese Aggression, many Chinese showed great heroism against a strong enemy. In one case, eight women soldiers, although seriously wounded, continued until they ran out of ammunition and then jumped into an adjacent river without fear. Five soldiers of the Eight-Route Army bravely resisted a Japanese advance, and then, with no way to retreat, leapt off a precipice rather than surrender.

Chinese history is full of such heroism too numerous to mention, which provides a certainty the nation will always continue as a colossus in the world.

文天祥宁死不屈，是南宋爱国名臣
Wen Tianxiang — the national hero in the Southern Song Dynasty — chose death over submission to his enemies.

勤劳俭朴
Diligence and Frugality

中国人生性勤劳，为家庭和社会创造财富
Diligent and frugal, Chinese bring prosperity to their
own homes as well as to the society.

中国人信奉一个朴素的道理：小到个人、家庭，大到民族、国家，凡是勤劳、俭朴的就能兴旺发达；凡是懒惰、浪费的就会破败灭亡。自古以来，中国人就尊重劳动，珍惜一切物质和劳动成果，并把勤劳俭朴视为一种美德。

早在人类的童年时期，中华民族的祖先就用自己勤劳的双手改造自然、创造文明。炼石补天的女娲（wā），教人种庄稼的后稷（jì），治理洪水的大禹……都是通过辛勤劳动为民造福的英雄。随着历史的发展，勤劳的美德成了中华民族的传家宝，无论做工、务农还是经商，人们都勤勤恳恳地努力劳作，并常常用"勤俭持家远，耕读继世长"，"遍地是黄金，单等勤劳人"等信条告诫后人：只有通过辛勤的劳动，才能开创美好的生活。

中华民族一向十分珍爱自己的劳动成果，以节俭朴素为荣，以奢侈浪费为耻。无论民间百姓还是统治者中的开明之士，都主张节俭，反对浪费。早在2,000多年前，孔子就把俭朴视为美德，他对齐国宰相晏婴一件皮袍穿30年的俭朴作风大加赞赏，认为齐国有这样的宰相执政，真是天大的幸运。三国时期的诸葛亮把俭朴生活和个人道德修养联系起来，提出了"俭以养德"的道德名言。意思是说，俭朴生活能够培养和增进人的高尚道德。劳动人民作为社会财富的创造者，更是珍惜自己的劳动果实，反对铺张浪费、暴殄(tiǎn)天物①。这种精神代代相传，就形成了中华民族崇尚俭朴的道德风尚。

千百年来，中华民族以其勤劳俭朴的美德著称于世，并凭借着这种精神，创造了光辉灿烂的华夏文明。

中国妇女素以勤劳见称
Chinese women are known to be diligent.

The Chinese people believe in a simple truth: diligence and frugality can bring prosperity, either for an individual or a family, a nation or a state; laziness and wastefulness can only lead to decline and destruction. Since ancient times, the Chinese people have highly valued labor, treasured the fruits of labor, and considered it a virtue to be diligent and frugal.

Legends about this go back to the dawn of civilization: Nuwa who melted down stones to patch up the sky, Houji who taught people to grow crops and Dayu who led people in curbing floods. In modern times, people work industriously, either as workers, peasants or businessmen; and often tell their offspring: "Being industrious and thrifty in managing a household, the family can last long; and part-time study and part-time farming can proceed in the future"; "The ground is covered with gold, which only awaits industrious people". These sayings reflect the belief that only through hard work can people enjoy a pleasant life.

Chinese have always cherished thrift and plain living, and been ashamed of extravagance and wastefulness. All people, be they civilians or enlightened personages among the rulers, advocate frugality and oppose wastefulness. As early as more than 2,000 years ago, Confucius deemed it a virtue to be frugal. He thought highly of Yan Ying, Prime Minister of the State of Qi, who wore a fur gown for 30 years, and believed the State of Qi was lucky to have such a prime minister. In the Three Kingdoms period (220-280 AD), Zhuge Liang related frugal life to personal moral characteristics, and put forward a famous dictum that "Thrift nourishes virtues①". Laboring people, as the creator of social wealth, cherish more of the fruit of their labor and oppose extravagance and reckless wasting of nature's bounties. This social ethic has been passed on from generation to generation.

 小注解 Footnotes

① 暴殄天物：任意糟蹋东西。

① "Thrift nourishes virtues" means that a frugal life can foster a person's noble morality.

勤奋好学
Diligent and Eager to Study

秋夜读书图
A portrait of a student studying at an autumn night

中华民族推崇的人生理想，是追求有所作为；看重的立身之本，是真才实学；认定的成才之路，是发愤学习。中国人重视读书、勤奋好学，已成为世代相传的优良传统。中国民间有许多关于学习的格言，如："少壮不努力，老大徒伤悲"、"书山有路勤为径，学海无涯苦作舟"、"活到老，学到老"等，也流传着很多古人珍惜时间、发愤苦读的故事。

战国时的苏秦，夜以继日地读书，实在太累了，就用锥子刺腿来使头脑清醒；汉代的孙敬，为了防止读书时瞌睡，便用一根绳子把自己的头发系在房梁上，只要一打瞌睡就会被扯醒。这就是历史上"刺股悬梁"的故事。

晋朝的车胤(yìn)、孙康、匡衡，家里都很穷，连点灯的油都买不起。夏天的晚上，车胤用纱布做成一个小口袋，捉一些萤火虫装进去，借着萤火虫发出的光亮看书；孙康在严寒的冬夜坐在雪地里，利用白雪的反光苦读；匡衡在墙上凿了个小洞，"偷"邻居家的一点灯光读书。成语"囊萤映雪"和"凿壁偷光"所讲的就是这几个故事。

东晋大书法家王羲之自幼苦练书法。他每次写完字，都到自家门前的池塘里洗毛笔，时间长了，一池清水变成了一池墨水。后来，人们就把这个池塘称为"墨池"。王羲之通过勤学苦练，终于成为著名的书法家，被人们称为"书圣"。

中国当代许多著名的学者和科学家，也是勤奋好学的楷模。数学家华罗庚，小时候在一家店铺里打工，工作非常辛苦。但他仍挤

出时间读书学习，最终成为享誉世界的数学家。

现在，人们的生活条件和学习条件好多了，不必再"囊萤映雪"、"凿壁偷光"，更不必模仿"刺股悬梁"的做法，但古人那种勤奋好学的精神却值得我们好好学习。

The ambition of life highly esteemed by Chinese is to be able to display one's talents and do well in life; the foundation of the way one conducts oneself in society is genuine knowledge or competence; the way to become an accomplished person is to put all one's energy into study. The Chinese people attach great importance to study, and it has become a fine tradition passed on from generation to generation to be diligent and eager to learn. There are many maxims on this. For instance: "If one does not work hard when young, it will be useless for him to regret when old"; "In the high mountain of books, industry is the only path leading to the peak; on the boundless sea of learning, diligence is one's own vehicle of passage"; and "One is never too old to learn". There are also many stories about ancient men valuing the time and studying industriously.

Su Qin of the Warring States Period (475-221 BC) read day and night. When he was too tired, he would jab his legs with an awl to keep himself awake. Sun Jing in the Han Dynasty (206 BC -220 AD) tied his hair to a ceiling beam to prevent him dozing off; thus, as he felt sleepy, he would be jerked back to wakefulness.

Che Yin, Sun Kang, and Kuang Heng in the Jin Dynasty (265-420 AD) were all very poor and could not buy kerosene to light a lamp. On summer nights, Che Yin made a small gauze bag to hold fireflies, and read books by their light. On cold winter nights, Sun Kang sat on the ground covered with snow and read by its reflected light. Kuang Heng bored a hole on the wall

1. 北京清华大学的学生正在图书馆温习
   The students of the Beijing Tsinghua University are studying at the library.
2. 北京大学未名湖博雅塔
   Peking University's Weiming Lake and Boya Pagoda
3. 北京大学是莘莘学子最想入读的学府
   Peking University is one of the most wanted schools in China.
4. 北京大学人才辈出
   Peking University has many outstanding alumni.

in order to get some light from the neighbor's house to read. Idiomatic expressions of "reading by the light of bagged fireflies or the reflected light of snow", and "boring a hole on the wall to make use of the neighbor's light to study" keep alive these old tales.

The great calligrapher Wang Xizhi of the Eastern Jin Dynasty (317-420 AD) practiced calligraphy from his childhood. Each time he finished writing, he would go to the pond in front of his house to wash his writing brush; as time passed, a pond of clean water became a pond of Chinese ink. Later, people called this stretch of water the "Chinese Ink Pond". As a result of diligent study and painstaking training, Wang Xizhi finally became a famous calligrapher, a "Calligrapher of the First Magnitude" as people called him. Many famous scholars and scientists in contemporary China were also models of diligence and eagerness to learn. Mathematician Hua Luogeng worked part-time in a shop and the job was quite laborious, but he tried to find time to read and learn, and finally became a mathematician enjoying a worldwide prestige.

Nowadays, the living and study conditions are better, so there is no need to "read by the light of bagged fireflies or the reflected light of snow", or "bore a hole on the wall to make use of the neighbor's light to study", and it is not even necessary to imitate ancient men to "jab one's side with an awl and tie one's hair onto the house beam to keep oneself awake", but the thought remains valid today.

谦虚礼让
Modesty and Comity

　　谦虚礼让作为中华民族的传统美德，主要包含以下内容：第一是正确地认识自己，能看到自己的不足，永不自满；第二是发现别人的长处，宽容别人的缺点，尊重别人；第三是正确对待个人的利益，懂得谦让，不居功，不争名夺利。古人把谦虚与成功的关系凝缩成"满招损，谦受益"这句话，告诫人们自满会招来损害，谦虚能得到益处。

　　春秋时期，有一次，孔子去拜访老子。虽然老子的年龄比孔子大，学问比孔子渊博，但他还是亲自驾车，赶到郊外去迎接孔子。这次见面，孔子虚心地向老子请教，老子耐心地一一解答。临别时，老子说，有道德修养的人要朴实，不能骄傲、贪婪、心存妄想。这些话给孔子留下了极深的印象。孔子后来说的"三人行，必有我师"，意思就是：只要有几个人在一起，其中就必定有值得我学习的老师。老子和孔子的言行对后人产生了很大影响。

　　战国时，赵国的蔺（lìn）相如因功被封为高官，大将军廉颇居功不服，处处和他过不去。而蔺相如毫不计较。有一次，蔺相如和廉颇在路上相遇，廉颇故意挡道，蔺相如就退到一边，让廉颇先过。蔺相如手下的人认为廉颇无礼，很不服气。蔺相如对他们讲，文臣武将之间应该谦恭礼让，加强团结，这样国家才能兴旺。后来廉颇知道了这件事，觉得很羞愧，就到蔺相如家请罪。蔺相如也深为廉颇勇于改正错误的精神所感动，从此两人同心协力治理赵国。

　　汉代的孔融四岁时，有一天，父亲买来一些梨让大家吃。孔融挑了一个最小的。父亲问他为什么挑最小的，他说自己年纪小，应该吃最小的，大的让给哥哥们吃。"孔融让梨"的故事在中国家喻户晓，家长们经常用这个故事教育孩子要学会谦让。

　　中华民族谦虚礼让的美德代代相传，至今仍然产生着积极的作用。

　　As traditional virtues of the Chinese nation, modesty and comity are mainly composed of the following elements: First, to know oneself accurately and see one's own limitations, and never become complacent. Second, to detect others' strong points, tolerate others' weaknesses, and respect others. Third, to correctly treat personal interests, give each other precedence, and not to claim credit oneself, or to scramble for fame and gain. Ancient men distilled the relationship between modesty and success into one sentence —— "Complacency spells loss, while modesty brings benefit".

In the Spring and Autumn Period (770-476 BC), Confucius once went to visit Lao Zi. Although Lao Zi was older and more knowledgeable, he drew a cart in person to welcome Confucius to his home. Confucius asked Lao Zi modestly for advice and Lao Zi explained various points patiently one by one. When they parted, Lao Zi said that a virtuous person should be sincere and honest, and not be proud and greedy or have vain hope. These words left a deep impression on Confucius. He later said, "If there are three men walking together, one of them is bound to be good enough to be my teacher." The words and deeds of Lao Zi and Confucius had great influence on later generations.

In the Warring States Period (475-221 BC), Lin Xiangru of the State of Zhao was given a title of senior official for having rendered outstanding service to the state, but General Lian Po claimed the credit for the work, and always tried to embarrass him. Lin Xiangru never argued with him. Once, Lin Xiangru met the general in the street and the latter deliberately blocked the way. Lin Xiangru withdrew and let Lian Po go first. His subordinates were angry, considering Lian Po had behaved impolitely. But Lin Xiangru told them that officials and officers should be modest and polite, give each other precedence and strengthen unity, and in this way the country could prosper. Later Lian Po got to know this, and, feeling ashamed, he went to Lin Xiangru's house to apologize. Lin Xiangru was also deeply moved that the general was brave enough to correct his mistakes. From then on, the two acted in concert to manage the State of Zhao.

When Kong Rong of the Han Dynasty (206 BC -220 AD) was four years old, one day his father bought some pears and Kong Rong chose the smallest one. His father asked him why; he said that he was the youngest and should eat the smallest and leave the bigger ones for his elder brothers. Every household in China knows the story of "Kong Rong yielding the bigger pears to his elder brothers", and parents often instruct their children through this story to learn comity.

1. 孔子虚心求学，树立良好的品德规范
   Sincere and modest, Confucius became the virtuous model for all.
2. 陕西宝鸡钓鱼台砖雕。传说周文王礼遇太公，为太公拉车
   Tile craving of Diaoyu Island, Baoji, Shaanxi Province. According to the legend, Emperor Zhou Wen was humble enough to steer the cart for his minister Taigong.

诚实守信
Honest and Trustworthy

　　诚实，就是忠诚正直，言行一致，表里如一。守信，就是遵守诺言、不虚伪欺诈。"言必信，行必果"、"一言既出，驷马难追"这些流传了千百年的古话，都形象地表达了中华民族诚实守信的品质。在中国几千年的文明史中，人们不但为诚实守信的美德大唱颂歌，而且努力地身体力行。

　　孔子早在2,000多年前就教育他的弟子要诚实。在学习中，知道的就说知道，不知道的就说不知道。他认为这才是对待学习的正确态度。

　　曾子也是个非常诚实守信的人。有一次，曾子的妻子要去赶集，孩子哭闹着也要去。妻子哄孩子说，你不要去了，我回来杀猪给你吃。她赶集回来后，看见曾子真要杀猪，连忙上前阻止。曾子说，你欺骗了孩子，孩子就会不信任你。说着，就把猪杀了。曾子不欺骗孩子，也培养了孩子讲信用的品德。

　　秦朝末年有个叫季布的人，一向重诺言，讲信用。人们都说"得黄金百斤，不如得季布一诺"。这就是成语"一诺千金"的由来。后来，季布遇到了灾祸，正是靠了朋友的帮助，才幸免于难。可见，一个人如果言而有信，自然会得到大家的尊敬和爱护。

　　旧时中国店铺的门口，一般都写有"货真价实，童叟 (sǒu) 无欺"八个大字。这说明，中国自古在商品买卖中，就提倡公平交易、诚实待客、不欺诈、不作假的行业道德。

　　在当代中国，诚实守信的美德也得到了发扬光大。这种美德表现在工作和学习上，就是专心致志，认真踏实，实事求是；表现在与人交往中，就是真诚待人，互相信赖；表现在对待国家和集体的态度上，就是奉公守法，忠诚老实。

Honesty is to be faithful and upright, think and act in the same way, and always practice what one says. Be trustworthy is to keep one's word and not to be hypocritical and deceitful. Old sayings having spread for thousands of years, such as "True in word and resolute in deed", and "A word once spoken cannot be overtaken even by a team of four horses" vividly manifest the need to be honest and trustworthy.

Confucius taught his disciples to be honest. In study, if you know a thing, say you know it; if you don't know, say so. He thought that it was the correct attitude towards study.

Zeng Zi was also an honest person. Once, his wife wanted to go to a market fair and their child cried and demanded to be taken along. His wife coaxed the child out of this by promising that, when she returned, she would kill a pig and cook pork for him. After she returned, she saw Zeng Zi was about to kill a pig and stopped him. But Zeng Zi said, "If you cheat the child, he will never trust you." He then went and killed the pig. Because Zeng Zi did not deceive the child, he fostered the spirit of keeping one's word in the child.

旧时中国店铺强调公平交易，诚实待客
The ancient Chinese shops advocated the ethics of fair trade.

In the late Qin Dynasty (221-207 BC), a man named Ji Bu always kept his word. People often said that "Better to get Ji Bu's promise than one hundred *jin* (Chinese weight measurement) of gold", thus creating the expression that a "promise is worth a thousand pieces of gold". Later, when Ji Bu met with catastrophe, he narrowly escaped due to the help of his friends. Hence, a person who keeps his word will naturally win respect and care from the people.

In olden times, the doors of Chinese shops had an inscription "Guarantee quality goods and reasonable prices for all customers". This shows that since ancient times China advocated the ethics of fair trade, honesty towards customers, no deception and no falsification.

In modern China, the virtue of being honest and trustworthy has been carried forward. It is to be single-minded, earnest and steadfast at work and study; it is to be sincere to friends and trust others when making friends; it is to be law-abiding, faithful and honest.

乐善好施
Be Glad to Give to Charities

乐善好施，在中国民间被称为"行善"和"义举"，它与同情、正义、善良、热情等优秀品质密切相连，是中华民族的一种传统美德。

中华民族历来把帮助别人当作一件快乐的事，提倡以真诚的同情心，主动去帮助和解救那些处于危难和困境中的人们。这种帮助，不计亲疏，不图回报。人们把帮助别人当作崇高的义务，也在帮助人的过程中获得幸福，使自己的精神、道德得到升华和完善。

2,000年前的汉将韩信，年轻时家境贫寒，经常吃不上饭。一天，一位在河边洗衣服的老妈妈看见韩信可怜，就拿饭给他吃。韩信非常感激，表示将来一定要报答。老妈妈说："我给你一点饭吃，并不是为了得到你的报答。"确实，这位老妈妈连名字都没有留下，但在她身上体现出来的乐于助人的美德却千古传颂。

宋朝的范仲淹做地方官时，一位下属病死，遗下年轻的妻子和两个孩子。范仲淹便拿出自己的钱接济他们。在他的带动下，其他官员也纷纷解囊相助。这种扶危济困的行为还感染、教育了下一代，范仲淹的儿子范尧夫也继承了这种美德，成为一个乐于助人的人。

旅居海外的许多华侨、华人，为兴教助学、扶助贫困地区慷慨解囊，义捐善款。他们的善举和美德，得到了家乡人民和海外侨胞的尊敬和爱戴。

乐善好施、扶危济困、助人为乐的美好品德，在今天的中国更是深入人心。一人受难，众人相帮；一方遭灾，八方支援，已成为一种普遍的社会风尚。

Being glad to give to charities, also called in China "doing good deeds" and "righteous deeds", is closely linked to outstanding qualities such as sympathy, justice, kindness, and warmheartedness, and is a traditional virtue of the Chinese nation.

Chinese have always considered it a happy deed to help others, and taking the initiative to help those in difficulties with sincere sympathy. This kind of help makes no distinction between those who are relatives or friends and those who are not, and requires no repayment. People deem it a noble obligation to help others, during which they become happy and thus promote and perfect their soul and morals of their own.

More than 2,000 years ago, Han Xin, who later became a general of the Han Dynasty, was so poor that he couldn't afford to eat. One day, an old woman washing clothes beside a river offered him some food. Han Xin was very grateful and said that he would reciprocate her kindness in the future. The old woman said, "I offered you food not to obtain your repayment". The old woman even did not tell Han Xin her name, but her virtue of being ready to help others has been handed down from generation to generation.

When Fan Zhongyan of the Song Dynasty (960-1279 AD) was a local official, one of his subordinates died of illness and left behind a young wife and two children. Fan Zhongyan gave financial aid to them. Encouraged by Fan, other officials also showed their generosity. Their act in helping those in distress had a positive influence on the offspring of Fan Zhongyan. His son, Fan Yaofu, inherited this virtue and always helped others.

Many overseas Chinese or foreign citizens of Chinese origin generously give financial aid and donate money to impoverished areas in order to provide educational opportunities and support and help those who want to learn. Their good deeds and virtues have won them respect and the love of people at home and abroad.

Virtues of being happy to do good and give alms, helping those in distress and aiding those in peril, and feeling happy to help others, have taken root in the hearts of the people in present China. It has become a common practice that whenever there is a problem, assistance comes from all quarters.

1. 中国的"希望工程"捐款活动，使贫困家庭的孩子圆了上学梦
   The "Hope Project" is organized by charity groups who help extend education to poor families.
2. 不少善心人捐款建校，还送出书簿文具予受助学童
   Many people donate to charities that provide schooling and give out free textbooks.

尊师重教
Honor the Teacher and Stress Education

重视教育，尊敬师长，在中国有着悠久的传统。自古以来，中华民族都把教育放在十分重要的地位。早在2,600多年前，管仲就说过：考虑一年的事情，要种好庄稼；筹划十年的目标，要种好树木；规划百年大事，就要培养人才。在中国第一部教育学专著《学记》中也提出了"教学为先"的思想，认为国家的首要任务就是教育。3,000多年前的周代，国家按行政区划，设立了不同规模、不同层次的学校，由官员兼任教师。到了春秋时期，孔子在他的家乡开办了私学，并提出人无论贵贱还是贫富，都有受教育的权利。

由于教育得到重视，在中国，读书人有较高的社会地位，有知识、有文化的人非常受人尊重。自古以来，无论贵族还是百姓，无论富人还是穷人，都千方百计地让子女上学读书，掌握知识。

对教育的重视，决定了教师的地位。中国民间有许多尊师的说法，如：尊师不论贵贱贫富；一日为师，终身为父等等。自古以来，从百姓到皇帝都十分敬重老师。如：在北京的孔庙里，有清代13位皇帝为孔子题写的牌匾，表达了帝王们对这位古代伟大教育家的景仰。

在中国，尊敬老师已成为一种源远流长的社会风尚，对老师的尊重，表现在社会生活的方方面面。教师见君王可以免掉许多礼节，反而当官的见到老师要躬身下拜。人们称老师为"恩师"、"先生"，在日常生活中以师为先，以师为尊。现在，中国还把每年的9月10日定为教师节，以表达对教师职业的尊重。

It is a tradition in China to attach importance to education and respect the teacher. Since ancient times, the Chinese nation has put education in a very important position. As Guan Zhong said over 2,600 years ago: it takes a year to grow crops, ten years to grow trees but a hundred years to rear people. And in China's first monograph on education —— *Record of Learning* —— an idea of "education first" was proposed, which holds that the prime task of a state is education. In the Zhou Dynasty more than 3,000 years ago, the government established schools of different scales at different levels according to administrative divisions, and officials acted as part-time teachers. In the Spring and Autumn Period (770-476 BC), Confucius opened a private school in his hometown, and put forward the idea that any person, whether of high or low social status, poor or rich, had the right to receive an education.

Since great importance is attached to education, intellectuals in China have high social status, and highly literate men are respected. Since ancient times, all levels of society have tried by every means to send their children to school.

The importance attached to education determines the status of the teacher. In China, there are many sayings about respecting the teacher. For example, the teacher, no matter of distinguished or humble origin, rich or poor, should be respected; a tutor for a day is a father for a lifetime. And since ancient times, people from the emperor down to the lowest subject have all shown great respect for the teacher. For instance, in the Confucian Temple of Beijing, there are boards inscribed with characters written by 13 emperors of the Qing Dynasty, showing imperial respect and admiration for this great educator of ancient China.

Respect for the teacher can be seen in all aspects of social life. The teacher could be excused from etiquette when meeting the emperor, and officials should bow down when meeting the teacher. People call the teacher "Honorable Master" or "Sir", and give them respect and priority in daily life. Now, China has a Teachers' Day on September 10, in order to demonstrate public esteem for them.

1. 教育家孔子的墓
   The mausoleum of the great educator: Confucius
2. 孔庙
   Confucius Temple

尊老爱幼
Respect the Aged and Care for the Young

1. 中国人有尊老爱幼的传统
   The Chinese have the fine tradition of respecting the elders and loving the youth.
2. 中国有法定的"老人节"和"儿童节"，继承和发扬尊老爱幼的道德教育
   The Elder's Day and Childern's Day in China demonstrate the fine moral teaching of respecting the aged and loving the young.

　　尊敬老人、爱护儿童是中华民族的优良传统。几千年来，人们一直把尊老爱幼作为一种社会责任和行为规范。战国时期的孟子就曾说过：要像尊敬自己的老人一样尊敬别人的老人，要像爱护自己的孩子一样爱护别人的孩子。在中国，违背了这种道德的人，不光会受到舆论的批评，严重的还要受到法律的惩处。

东汉时有个叫黄香的人，从小孝敬父亲。为了让父亲睡得舒服，他夏天用扇子为父亲扇凉席子，冬天用身体为父亲温暖被窝。汉文帝的母亲生病时，文帝每次都要亲口尝过汤药的冷热，才端给母亲。早在汉朝时，政府就曾多次发布命令，提倡、奖励孝敬老人的行为。当时政府发给70岁以上的老人一种拐杖，用这种拐杖的老人，在社会上可以得到特殊的优待和照顾。清朝康熙、乾隆年间都举行过大型的尊老敬老活动，皇帝亲自在宫里宴请65岁以上的老人，每次人数都多达千人。

中国人对后代的关怀爱护是爱中有教，慈中有严，包含着强烈的道德责任感。古人留下的《诫子书》、《家训》等大量有关教育子女的著作，是中华民族一笔宝贵的道德教育财富。著名的故事《孟母三迁》，就说明了中华民族非常重视对子女的教育。孟子小的时候，母亲担心住家周围杂乱的环境对他的成长不利，连续搬了三次家，直到把家搬到了学校的旁边，孟母才放下心来。

尊老爱幼的传统在当代得到了继承和发扬。现在，中国的老人和儿童有自己的法定节日"敬老节"和"儿童节"；政府还专门制定了保护妇女儿童的法律；法律中也明文规定了公民必须履行赡养父母、抚养子女的义务。

尊老爱幼这种传统的美德保证了家庭的和睦和社会的稳定，也为中华民族繁衍发展提供了坚实的社会基础。

It is a fine tradition of the Chinese nation to respect the aged and love the young. For thousands of years, people have always considered it a social responsibility and behavioral norm to respect the aged and care for the young. Mencius in the Warring States Period (475-221 BC) said that one should respect the elderly relatives of other people as one's own, and take good care of others' children as one loved one's own. In China, a person who ignores these moral tenets will not only be criticized by public opinions, but also punished by law.

Huang Xiang of the Eastern Han Dynasty (25-220 AD)

毛麻绣——母与子
The embroidery depicting a mother's love

treated his father with filial respect from childhood. In order to let his father sleep more comfortably, he cooled his sleeping mat with a fan in summer and warmed the quilt by himself in winter. When the mother of Emperor Wendi of the Han Dynasty (206-220 AD) was ill, the emperor would taste the decoction of medicinal ingredients and then carry it to his mother himself. As early as the Han Dynasty, the government issued orders many times advocating and encouraging and rewarding behavior related to treating the old with filial respect. At that time, the government distributed a kind of walking stick to those over 70, and those with the stick could get special treatment and care. In the Qing Dynasty (1644-1911 AD), when Emperor Kangxi and Emperor Qianlong reigned, they held large-scale activities to show respect for the aged; each time, the emperor held a banquet for more than 1,000 men aged 65 and over in his palace.

The Chinese people treat their offspring with love and education, with kindness and strictness, embodying a strong sense of moral responsibility. A number of books on educating children left by ancient men, such as *Advice to My Son* and *Parental Instruction*, are precious tracts on moral education. The famous story *Mencius' Mother Moved Three Times* shows the great stress laid on educating children. When Mencius was young, his mother was afraid that the chaotic surroundings of their house would have an unfavorable impact on his growth, and thus moved three times. Only when they finally moved close to a school was her mind at rest.

The tradition of respecting the old and caring for the young has been carried forward in modern times. At present, the old and the young in China have their own legal holidays —— Elders' Day and Children's Day. The government has promulgated specific laws to protect women and children; and the law also stipulates in explicit terms that Chinese citizens have the obligation to support parents and rear children.

概述
Introduction

中国是世界上四大文明古国之一。在相当长的一个历史时期内，中华民族在科学技术方面的成就，一直保持着世界领先的地位。世界上第一台地震观测仪的发明，数学领域里对圆周率的精确推算，第一架测天仪的诞生……都遥遥领先于西方千百年。著称于世的古代四大发明、先进发达的农业科技，举世闻名的水利工程、神奇奥妙的中医中药……中华民族在科学技术方面所创造的奇迹，犹如闪烁的繁星，数不胜数。

China is one of the four ancient civilizations. In a relatively long historical period, its achievements in the fields of science and technology were advanced. The invention of the first seismograph, accurate calculation of *pi* in mathematics, creation of the first astronomical instrument, etc. were all centuries ahead of the West. Ancient China's four great inventions — the compass, gunpowder, papermaking and printing, advanced agricultural science and technology, water conservancy projects enjoying worldwide prestige, profound traditional Chinese medical science and traditional Chinese medicine were among many proud achievements.

指南针
Compass

1

2

1. 指南针
   Compass
2. 罗盘
   Ancient compass
3. 司南
   Magnetic spoon

指南针是中国古代"四大发明"之一。

在指南针发明以前，人们在茫茫大海上航行，只能靠太阳和星星的位置辨认方向，如果遇上阴雨天，就会迷失方向。是中国人发明的指南针，帮助人们解决了这个难题。

指南针是指示方向的仪器。早在战国时期，中国人就发现了磁石指示南北的特性，并根据这种特性制成了指示方向的仪器——司南。司南由一把光滑的磁勺和刻着方位的铜盘组成，勺把指示的方向是南方，勺头指示的方向是北方。到了宋代，人们把经过人工磁化的指南针和方位盘结合起来，制成了"罗盘"。有了罗盘，无论在什么情况下，人们都能准确地辨认方向了。

北宋时，指南针已开始应用于航海事业上。南宋时，指南针经由阿拉伯传到欧洲，当时的阿拉伯人亲切地称指南针为"水手之眼"。

指南针的发明，给航海事业带来了划时代的影响，世界航运史也由此翻开了新的一页。明朝初期郑和率领船队七下西洋，15世纪哥伦布发现新大陆和麦哲伦环绕地球航行等壮举，都是指南针用于航海事业的结果。

The compass is one of the four great inventions of ancient China.

Before the compass was invented, people depended upon the position of the sun and stars to tell them the direction when at sea, which only worked when it wasn't cloudy.

As early as the Warring States Period (475-221 BC), Chinese discovered that a magnet could indicate south and north, and, on the basis of this feature, made a southward-pointing instrument that was the prototype of the compass. The instrument comprised a smooth magnetic spoon and a copper plate carved with directions; the handle of the spoon points south. In the Song Dynasty, people combined an artificially magnetized compass with an azimuth plate to create a proper compass.

In the Northern Song Dynasty (960-1127 AD), the compass was being used for navigation at sea. In the Southern Song Dynasty, its use spread to Europe via Arabia, and Arabs called it affectionately "the Eye of Sailors".

The invention of the compass had epochal influence on navigation, opening up a new chapter in the history of world navigation. Thus, Admiral Zheng He made seven voyages across seas to Southeast Asia and around Indian Ocean in the early Ming Dynasty (1368-1644 AD), Christopher Columbus discovered the New World, and Ferdinand Magellan sailed round the world.

3

古代造纸术
Papermaking

造纸术是中国古代"四大发明"之一。

在造纸术发明以前，人们把字刻写在龟甲、兽骨、竹片、木片和绢帛①(juànbó)上。甲骨、木片很笨重，用起来不方便；绢帛太贵，一般人用不起。大约在西汉初期，人们用大麻和苎麻②(zhùmá)造出了纸。这种早期的纸比较粗糙，不太适合写字。

到了东汉时期，在朝廷做官的蔡伦，经过长期的试验，改进了造纸方法。他用树皮、破布、破鱼网等多种植物纤维作原料，加水蒸煮，捣烂成浆，再均匀地摊在细帘子上晾干，造成了一种薄薄的纸。这种纸便于写字，而且便宜，受到了人们的欢迎。所以说蔡伦在造纸术方面的贡献是巨大的。

东汉以后，造纸技术得到不断的改进，竹子、稻草、甘蔗渣等都逐渐成为造纸原料。因为原料不同，纸也有了各种不同的种类和用途。安徽省宣州生产的宣纸，就是闻名中外的上等纸张，是用于中国书法、绘画的珍品。

中国的造纸术于隋末唐初传到朝鲜和日本，后来又传到阿拉伯地区和其他国家，纸的发明，极大地方便了信息的储存和交流，对于推动世界文明的发展具有划时代的意义。

1

2

1. 西汉早期麻纸地图
   The plant-fiber map of the early Western Han
2. 古代造纸流程图
   The ancient procedure of papermaking
3. 广东肇庆邓村至今仍沿用传统的造纸技术
   The people in Deng Village, Zhaoqing, Guangdong Province, still adopt the traditional method of papermaking

Before the papermaking technology was invented, people carved or wrote Chinese characters on tortoise shells, animal bones, bamboo slices, wooden plates, and thin tough silks[1]. Tortoise shells, animal bones and wooden plates are too heavy to use while silks are too expensive. Around the early period of the Western Han Dynasty (206 BC-25 AD), people made paper from hemp and ramie[2]. Initially, this was very rough and not suitable for writing characters on.

During the Eastern Han Dynasty (25-220 AD), an official named Cai Lun improved the technique after years of experimentation. He used many plant fibers such as bark, rags, torn fishing nets as raw materials, steamed and cooked them with water, then pounded them into pulp, and then spread the pulp evenly on a fine screen and dried it into a kind of thin paper. The paper was suitable for writing and also very cheap so it became very popular.

Papermaking technology gradually improved so that various types of paper were created for different uses. For example, the *Xuan* paper made in Xuanzhou of Anhui Province is a high quality paper adapted for use in Chinese calligraphy and painting.

The technology spread to Korea and Japan in the late Sui (581-618 AD) and early Tang (618-907 AD) dynasties, and later to Arabia and other countries. The invention of paper made it more convenient for information storage and communication and had a great significance in promoting the development of international civilization.

小注解 Footnotes

① 绢帛：一种丝织品。
② 苎麻：一种草本植物，是纺织工业的重要原料。

① It is a kind of silk fabric.
② As a kind of herb, ramie is an important raw material for textile industry.

古代印刷术
Printing

印刷术是中国古代"四大发明"之一。

印刷术发明以前，读书人要得到一本新书，只有一个字一个字地抄写。隋唐时，发明了雕版印刷术①，提高了印书的速度。但是每印一本书都要雕大量的版，还是十分费事。到了900多年前的北宋时期，平民发明家毕升，经过反复试验，发明了活字印刷术。他把字刻在一小块一小块的胶泥上，放进火里烧硬，做成一个个活字。印书时，把活字按书稿排列，排成整版后印刷。印完后，把这些活字拆下来，以后还可以再用。毕升发明的活字版印刷术，既经济又省时，使印刷技术进入了一个新时代。

中国的活字印刷术先向东传到了朝鲜、日本，接着向西传到波斯、埃及，最后传遍了全世界。印刷术的发明大大加快了世界各国文化发展、交流的速度。活字印刷术是中国对世界的一大贡献。

🔍 小注解 Footnotes

① 雕版印刷术：把字一个一个地刻在一块木板上，涂上墨，用纸覆在上面进行印刷。

① Chinese characters are engraved on a wooden plate and coated with Chinese ink, and then covered with paper to print.

Before printing was invented, a scholar had to copy characters one by one if he wanted to create a new book. In the Sui and Tang dynasties, block technology① was invented, which improved the speed of printing. But to print a book, many blocks had to be engraved, which was troublesome. During Northern Song Dynasty more than 900 years ago, Bi Sheng invented movable-type printing after years of experimenting. He engraved the characters on small pieces of clay, and heated them until they became hard movable characters. When printing a book, people placed the moveable characters in order into a whole block and then run off a print. After printing, they could take the block apart and reuse the characters later. This method was both economical and timesaving.

China's movable-type printing first spread eastward into Korea and Japan, and then westward into Persia and Egypt, and, at last, around the world. The invention of printing greatly speeded up the development of exchanges between cultures of all the countries throughout the world.

江苏苏州曲园木刻原版
The original wooden print block made in Suzhou, Jiangsu Province

火药
Gunpowder

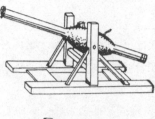

火药是中国古代的"四大发明"之一。

火药的配方最初是由中国古代炼丹家在炼制丹药的过程中发现的。后来，人们根据这个配方，将硝石、硫磺、木炭按一定比例配制在一起，制成了黑火药。唐朝中期的书籍里，就记载了制造这种火药的方法。火药发明后，先是被制成了爆竹和焰火，到了唐朝末年，开始用于军事。北宋时，火药在军事上大量使用，那时候的火药武器有突火枪、火箭、火炮等。

公元1225－1248年之间，火药和火药武器经由阿拉伯传到欧洲。因为制造火药的主要原料硝石洁白如雪，所以火药被阿拉伯人称为"中国雪"和"中国盐"。火药传到欧洲后，被各国用来制造兵器，还在开山、修路、挖河等工程中广泛使用，火药的使用促进了工业革命的到来。

The formula of the gunpowder was first discovered by Taoist alchemists of ancient China when trying to make pills of immortality. Later, people made up black gunpowder with niter, sulfur and charcoal of certain proportions on the basis of the formula. Books of the middle Tang Dynasty (618-907 AD) recorded the method of producing this kind of gunpowder. It was first used to make firecrackers and fireworks, and then used in military affairs in the late Tang Dynasty. In the Northern Song Dynasty (960-1127 AD), gunpowder-based weapons such as rockets and cannon were widely used.

Between 1225 and 1248, gunpowder and the related weapons spread to Europe via Arabia. Since the major raw material of gunpowder niter is as white as snow, Arabians called gunpowder "Chinese Snow" and "Chinese Salt". After gunpowder spread into Europe, it was not only used in weapons, and also for cutting through mountains, constructing roads, and digging rivers. The invention of gunpowder accelerated the coming of the Industrial Revolution.

张衡和地动仪
Zhang Heng and the Seismograph

在北京中国历史博物馆的展览大厅里，陈列着世界上第一架地动仪的复原模型。这架地动仪的发明者是中国东汉时著名的科学家张衡。

张衡（公元78－140年），河南南阳人。他勤学好问，博览群书，特别爱好天文、历法和数学，是一位博学多才的科学家。

公元132年，张衡在京城洛阳制成了可以测定地震方向的"候风地动仪"。地动仪全部用精铜铸成，外形像一个带盖的大茶杯。仪器表面铸有八条垂直向下的龙，龙头分别对准东、南、西、北、东南、东北、西南、西北八个方向，每条龙的嘴里都含着一个铜球。在对着龙嘴的地上，蹲着八个仰着头、张着嘴的铜蟾蜍（chánchú）。地动仪的内部结构非常精细巧妙，当某个方向发生地震时，仪器上对着那个方向的龙嘴就会张开，铜球就会掉进铜蟾蜍的嘴里，自动报告发生地震的方向。公元138年的一天，地动仪西边的龙嘴吐出了铜球。果然，远在千里之外的陇西（今甘肃省）在这一天发生了地震。这是人类第一次用仪器测报地震。在欧洲，直到1,700多年后，才发明了同类的仪器。

张衡还制造出了世界上第一架测量天体位置的水运浑天仪，凡是已知的重要天文现象，都刻在这架仪器上。人们可以通过浑天仪观测到日月星辰运行的情况。张衡又是一位机械工程师，制造过能飞的"木雕"和能计算里程的"计里鼓车"等。

人们非常敬重张衡这位1,800多年前的大科学家，经常举行纪念活动，表示对他的敬意。月球上有一座环形山是以他的名字命名的，这也是世界人民对他的纪念。

In the Exhibition Hall of the Museum of Chinese History in Beijing, there is a restored model of the first seismograph. The inventor was Zhang Heng, a famous scientist in the Eastern Han Dynasty (25-220 AD).

Zhang Heng (78-140 AD) was from Nanyang of Henan Province. He studied diligently, and was especially fond of astronomy, calendar and mathematics.

In 132 AD, in the then national capital of Luoyang, Zhang Heng made the ancient seismograph to determine the direction of an earthquake. It was made of fine copper, and looked like a big cup with a lid. The instrument was cast with eight dragons on the surface, whose heads pointed in eight directions — east, south, west, north, southeast, northeast, southwest, and northwest; and each dragon had a copper ball in the mouth. On the ground below the dragons there were eight copper toads raising their heads and opening their mouths opposite the dragons' mouths. The inner side of the seismograph was ingeniously constructed. When an earthquake occurred, the dragon facing that direction would open its mouth, and the ball would fall into the toad's mouth, automatically indicating the direction of the earthquake. One day in 138 AD, the dragon in the west expelled its ball. As expected, an earthquake had occurred that day in Longxi (present-day Western Gansu Province) a thousand kilometers away. It was the first time that mankind had used an instrument to detect an earthquake. It was over 1,700 years later that a similar instrument was invented in Europe.

Zhang Heng also made the first water-driven celestial globe in the world to measure the position of celestial bodies, which was carved with known important astronomical phenomena. People could observe the movement of the sun, moon and stars. Zhang Heng was also a mechanical engineer, and made a flying "wooden eagle" and a "mileage-counting drum-cart".

People highly esteem Zhang Heng, a great scientist living more than 1,800 years ago, and they often hold commemorative activities to show respect for him. A ring of hills on the moon was named after him.

1. 张衡 (右)是东汉的著名科学家
   Zhang Heng (right) is the famous scientist in the Eastern Han Dynasty.
2. 浑天仪
   Celestial globe
3. 地动仪
   Seismograph

祖冲之和圆周率
Zu Chongzhi and *Pi*

月球背面有一座环形山，被命名为"祖冲之环形山"。

祖冲之 (公元429－500年) 是中国南北朝时著名的数学家、天文学家和机械制造家。他从小聪明好学，爱好自然科学、文学和哲学，经过刻苦的学习钻研，终于成为一位享誉世界的科学家。

祖冲之在数学方面的成就为世界所公认。远在1,500多年前，祖冲之就计算出了精确的圆周率[①]。圆周率通常用"π"来表示，求算圆周率的值是数学中一个非常重要也是非常困难的研究课题。中国古代许多数学家都为研究这个课题付出了心血，并取得了喜人的成果。祖冲之在前人研究的基础上，继续进行了深入系统的研究，经过1,000多次的计算，得出圆周率在3.1415926和3.1415927之间，成为世界上第一个把圆周率推算到小数点后七位数字的科学家。祖冲之还提出 π 的近似值为355/113，称为"密率"，把数学中关于圆周率的计算推进到一个新阶段，成为当时世界上最精确的圆周率。日本数学家尊称它为"祖率"。直到1,000多年以后，西方的数学家才达到和超过了祖冲之的成就。

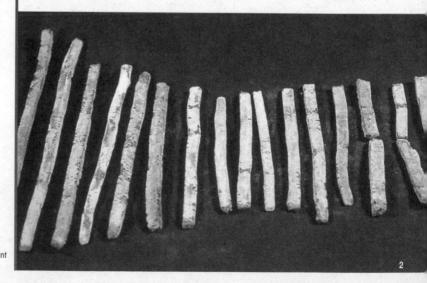

1. 数学家祖冲之像
   A portrait of the mathematician Zu Chongzhi
2. 古代算筹(中国最古老的计算工具)
   Chips used for counting (the most ancient tabulating device of China)

圆周与直径的关系图
Circumference versus Diameter Graph

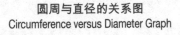
圆周 Circumference

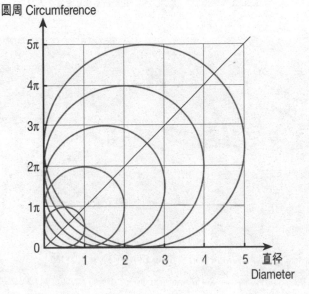

Zu Chongzhi (429-500 AD) was a famous mathematician, astronomer and mechanic in the Southern and Northern Dynasties (421-581 AD). Smart and fond of learning since childhood, he liked natural science, literature and philosophy, and later became a world-famous scientist.

The achievements Zu Chongzhi made in mathematics have been universally acknowledged. He worked out an accurate value of pi[1]. Pi is usually represented by π, and it has always been a very important yet difficult research topic for mathematics to calculate the value of pi. Many mathematicians of ancient China made painstaking efforts in this research with satisfactory results. Based on earlier research, Zu Chongzhi continued to carry out systematic study. After calculating more than 1,000 times, he concluded that the value of pi falls between 3.1415926 and 3.1415927; and therefore he became the first scientist in the world who calculated the value of pi to seven decimal places. Zu Chongzhi also put forward the thesis that the approximate value of pi was 355/113, which was called milü (close ratio), pushing the calculation of pi to a new stage. The value was the most accurate in the world at that time, and Japanese scientists respectfully called it the "Zu Chongzhi Ratio". Not until more than 1,000 years later, did scientists in the West come up to and surpass the achievements of Zu Chongzhi.

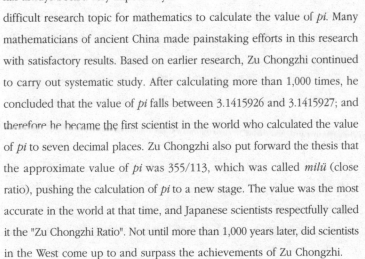

小注解 Footnotes

① 圆周率：圆周长度与圆的直径长度的比。

[1] Pi is the ratio of the circumference of a circle to its diameter.

黄道婆改革纺织术
Huang Daopo Innovating Textile Technique

　　黄道婆生活在宋末元初，是松江乌泥泾人。她年轻时因为受不了公婆的虐待，离开家乡流落到海南岛。海南岛盛产棉花，那里的黎族同胞很早就从事棉纺织业。黄道婆和黎族姐妹一起生活，结下了深厚的友谊，也学到了一整套种植和纺织棉花技术。

　　30年后，两鬓斑白的黄道婆回到家乡。她把在海南岛学会的纺织技术教给松江的兄弟姐妹，同时还推广和改进了很多纺织机械，大大提高了劳动效率。她改进了弹棉花的弹弓，并成功地制成了当时世界上最先进的纺纱工具——三锭脚踏纺棉车；她还把黎族先进的纺织技术和汉族传统的织造工艺结合在一起，织成了配有各种图案的被褥等物品，被人们称为"乌泥泾被"。

　　黄道婆逝世后，当地人民把她安葬在乌泥泾镇旁，还编了歌谣来纪念这位平凡而伟大的古代巧妇。这首广为流传的歌谣是："黄婆婆，黄婆婆，教我纱，教我布，两只筒子两匹布。"

Huang Daopo of late Song Dynasty (960-1279 AD) and early Yuan Dynasty (1271-1368 AD) was from Wunijing of Songjiang. Since she could not bear her parents-in-law when she was young, she left her hometown and wandered to Hainan Island. The area is abundant in cotton, and the Yi people there had started a textile industry long ago. Huang Daopo lived with Yi women and learnt from them the techniques of planting and spinning and weaving cotton.

1. 纺织图
   A portrait of spinning and weaving
2. 江南一带仍可见弹棉花的传统工艺
   The traditional art of cotton fluffer can be found in the region south of Yangtze River.

Now gray at the temples, Huang Daopo came back to her hometown 30 years later. She taught people in Songjiang the textile technique she had learnt in Hainan. At the same time she also popularized and innovated textile machines that greatly increased efficiency. She improved on the cotton fluffer and successively made the most advanced textile tool of the time, a pedal spinning wheel with three spindles. Combining the advanced textile technique of the Yi ethnic group with the traditional weaving techniques of the Han ethnic group, she also produced textiles such as bedding with various patterns called "Wunijing Bedding".

After Huang Daopo died, local people buried her near Wunijing Town, and also compiled a ballad to commemorate this ordinary but also great ancient clever woman. The popular ballad is as follows: "Granny Huang, Granny Huang, teach me spinning, teach me weaving, two spindles and two bolts of cloth."

日晷和铜壶滴漏
Sundial and Copper Clepsydra

今天，各式各样的钟表为人们计时提供了方便。在没有钟表的古代，中国人用什么工具计时呢？

最初，人们根据日月星辰在天空中的位置来判断时间，但是这种判断并不准确。后来，人们设计了一种利用太阳测定时刻的计时器——日晷 (guǐ)。秦汉时，日晷已在民间流行。日晷是个大圆盘，晷面上刻着"子丑寅卯辰巳午未申酉戌亥"12个时辰，晷面中间插着一根铜针。在太阳的照射下，铜针的影子随着太阳的移动在晷面上慢慢地移动。移到哪个刻度上，就是到了哪个时辰。这样，计算时间就准确多了。

但是到了阴天和夜晚，日晷就起不了作用了。后来，人们又用滴水、漏沙的方法计时，发明了一种新的计时工具——铜壶滴漏。

铜壶滴漏又叫"漏刻"、"刻漏"、"壶漏"、"漏壶"。最早的漏壶用一只铜壶盛水，壶底有一个小洞，壶中插一根刻有刻度的标杆，水从小洞滴出后，人们根据水位降低后标杆上的刻度来判断时间。这种漏壶计时的准确性仍然比较差。

漏壶历代相传，由单只逐渐发展成为后来四只一套的漏壶。人们把四只漏壶依次放在一个四级木架上，上面的一只叫日壶，下面的三只分别叫月壶、星壶、授水壶。日壶、月壶、星壶的下面各有一个滴水的铜嘴，授水壶内有一个标尺。水从日壶滴入月壶，再到星壶，最后滴入授水壶。授水壶内的水越来越多，标尺受到水的浮力作用逐渐上升，人们通过标尺浮出水面的刻度，就可以知道时间了。漏壶的级数越多，计时就越准确。现在，在北京的中国历史博物馆和故宫博物院里还分别保存着元代和清代的四级漏壶，供人们参观。

日晷和铜壶滴漏是中国古人聪明才智的结晶，它们不仅告诉了我们古人计时的方法，也留下了中国古代科学技术发展的宝贵资料。

Today, all kinds of clocks and watches bring convenience to daily life. But in ancient times, how did Chinese people measure time?

At first, they judged the time according to the position of the sun, the moon and stars in the sky, which was not very accurate. Later, people designed a kind of hour counter using the sun to determine the time — the sundial. In the Qin (221-207 BC) and Han (206 BC-220 AD) dynasties, the sundial had become popular. The sundial is a round plate, the surface is carved with 12 hours (*zi, chou, yin, mao, chen, si, wu, wei, shen, you, xu* and *hai*), with a copper needle embedded in the center of the surface. Under the sun, the shadow of the copper needle moves slowly on the surface of the sundial to provide an accurate indication of time.

But when it is cloudy or at night, the sundial does not function. Later, people used the method of dropping water or sand to measure time, and invented a new tool — the copper clepsydra.

The copper clepsydra was also called a water clock, hourglass, and sandglass. The earliest clepsydra was a copper pot holding water with a small opening at the bottom and a pole with scales standing in the center. When the water dropped through the small hole, people determined time by the scale on the pole as the water level decreased. This method of measuring time through clepsydra was still not accurate.

As the clepsydra was passed on from generation to generation, it gradually evolved into a set of four pots. These are placed in order on a four-level wooden stand, the one on the highest level called the Sun Pot, and below it the Moon Pot, Star Pot and Water-receiving Pot, respectively. The Sun Pot, Moon Pot and Star Pot all have an opening at the bottom for water to drop, and the Water-receiving Pot has a gauge inside. The water drops from the Sun Pot into the Moon Pot and then into the Star Pot and at last into the Water-receiving Pot. As more and more water drops into the Water-receiving Pot, the gauge gradually increases with the buoyancy of water. And thus people could tell the time through the scale above the water. The more levels the clepsydra has, the more accurate it is to measure time. Now, the four-level clepsydra of the Yuan (1271-1368 AD) and Qing (1644-1911 AD) dynasties are preserved respectively in the Museum of Chinese History and the Palace Museum in Beijing.

The sundial and copper clepsydra are the crystallization of ancient Chinese' wisdom and creativeness. They not only tell us how ancient Chinese measured time, but also provide precious materials on the development of science and technology in ancient China.

1. 日晷
   Sundial
2. 铜壶滴漏
   Copper clepsydra

2

算盘和珠算
Abacus and Calculation with an Abacus

算盘是中国古代一项伟大的发明。

算盘是中国人在长期使用算筹 (chóu) 的基础上发明的。古时候，人们用小木棍进行计算，这些小木棍叫"算筹"，用"算筹"作为工具进行的计算叫"筹算"。后来，随着生产的发展，需要计算的数目越来越大，用小木棍计算受到了限制，于是，人们又发明了更先进的计算器——算盘。

算盘是长方形的，四周是木框，里面固定着一根根小木棍，小木棍上穿着木珠，中间有一根横梁把算盘分成两部分：每根木棍的上半部有两个珠子，每个珠子代表五；下半部有五个珠子，每个珠子代表一。

随着算盘的使用，人们总结出许多计算口诀，使计算的速度更快了。这种用算盘计算的方法，叫珠算。到了明代，珠算已能进行加减乘除的运算，广泛用于计算物体的重量、数量、面积、体积等。

由于算盘制作简单，价格便宜，珠算口诀便于记忆，运算又简便，所以算盘在中国被广泛使用。中国各行各业都有一批打算盘的高手，而且有的人能用左右两只手同时打算盘。

算盘后来陆续流传到了日本、朝鲜、美国和东南亚等国家和地区。人们在使用过程中发现，使用算盘，除了运算方便以外，还有锻炼思维能力和动手能力的作用。因为打算盘需要脑、眼、手的密切配合，是训练综合反应能力的一种好方法。

The abacus was invented on the basis that Chinese used the counting-rod for a long period. In ancient times, people used small rods to count. Later, with the development of productivity, the amount requiring calculation was greater, and calculation with counting-rods limited the calculation. Thus, people invented a more advanced counter — the abacus.

The abacus is rectangular with wooden frame on the four sides and small rods fixed inside strung with wooden beads; a girder across the middle separates the abacus into two parts: Each rod has two beads on its upper part, each representing five, and five beads on the lower part, each representing one.

With the application of the abacus, people summarized many abacus rhymes, increasing the calculating speed. By the time of the Ming Dynasty (1368-1644 AD), people could use the abacus in addition, subtraction, multiplication and division, which were widely used in calculating weight, amount, space and volume.

1. 中国一些庙宇把算盘放在显著位置，打出6、8等幸运数字，保佑善信
   Some Chinese temples would place an abacus which displays lucky numbers such as "6" and "8" at an obvious location to bless the worshippers.

2. 手工精细的小算盘
   A delicate abacus

3. 不同种类的算盘
   Different types of abacus

Since it is simple to make an abacus and cheap to buy one, and it is easy to remember abacus rhymes, simple and convenient to calculate with an abacus, it is widely used in China. There are many experts in the use of the abacus in all trades and professions, and some people can use an abacus with two hands at the same time.

Later the abacus gradually spread into Japan, Korea, America, and countries and regions in Southeast Asia. People find that using an abacus can improve thinking and practical abilities in addition to providing convenient calculation. Since it requires cooperation of the mind, eyes and hand, it is a good way to improve the comprehensive reaction ability.

针灸术
Acupuncture and Moxibustion Therapy

针灸术在中国已有几千年的历史，是中国医学宝库中一颗璀璨的明珠。

针灸术包括中国两种古老的治病方法：针法和灸法。针法是用特制的不同长度的金属针，按一定穴位，刺入病人体内，用捻、提等手法治疗疾病。灸法是把烧着的艾绒[①]按一定的穴位，靠近皮肤或放在皮肤上，利用热的刺激来治疗疾病。

中国古代有很多用针灸术为人治病的名医，像春秋时的扁鹊、东汉时的华佗等，他们治过不少疑难杂症，被誉为能使人起死回生

1. 扁鹊像
   A statue of Bian Que
2. 针灸铜人模型
   A bronze human figure marked with acupuncture points

的"神医"。公元1027年，宋代针灸医官王惟一，创造了针灸史上一大奇迹。他设计铸造了两具针灸铜人模型，在铜人体上精细地刻了十二经脉和354个穴位，供人学习针灸时使用。这是中国最早的医用铜人模型，也是中国针灸教育事业上的一个创举。

今天，古老的针灸术不但在中国广泛使用，为人们解除病痛，而且还漂洋过海，传到了全世界各个地方。

小注解 Footnotes

① 艾绒：艾是一种植物，叶子可入药。

① Moxa is a kind of plant, whose leaves can be used as medicine.

Acupuncture and moxibustion therapy, with a history of thousands of years in China, is at the core of Chinese medicine.

Acupuncture therapy involves jabbing specially made metal needles of different length into the patient's body at certain acupuncture points, treating the patient by twirling or lifting the needles. Moxibustion therapy requires the placement of burning crushed dry moxa[①] near or on the skin at certain acupuncture points, treating by the irritation of heat.

In ancient China, there were many well-known doctors using acupuncture and moxibustion therapy to treat patients, such as Bian Que of the Spring and Autumn Period (770-476 BC) and Hua Tuo of the Eastern Han Dynasty (25-220 AD), who had treated some difficult and complicated cases, and thus were acclaimed as miracle-workers. In 1027 AD, a medical official of acupuncture and moxibustion of the Song Dynasty (960-1279 AD) Wang Weiyi designed and made two bronze human figures marked with acupuncture points, carefully carved 12 channels and vessels and 354 acupuncture points on the figures for people to use when learning the therapy. This was the earliest bronze human figure for medical use in China.

Nowadays, acupuncture and moxibustion therapy is not only widely used in China to relieve people of their diseases, it has also spread around the world.

2

麻醉术
Narcotherapy

麻醉术就是用药物或针刺等方法使人的全身或某一部分暂时失去知觉，医疗上一般在实施外科手术时使用。世界上第一个发明麻醉手术的人是中国东汉时的"神医"华佗。

早在春秋战国时期，中国的民间医生就懂得并记载了某些药物所具有的麻醉作用。东汉名医华佗在认真研究古书的基础上，亲自去山野里采集具有麻醉作用的曼陀罗等药草，经过炮制加工，制成了麻醉药"麻沸散"。

一天，人们抬来一个危重病人。华佗让病人喝下"麻沸散"，然后打开他的腹腔，清理了腐烂的肠子，在病人毫无痛苦的情况下完成了剖腹手术。这次手术是中国也是世界上有文字记载的最早的大型剖腹手术病例。

现代医学已经广泛地使用麻醉术，人们永远不会忘记麻醉术的先驱者——华佗。

华佗像
A portrait of Hua Tuo

Narcotherapy is to disable the body or one part temporarily by drugs or acupuncture, which is usually used in surgical operations.

As early as the Spring and Autumn and the Warring States periods (770-221 BC), some Chinese doctors had known and recorded the anesthesia function of some drugs. The famous doctor Hua Tuo of the Eastern Han Dynasty (25-220 AD), on the basis of carefully studying ancient books, went to the mountains and plains to collect herbs with an anesthesia function, such as jimsonweed, which were made into narcotic drugs after being roasted and processed.

One day, people carried a seriously ill patient to Hua Tuo. He let the patient drink the drug and then opened his abdominal cavity and cleared away his rotten intestines, completing the operation while the patient felt no pain. This operation was the earliest recorded large-scale laparotomy both in China and in the world.

中医中药
Traditional Chinese Medical Science and Medicine

中国人很早就懂得用医药来保障自己的健康。中国的医药学是一座神奇的知识宝库，中医中药是世界上独树一帜的科学。

相传上古时候的神农氏①，曾经亲自品尝百草，识别药用植物。现存最早的一部医书《黄帝内经》，比较系统地总结了春秋战国以前的医疗经验，为中医学奠定了理论基础。战国时期的著名医生扁鹊，最早用望、闻、问、切四种方法诊断病情。这四种方法一直沿用到今天，成为中医的传统诊断法。望，是观察病人的外表和精神状态；闻，是听病人喘息的声音；问，是询问病人的发病过程、自我感觉和饮食起居状况；切，是摸查病人脉搏跳动的情况。

中药的来源主要是植物，也有一些动物和矿物。这些东西经过特殊的炮制，被制成内服、外用的药剂。汉代著名的药物学著作《神农本草经》，记载了365种药物。南北朝时期的名医陶弘景，又添加了365种，写成《本草经集注》。明代名医李时珍编著的《本草纲目》，收录了近2,000种药物和10,000多个药方。

中国历史上的名医多不胜数，像扁鹊、华佗、张仲景、孙思邈(miǎo)、李时珍等，都以他们精湛的医术为病人解除了痛苦。现代中国也有很多著名的医生，他们努力攻克医学难关，为人民造

1. 张仲景像
   A statue of Zhang Zhongjing
2. 中药店仍按古法配药
   Chinese herbal medicine shop prescribes traditional herbal formulas.

1. 中药材
   Herbal medicine
2. 草药田
   Herbal field

福。中国少数民族医学也有它的独到之处，像蒙医、藏医、维医、傣医等，都为各民族人民的健康幸福作出了自己的贡献。

现在，中医中药已传到了世界许多地方。

Chinese people knew how to safeguard their health by medical science and drugs long ago. Legend has it that Shennong Shi① of ancient times once tasted 100 herbs in person to distinguish herbal plants. China's earliest extant medical book *Canon of Medicine of the Yellow Emperor* systematically summarized medical experience before the Spring and Autumn and the Warring States periods (770-221 BC), laying a theoretical foundation for traditional Chinese medical science. The famous doctor of the Warring States Period Bian Que was the first to use observation, auscultation and olfaction, interrogation, and palpation for diagnosis. Observation is to observe the patient's appearance and mental state; auscultation and olfaction are to listen to the patient's breathing; interrogation is to inquire about the onset of the problem and the patient's own feelings, his diet and daily life; and palpation is to feel the pulse of the patient.

Traditional Chinese medicine mainly comes from plants, and also some animals and minerals. These are made into oral or external medicines after being specially prepared. The famous medical book of the Han Dynasty (206 BC-220 AD) *Shennong's Materia Medica* recorded 365 herbs. The well known doctor Tao Hongjing of the Southern and Northern dynasties (421-589 AD) added another 365 herbs and wrote *Variorum of Shennong's Materia Medica*. *Compendium of Materia Medica*, written by the famous doctor Li Shizhen of the Ming Dynasty (1368-1644 AD), included nearly 2,000 medicines and 10,000 prescriptions.

There are numerous famous doctors in Chinese history, such as Bian Que, Hua Tuo, Zhang Zhongjing, Sun Simiao, Li Shizhen, who relieved patients of pain with their consummate medical skills. In modern China, there are also many famous doctors who try hard to resolve serious difficulties and work for the well-being of the people. The medical sciences of China's ethnic minority groups, with distinctive features, have also contributed much, including that of the Mongolian, Tibetan, Uygur and Dai groups.

龕

龗

龓 龏

隸 辨

唐 欧陽通
道因法師碑

漢 礼器碑陰

漢 龜池五瑞図題字

龕

龍

龒

龕

龍

說 文

龐

龐

古龐字
虘鐘

說文古籀補

龐

說 文

邸鐘

文

唐褚遂良 伊闕仏龕碑

毛公鼎

龔

龍

龐

龕

龕

東晉郗超
淳化閣帖

龍

毋宇

龍

龍伯戡

龕

唐褚遂良倪寬贊

草書韻会

龐

龐

說文古籀補

東晉庾翼
淳化閣帖

唐褚遂良
淳化閣帖

龍

龍

隸 辨

概述
Introduction

　　历史悠久的汉语，是世界上使用人数最多的语言之一；古老的汉字，是世界上使用时间最长的文字之一。丰富、发达、历史悠久的汉语言文字，不仅是中华文化的载体，而且本身就是一种灿烂的文化。

　　The Chinese language is one of the languages with a written script that has the longest history and is used by the most number of people in the world. The language is not only a carrier of Chinese culture, but also a kind of culture in its own right.

汉语
The Chinese Language

汉语是中国汉民族使用的语言。汉语历史悠久，在3,000多年前就有了相当成熟的文字。

汉语是使用人数最多的一种语言，全世界大约有12亿人使用汉语。除中国大陆、台湾省和香港、澳门特区外，新加坡、马来西亚等国也有相当一部分人使用汉语，分布在世界各地的几千万华侨、华裔，也以汉语的各种方言[①]作为自己的母语。

汉语是中国人使用的主要语言，也是联合国的工作语言之一。汉语的标准语是"普通话"，在台湾省被称作"国语"，在新加坡、马来西亚等国被称作"华语"。汉语目前有七大类方言：北方话、吴语、湘语、赣（gàn）语、客家话、粤（yuè）语、闽（mǐn）语。汉语的普通话既是汉民族的共同语，也是汉民族的标准语。

中国除了汉语以外，还有几十种其他语言。

Used by the Han people in China, the Chinese language has a long history, having established a fairly mature written language more than 3,000 years ago.

The Chinese language has more than 1.2 billion users. In addition to the Chinese mainland, Taiwan Province, Hong Kong and Macao special administrative regions, some people in Singapore and Malaysia use Chinese, and millions of overseas Chinese and foreign citizens of Chinese origin distributed around the world use various Chinese dialects[①] as native language. It is also one of the working languages of the United Nations.

The standard language of Chinese is *putonghua* (Mandarin) which is called *guoyu* (national language) in Taiwan Province and *huayu* (Chinese language) in Singapore and Malaysia. The Chinese language presently has seven dialects: northern dialect, Wu dialect, Xiang or Hunan dialect, Gan dialect, Hakka, Yue or Guangdong dialect and Min dialect. Mandarin is the standard language as well as the common one of the Han people.

🔍 小注解 Footnotes

① 方言：一种语言中跟标准语有区别的，只在一个地区使用的话，如汉语的粤方言、吴方言等。

① Dialect differs from the standard language and is only used in one area, such as Guangdong and Wu dialects of the Chinese language.

普通话和方言
Mandarin and Dialects

中国的学校全部采用普通话授课
All schools in Mainland are taught in Mandarin.

🔍 小注解 Footnotes

① 白话文：指现代汉民族共同语的书面语言。

② 北方方言：以北京话为代表，通行于中国的东北、华北、西北、西南、江淮地区。

③ 吴方言：以上海话为代表，通行于中国的江苏省、浙江省的部分地区。

④ 湘方言：以长沙话为代表，通行于中国的湖南省大部分地区。

⑤ 赣方言：以南昌话为代表，通行于中国的江西省和湖北省东南一带。

⑥ 客家方言：以广东的梅县话为代表，主要通行于中国的广东省东北部、福建省西部和北部、江西省南部。

⑦ 闽方言：通行于中国的福建省、广东省潮汕地区、海南省、台湾省。

⑧ 粤方言：俗称广东话。以广州话为代表，通行于中国的广东省中部和西南部、广西省东部和南部、香港及澳门。

现代汉语是现代汉民族的语言，它包括普通话和多种方言。

普通话是现代汉民族共同语。它以北京语音为标准音，以北方话为基础方言，以典范的现代白话文①作为语法规范。普通话为中国不同地区、不同民族人们之间的交际提供了方便。

中国地域广阔，人口众多，即使都使用汉语言，各地区说的话也不一样，这就是方言。方言俗称地方话，是汉语在不同地域的分支，只通行于一定的地域。汉语目前有七大类方言：北方方言②、吴方言③、湘方言④、赣方言⑤、客家方言⑥、闽方言⑦、粤方言⑧。其中，北方方言是通行地域最广，使用人口最多的方言。客家话、闽语、粤语还在海外的华侨华人中使用。

汉语方言十分复杂。各方言之间的差异表现在语音、词汇、语法三个方面，其中语音方面的差异最明显。在中国东南沿海地区就有"十里不同音"的说法。如果各地人之间都用方言土语说话，就会造成交际上的困难。

早在2,000多年前，中国人就认识到，社会交际应该使用一种共同语。与"十里不同音"的方言相比，各地人都能听得懂普通话。

因为讲普通话有利于各民族、各地区人民之间的文化交流和信息传递，所以中国政府十分重视推广普通话的工作，鼓励大家都学普通话。

Mandarin has Beijing pronunciation as its standard pronunciation, northern dialect as its basic dialect, and the typical modern vernacular Chinese[1] as its grammatical standard. Mandarin offers convenience for communication between people at different areas or of different ethnic groups in China.

China has a vast territory and a large population. Even though people all use the Chinese language, they speak in different ways in different areas, which are called dialects. Generally called local languages, dialects are branches of the Chinese language in different regions, and are only used in certain areas. At present, the Chinese language has seven dialects: northern dialect[2], Wu dialect[3], Xiang dialect[4], Gan dialect[5], Hakka[6], Min dialect[7] and Yue or Guangdong dialect[8]. Among them, northern dialect is one used most widely. Hakka, Fujian dialect and Guangdong dialect are also used by overseas Chinese.

Dialects of the Chinese language are very complicated. Various dialects differ from each other on three aspects: pronunciation, vocabulary and grammar. And the difference in pronunciation is the most outstanding. There is a saying in coastal areas of southeastern China — "Pronunciations differ within 10-*li* (Chinese unit of measurement, 1 li=0.5 km) area". If all people in different areas speak in local dialects, it will lead to the trouble in communications.

More than 2,000 years ago, Chinese people had realized that a common language should be used in social intercourse. Compared with dialects "differing within 10-*li* area", Mandarin can be understood by all people. Since it is beneficial to cultural exchange and information transmission between ethnic groups and people in different places, the Chinese government attaches great importance to popularizing Mandarin and encourages people to learn Mandarin.

小注解 Footnotes

[1] Vernacular Chinese is the written language commonly used by modern Han people.

[2] Northern dialect, represented by Beijing dialect, is commonly used in northeastern China, northern China, northwestern China, southwestern China and areas along the Yangtze and Huaihe rivers.

[3] Wu dialect, represented by Shanghai dialect, is commonly used in some areas in Jiangsu and Zhejiang provinces of China.

[4] Xiang or Hunan dialect, represented by Changsha dialect, is commonly used in most areas of Hunan Province.

[5] Gan dialect, represented by Nanchang dialect, is generally used in Jiangxi Province and southeastern Hubei Province.

[6] Hakka, represented by Meixian dialect of Guangdong Province, is mainly used in northeastern Guangdong Province, western and northern Fujian Province, and southern Jiangxi Province.

[7] Min dialect is generally used in Fujian Province, Chaoshan area of Guangdong Province, Hainan Province and Taiwan Province.

[8] Yue or Guangdong dialect, represented by Guangzhou dialect, is generally used in central and southwestern Guangdong Province, eastern and southern Guangxi Province, Hong Kong and Macao.

汉字
Chinese Characters

汉字是世界上最古老的文字之一，也是世界上使用人数最多的文字。汉字的数量很多，总数约6万个，其中常用字约6,000个。

汉字有悠久的历史。目前发现的最古老的汉字，是距今3,400多年前的甲骨文，它们已是很成熟的文字。据科学家推算，汉字的历史有5,000年左右。

甲骨文 *Jiaguwen*	金文 *Jinwen*	篆书 *Xiaozhuan*	隶书 *Lishu*	楷书 *Kaishu*

汉字起源于记事图画。从古到今，汉字的形体发生了很大的变化，经历了甲骨文、金文、小篆①(zhuàn)、隶(lì)书②、楷(kǎi)书③等字体的演变。现行汉字的通行字体是楷书。

汉字的造字方法，主要有以下四种：

象形：是指画出事物形状的造字法。如："月"〔☽〕、"羊"〔𦍌〕。

指事：在象形字上加指事符号，或完全用符号组成字的造字法。如："刃"〔刃〕，在刀锋上加一点儿，指出刀刃所在。

会意：把两个或两个以上的符号组合起来，表示一个新的意义的造字法。如："休"〔休〕，一个人靠在树旁，表示休息的意思。

形声：用形旁和声旁组成新字的造字法。形旁，是表示字的意义和属性的偏旁。声旁，是表示字音的偏旁。如："湖"字，水是形旁，胡是声旁。大多数汉字都是形声字。

历史上，汉字曾被朝鲜、日本、越南等国家长期借用，促进了国际交流。在当代，中国人以多种方式解决了汉字进入计算机、为信息处理服务的问题。历史证明，汉字具有旺盛的生命力。

篆隶《千字文》
Thousand Character Essay in seal script

The Chinese characters constitute one of mankind's oldest systems of writing, and have the most users in the world. There are many Chinese characters, totaling about 60,000, with about 6,000 basic ones.

Chinese characters have a long history. The oldest Chinese characters discovered till now are *jiaguwen* (ancient Chinese characters carved on tortoise shells or animal bones), dating back 3,400 years, which were already mature characters. As scientists estimate, Chinese characters have a history of about 5,000 years.

Chinese characters originate from pictures for keeping records. From ancient to modern times, the form and structure of Chinese characters has changed a lot, evolving from *jiaguwen*, *jinwen* (ancient language used in inscriptions on ancient bronze objects), *xiaozhuan*[1] (small seal character), *lishu*[2] (official script), and *kaishu*[3] (regular script). The current script of Chinese characters is *kaishu* (regular script).

There are mainly four word-formation methods as follows:

Pictography refers to the method to draw the form of a thing, such as 月 (☽), 羊 (羊).

Self-explanatory characters are made up by adding self-explanatory symbols on pictographs, or totally made up of symbols, such as 刃 (刃), which is made up by adding a point on the cutting edge of a knife, pointing out the position of the blade.

Associative compounds are combination of two or more symbols to represent a new character of a new meaning. For instance, 休 (休) is a person leaning against a tree, meaning "rest".

Pictophonetic method is a word-formation method combining one element of a character indicating meaning and the other, sound, into a new word. Form element indicates the word's meaning and characteristic. Phonetic element indicates the pronunciation of the word. For example, 湖(lake) is composed of three dots indicating water and 胡, indicating the sound.

In history, Chinese characters were borrowed by Korea, Japan, and Vietnam, thereby promoting international communication. In modern times, Chinese people have by many means solved the problem of inputting Chinese characters into computers to serve information processing. It has been borne out that Chinese characters are of vigorous vitality.

甲骨文
Jiaguwen

中国现存最早的文字是甲骨文。甲骨文就是刻在龟甲或兽骨上的文字。主要是商代的文字。

商代甲骨文是1899年由清代学者王懿 (yì) 荣发现的，出土地点主要在河南安阳，那里曾经是商代晚期的都城。

在这之前，河南安阳小屯村的农民，经常发现刻着奇怪文字的龟甲和兽骨，他们不认识上面的字，就把甲骨当作药材卖给了药店。王懿荣从买来的中药中发现了这些龟甲、兽骨，经过研究，他认为，刻在甲骨上的文字，是3,000多年前商代的文字。

到目前为止，从河南安阳出土的有字甲骨共10多万片，发现甲骨文单字4,500个左右，已经确认的约有1,700字。这些文字，大都是商代统治者占卜祭祀时的祝辞和简单记事。甲骨文以象形字为主，笔画匀称，字形美观，这说明，甲骨文的形成，已经经过了相当长的发展过程。甲骨文是中国最早的、成熟的汉字，它为研究汉字的起源提供了重要的实物资料。

过去，人们一般把商代甲骨文当作中国最早的文字。20世纪80年代，又从西安市郊区出土了少量的有字甲骨，经过考古学家研究证明，这些甲骨文比商代甲骨文还要早，距今已有4,000年左右的时间。

The earliest extant characters in China are *jiaguwen* carved on tortoise shells or animal bones, mainly during the Shang Dynasty (17th-11th century BC).

Jiaguwen of the Shang Dynasty was discovered in 1899 by Wang Yirong, a scholar of the Qing Dynasty. The inscriptions were unearthed in Anyang of Henan Province that was the capital in the late Shang Dynasty.

Before the discovery, villagers of the Xiaotun Village in Anyang of Henan Province often found tortoise shells and animal bones carved with strange characters. They did not know what they were and sold them as medical materials to drugstores. Wang Yirong discovered these tortoise shells and

刻有文字的兽骨
The animal bone inscribed with the ancient language *jiaguwen*

1. 河南安阳殷墟是3,000多年前商代的都城，出土了许多刻有文字的龟甲和兽骨
   The 3,000-year-old ancient capital of Shang Dynasty (Yinxu, Anyang, Henan Province) unearthed many tortoise shells and animal bones that were carved with the oldest characters.

2. 古人把文字刻在兽骨上
   The animal bone inscribed with the ancient language *jiaguwen*

animal bones among some Chinese medicine he had bought. After research, he believed that the characters carved on tortoise shells and animal bones were those of the Shang Dynasty more than 3,000 years ago.

So far, altogether more than 100,000 pieces of tortoise shells and animal bones have been excavated from Anyang; about 4,500 Chinese characters have been discovered on tortoise shells and animal bones, among which 1,700 have been affirmed. These characters were mostly prayers by Shang rulers at divination and sacrificial rites, as well as simple records. *Jiaguwen* is mainly the pictograph with regular strokes and beautiful form, showing it had undergone a long development process. They provide important materials for research into the origin of Chinese characters.

In the past, people generally considered *jiaguwen* of the Shang Dynasty as the earliest kind of Chinese characters. In 1980s, a few tortoise shells and animal bones carved with characters were unearthed in suburban Xi'an. Archaeologists confirmed these characters were about 4,000 years ago, even earlier than *jiaguwen*.

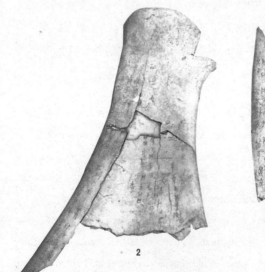

2

繁体字和简化字
Original Complex Chinese Characters and Simplified Chinese Characters

难学开习医.后丑云尘

難學開習醫後醜雲塵

千百年来，中国人用繁体字书写了浩如烟海的古籍，繁体字为记录历史、传播文化曾经立下过汗马功劳。

但是，笔画繁多的繁体字，难认、难记，也难于书写。因此，历史上各个时期，民间都创造了不少简体字，历代政府也不断地对汉字进行整理和规范。秦始皇推行的"书同文"[①]，就是中国历史上第一次大规模进行的汉字整理和规范工作。从汉字几千年的发展过程可以看出，汉字演变的总趋势是简化。

简化字，是汉字中由笔画繁多的字改写成的笔画简单的字。1949年以后，为了普及教育的需要，中国政府统一对汉字进行了较大规模的简化工作，先后有2,000多个繁体字被简化字取代。汉字简化的主要方法有：1.用简单的符号代替复杂的偏旁。如：难—難、学—學。2.保留繁体字的一部分。如：开—開、习—習、医—醫。3.用笔画简单的同音字代替。如：后—後、丑—醜。4.借用古字。如：云—雲、尘—塵。5.草书[②]楷化。如：书—書、乐—樂、当—當。"书"、"乐"、"当"都是古时的草体字。6.改换形声字的声旁。如：拥—擁、怜—憐。7.用传统方法造新字。如：形声字"护—護"、"响—響"；会意字"笔—筆"、"岩—巖"。

现在，简化字是联合国的工作文字之一，而在台湾、香港等地区仍然通行繁体字。

For thousands of years, Chinese people wrote with original complex Chinese characters ancient books as vast as the open sea, which rendered great service to the recording of history and the spreading of culture.

However, these characters, with many strokes, are hard to recognize,

书　書
乐　樂
当　當
拥　擁
怜　憐
护　護
响　響
笔　筆
岩　巖

remember, and write. Thus, people created some simplified Chinese characters during each historical period, this process continued through time to sort out and regulate them. The First Emperor of the Qin Dynasty introduced *shutongwen*[1], which was the first large-scale sorting and standardization. From the development of Chinese characters for thousands of years, we can see that the overall evolving trend of Chinese characters is simplification.

Simplified Chinese characters are those with fewer strokes adapted from complex ones with many strokes. After 1949, in order to make education universal, the Chinese government simplified Chinese characters in a unified and relatively large-scale way, when more than 2,000 original complex Chinese characters were successively replaced by simplified ones. Major methods to simplify Chinese characters are as follows: 1. Replace complicated basic components with simple symbols, such as 难—難, and 学—學. 2. Retain part of original complex Chinese character, such as 开—開, 习—習, and 医—醫. 3. Replace original complex Chinese character with its homophone of simple strokes, such as 后—後, and 丑—醜. 4. Borrow ancient Chinese characters, such as 云—雲, and 尘—塵. 5. Transform *caoshu*[2] (cursive or grass script) into *kaishu* (regular script), such as 书—書, 乐—樂, and 当—當. 6. Replace the phonetic element of pictophonetic characters, such as 拥—擁, and 怜—憐. 7. Form new characters by traditional methods, such as pictophonetic ones 护—護, and 响—響, and associative compounds 笔—筆 and 岩—巖.

At present, simplified Chinese characters are one of the working languages of the United Nations, while original complex ones are still in common use in Taiwan Province and Hong Kong.

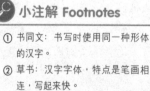

小注解 Footnotes

① 书同文：书写时使用同一种形体的汉字。
② 草书：汉字字体，特点是笔画相连，写起来快。

① *Shutongwen* is a kind of Chinese characters using the same form when written.
② *Caoshu* is a kind of script of Chinese characters, which features in flowing strokes and quick writing.

概述
Introduction

　　中国文学是中国文化中最有活力、最辉煌灿烂的一部分。在历史发展的长河里，中国文学体现了中华文化的基本精神，体现了中华民族的理想信念和美学追求。表现出了自己独特的个性和精神风采，从瑰丽奇特的远古神话到《诗经》、《楚辞》、唐诗、宋词、元杂剧、明清小说……各种文学形式此起彼伏，高潮迭起，连绵数十年，不断地创造出反映人民生活和时代精神的文学大观，涌现出了许多古今闻名的文学家。

Chinese literature is a most dynamic and glorious part of Chinese culture in manifesting its basic spirit and the aspirations and aesthetic pursuits of the Chinese nation with a unique nature and charm. From myths of remote antiquity to *The Book of Songs*, *Chu Ci* poems, Tang Dynasty poems, Song Dynasty *Ci* poems, Yuan Dynasty *Zaju* (poetic drama set to music), works of fiction of the Ming and Qing dynasties... those different forms of literature have spanned thousands of years and represent the cream of the output of a large number of famous men of letters.

远古神话
Myths of Remote Antiquity

中国远古神话，大多是原始社会劳动人民的集体创作。它们经历了口头流传的漫长岁月，直到文字发明以后，才被记载下来。

中国远古神话，以丰富神奇的想像，反映了远古社会丰富多彩的历史内容，其中有：解释世界起源的《盘古开天地》、《女娲造人》、《女娲补天》；反映人类与自然作斗争的《后羿射日》、《夸父追日》、《精卫填海》；歌颂献身精神的《神农尝药》、《鲧（gǔn）禹治水》等等。

《女娲补天》讲的是：远古时候，天空突然塌下半边，出现了一个大洞，大地上洪水泛滥，猛兽横行，人类面临着巨大的灾难。这时，人类的母亲女娲挺身而出，炼出五彩石修补天空，拯救了人类。

《鲧禹治水》讲述了鲧、禹父子两代治理洪水的故事。远古时候，大地被洪水淹没，大神鲧偷了天帝的宝贝"息壤"——一种能自己生长的土，去堵塞洪水，事后被天帝处死。三年后，禹从鲧的肚子里跳出，继承父亲的事业，继续治水。八年之中，大禹三过家门而不入，终于疏通了河道，使洪水流进了大海。

这些美丽动人的神话，不仅反映了远古先民对自然现象的认识和征服自然的愿望，也体现了中华民族祖先不怕困难、英勇顽强地与自然灾害作斗争的伟大精神。

中国远古神话在民间流传很广，它给人以鼓舞和启发，促使人们把神奇的幻想变为现实。远古神话对中国文学的发展影响很大，后世的许多著名作家都从古代神话中吸取营养，创作出了优美、动人的文学篇章。

Chinese myths of remote antiquity were mostly created collectively by the laboring people of the primitive society, circulated and handed down orally until written script was invented to provide a more permanent record.

Drawing on the powerful imagination of their creators, these myths reflect the rich and colorful life of ancient society. The best-known include *Pangu Separates the Sky from the Earth, Nu Wa Makes Men, Nu Wa Mends the Sky,* describing how the world came into being; *Hou Yi Shoots down Suns, Kua Fu Chases the Sun, Jing Wei Determines to Fill up the Sea,* reflecting mankind's incessant struggle against nature; *Shennong Shi Tastes Medicine, Gun and Yu Harness Water,* written in praise of selfless devotion.

Nu Wa Mends the Sky: Long, long ago, half of the sky suddenly collapsed and a huge hole appeared. Floods ravaged the land and beasts ran amok, so that the human race was in great danger. Just then, a woman named Nu Wa came out to mend the sky with five colored rocks that she had previously tempered, and thus saved mankind.

Gun and Yu Harness Water: Long, long ago, the land was flooded. A deity named Gun stole the Heavenly Emperor's treasure, *xirang,* a kind of earth that could grow to block floods. He was later tracked down and put to death. Three years later, Yu leapt out of Gun's stomach. He succeeded to his father's work and continued to harness the waters. He was so devoted to the task that in eight years he never once entered his own home, although he passed the front door three times. The river was harnessed at last, and the floodwaters poured safely into the sea through the watercourses they had dredged.

Such fascinating myths not only reflected ancient people's understanding of nature and their wish to tame it, but also their dauntless spirit and tenacity in the struggle against natural disasters.

Chinese myths of remote antiquity continue to circulate, giving people courage and providing them with enlightenment to help them turn their dreams into reality. The ancient fantasies had a great impact on the development of Chinese literature. Many renowned writers of later generations drew inspiration from them in their own outstanding works.

1. 龙凤仕女图
   A portrait of the mythic dragon, the phoenix and the lady
2. 大禹像
   A portrait of Yu

《诗经》
The Book of Songs

　　《诗经》是中国第一部诗歌总集。它收录了从西周初年到春秋中叶大约500年间的305首诗。相传,周代的采诗官经常到民间收集诗歌,也有官员们向天子献诗的制度。这些诗歌经过乐官的整理编订后,形成了这部诗歌总集。《诗经》最初叫《诗》或《诗三百》,后来,孔子把《诗三百》作为教科书传授给弟子。汉代以后又被称为《诗经》。

　　《诗经》以四字句为主,语言清新,音韵和谐,风格朴素。如:

……

彼采萧 (xiāo) 兮 (xī),

一日不见,

如三秋兮。

……

　　这首名叫《采葛 (gé)》的诗,表达了一位男子思念情人的焦急心情。诗的大意是:她去采集香草了,一天没见,好像隔了三年那么长。成语"一日不见,如隔三秋"就是由此而来的。

　　《诗经》中的很多作品都真实地描写了当时的社会风貌,其中表现青年男女爱情、婚姻生活的特别多。除此以外,有的诗歌描写了下层人民的劳动生活;有的反映了人民反抗压迫,追求自由幸福的愿望;有的控诉了战争造成的苦难;有的直接揭露了统治者的丑恶。

　　《诗经》是中国文学的光辉起点。它所取得的思想和艺术成就,对后世诗歌的发展产生了巨大而深远的影响。

1

The Book of Songs is the earliest collection of poems in China. It contains 305 poems created over a period of some 500 years from the early Western Zhou Dynasty (11th century-771 BC) to the middle of the Spring and Autumn Period (770-476 BC). It was said that, in the Zhou Dynasty, there were officials whose job was to collect poems from the public. There was also a rule requiring officials to compose poems and present them to the emperor for eventual editing and compilation in this anthology. At first, *The Book of Songs* was known as *Poems* or *Three Hundred Poems*. Confucius used it as a textbook for teaching his disciples. Eventually, after the Han Dynasty, more than 2,000 years ago, it became known officially as *The Book of Songs*.

Poems in *The Book of Songs* are made up of four-character verses. The language used is in the form of concise and refreshing rhymes. They are simple in style. For instance:

There she is gathering vine/ A day without seeing her/ Is like three seasons.

This poem entitled *Gathering Vine* expresses a young man's anxiety in the absence of his woman. The popular idiom "a day without seeing is like three seasons" originated from this poem.

Many poems in *The Book of Songs* truthfully mirror the life and society of that time. A large number are about love and marriage. Others depict the hard work of laborers at the bottom of society, while some reflect people's wishes for a free and happy life, denounce wars that caused sufferings, and directly expose the evil acts of rulers.

The Book of Songs' ideological and artistic achievements had great influence on the evolvement of poetry of later generations.

1. 《诗经》
   The Book of Songs
2. 《鹿鸣之什图》展示《诗经》的意境
   A portrait inspired by The Book of Songs

楚辞
Chu Ci

1. 《九歌》：山鬼图
   An illustration of *Nine Songs*: "Mountain Ghost"
2. 屈原是中国著名爱国诗人，他的作品华美浪漫，想像奇特
   Qu Yuan was a famous patriotic poet, and his works were romantic and imaginative.
3. 《九歌》：湘君图
   An illustration of *Nine Songs*: "The Goddess of the Xiang River"

"楚辞"是在《诗经》之后出现的一种新诗体，公元前4世纪诞生在中国南方的楚国。"楚辞"在形成过程中，受到了楚地民歌、音乐及民间文学的影响，带有浓厚的楚国地方色彩。

"楚辞"的代表作家屈原，是中国历史上最受尊敬的伟大诗人之一，每年端午节，中国人都要举行赛龙舟等活动纪念他。20世纪50年代，屈原被推举为世界文化名人，受到了全世界人民的敬仰。他的主要作品有《离骚》、《天问》[①]、《九歌》[②]等。

《离骚》是一篇宏伟壮丽的政治抒情诗。全诗共370多句，2,400多字。诗人用血和泪的文字，讲述了自己的身世、品德和遭遇，倾诉了他对楚国命运的关怀和坚持理想的决心。他在诗中驾起玉龙，乘上彩车，在月神、风神和太阳神的护卫下，神游天上，追求理想，最后不得不离开他深爱的楚国。屈原的爱国热情和不屈精神，激励了一代又一代的作家。

"楚辞"中神话传说的运用，奇特的想像，奔放的情感，华美的词章，展现了独特的浪漫色彩，为中国文学开辟了一条新路。

Chu Ci was a new style of poetry to emerge after *The Book of Songs*. It originated in the State of Chu in southern China in the 4th century BC. In the course of the formation of this genre, it was much influenced by folk songs, music and the folk literature of the State of Chu, and so it was characterized

2

by a strong local color.

The best representative poet of *Chu Ci* was Qu Yuan, who is held in the highest esteem in China. On the Dragon Boat Festival every year, Chinese people hold dragon boat race to commemorate him. In the 1950s, Qu Yuan was recommended and cited as an outstanding cultural figure in the world for all people to respect. His main works include *Sorrow After Departure* (*Li Sao*), *Asking Heaven* (*Tian Wen*)[1], *Nine Songs* (*Jiu Ge*)[2], etc.

Sorrow After Departure (*Li Sao*) is a colossal political lyric made up of over 370 lines with 2,400 characters. With deep grief, the poet recounts his life, his beliefs and misfortunes, expresses his concern over the fate of the State of Chu and his determination to maintain his lofty aspirations. In this poem, he rode on a jade dragon and a colorful chariot, traveled to Heaven in search of his ideals under the protection of the God of the Moon, the God of Wind and the God of the Sun. Finally he was forced to leave his most beloved State of Chu. Qu Yuan's patriotism and unyielding spirit has encouraged many writers down through the generations.

The use of myths and fantasies, the strange twists of imagination, the vigorous surge of feelings and beautiful verses in *Chu Ci* demonstrate a unique romanticism that has never faded.

🔍 小注解 Footnotes

① 《天问》：是一首十分奇特的长诗。它用诗歌的形式，一口气提出了170多个问题。

② 《九歌》：是屈原根据楚国民间神话故事，并利用民间祭歌的形式写成的一组抒情诗。包括《东皇太一》、《云中君》、《湘君》、《湘夫人》等。

① *Asking Heaven* (*Tian Wen*) is a very unique long poem that asks 170 questions in rapid succession.

② *Nine Songs* (*Jiu Ge*) is a group of lyrics based on local folk tales and myths, including "The Great Emperor of the East", "The Lady of the Clouds", "The Goddess of the Xiang River" and "The Lady of the Xiang River".

汉乐府
Yuefu Songs of the Han Dynasty

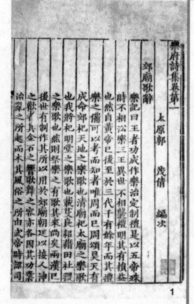

"乐府"原指汉代的音乐机构，它的职责是收集、采撷文人诗和民间歌谣，并配上乐曲。后来，由乐府收集、编制的诗也被称为乐府。汉乐府中的精华是汉乐府民歌[①]。

江南可采莲，莲叶何田田。鱼戏莲叶间。鱼戏莲叶东，鱼戏莲叶西，鱼戏莲叶南，鱼戏莲叶北。

这首名为《江南》的民歌，表现了江南百姓采莲的情景和劳动时的愉快心情。诗的大意是：江南大湖里的莲蓬到了可以采摘的季节，湖里长满了莲花荷叶，小鱼儿在莲叶间游来游去……

汉乐府民歌大多是叙事诗，这些诗真实地表达了人民的喜怒哀乐。有的反映了劳动人民的穷困生活；有的揭露了战争给人民带来的痛苦；有的表现了反对封建婚姻、追求美好爱情的愿望；有的揭露了贵族的腐朽生活和社会的黑暗。

《孔雀东南飞》是汉乐府中最有名的诗篇，也是中国历史上第一部长篇叙事诗，它生动地叙述了一个封建家庭的爱情悲剧故事：

孔雀东南飞，五里一徘徊。十三能织素，十四学裁衣，十五弹箜篌 (kōnghóu)，十六诵诗书……

聪明、美丽、善良的刘兰芝和焦仲卿结婚后，互敬互爱，感情深厚。但是，焦仲卿的母亲却狠毒地拆散了这对夫妻。刘兰芝、焦仲卿双双自杀，变成了一对永不分离的鸳鸯，"仰头相向鸣，夜夜达五更"。这首长诗，通过刘兰芝、焦仲卿的悲剧，控诉了封建礼教、家长统治的罪恶，表达了青年男女追求婚姻自由的愿望。

汉乐府真实反映社会现实的精神和伟大的艺术成就，对后世诗歌的发展产生了直接和巨大的影响。

Yuefu originally referred to the musical bureau in the Han Dynasty (206 BC-220 AD) in charge of collection of folk ballads and poems created

小注解 Footnotes

① 民歌：采集于民间的诗歌。

① Songs that are popular among local people.

1. 《乐府诗集》书影
   The collection of *Yuefu* songs and poems
2. 采莲图
   A portrait depicting a lotus-picking scene

by literati, which would then be set to music. Later, poems and folk ballads collected and compiled by the *Yuefu* were given this generic name. Folk songs^① form the best part of the *Yuefu* songs of the Han Dynasty.

Time to gather lotus in the Yangtze Valley, / As lotus leaves are fair and lusty. / Fish frolic amidst the lotus leaves. / Fish frolic to the east of the lotus leaves, / Fish frolic to the west of the lotus leaves, / Fish frolic to the south of the lotus leaves, / Fish frolic to the north of the lotus leaves.

This folk song entitled *Jiangnan* (south of the Yangtze River) depicts the joyous mood of local people gathering lotus.

Most of the *Yuefu* songs of the Han Dynasty are narrative poems, which truthfully reflected people's feelings. Some mirror the poverty-stricken life of laboring people; some expose the misery caused by war; some express opposition to feudal marriage customs and express a wish for true love; some reveal the decadent life of noblemen and the seedy side of society.

The best known is *The Bride of Jiao Zhongqing* (*Kong Que Dong Nan Fei*), which is also the earliest long narrative poem in Chinese history. It gives a vivid account of a tragedy of two lovers in a feudal family.

Southeast the lovelorn peacock flies. Alack, / At every mile she falters and looks back! / At thirteen years Lanzhi learned how to weave; / At fourteen years she could embroider, sew; / At fifteen music on her lute she made; / At sixteen knew the classics, prose and verse....

Liu Lanzhi, a smart, pretty and kind hearted girl, and her husband Jiao Zhongqing, loved each other deeply, But Jiao's mother was so cruel that she forced them to separate. As a result, both Jiao and Liu committed suicide and turned into a pair of lovebirds. *"They cross their bills and sing to one another / Their soft endearments all night long till dawn."* The tragedy condemned the feudal ethics and evil clan rule, and expressed the wishes of the young for free marriage.

The pursuit of faithful reflection of social reality by *Yuefu* songs of the Han Dynasty and the artistic merits they achieved had great impact on the development of poetry in later generations.

南北朝民歌
Folk Songs of the Northern and Southern Dynasties

从东晋灭亡到隋朝统一的100多年间，是中国历史上南北对峙的南北朝时代。

南北朝民歌也是人民的口头创作，是汉乐府民歌之后出现的又一批民歌。

南朝民歌大多是情歌，而且多数是从女子的口中唱出的。《西州曲》是南朝民歌中的代表作，描写了一个女子一年四季对情人的思念。南朝民歌语言清新自然，诗中喜欢用双关语①，显示出了丰富的想像力。保留到今天的南朝民歌大约有500首。

北朝民歌大部分是少数民族人民创作的。这些民歌从多方面反映了北方各民族的社会生活面貌。由于北朝战争频繁，因此，民歌中反映战争的作品比较多。长篇叙事诗《木兰辞》是北朝民歌中最杰出的作品。它歌颂了女英雄花木兰女扮男装代父从军，奋战疆场，杀敌立功的英雄气概。这在重男轻女的封建社会，具有特殊的意义。这首诗深受人民喜爱，木兰从军的故事还被搬上了银幕、舞台，一直流传到今天。北朝民歌风格豪放，语言朴素，和南朝民歌形成了鲜明的对比。

南北朝民歌对后来唐朝的诗人有很大的影响。

The one hundred years from the fall of the Eastern Jin (317-420 AD) to the founding of the Sui Dynasty (581-618 AD) was a period of confrontation between two powers, one in the north and the other in the south. This period is known in Chinese history as the Northern and Southern dynasties (421-581 AD).

Folk songs of the Northern and Southern dynasties were created orally by people in the wake of *Yuefu* songs.

Songs of this genre are mostly love songs. It is worth noting that most were created by women. *Ode to Xizhou* is a representative work that describes a young woman missing her man in the four seasons of the year. The language used in these songs is refreshing and natural. Puns[1] are often used, which show the powerful imagination of authors. To date, about 500 folk songs of the Northern and Southern Dynasties have been preserved.

Folk songs of the Northern Dynasty were mostly created by ethnic groups and reflected the society and their lives. As the Northern Dynasty was riven by wars, most folk songs had something to do with this aspect. The long narrative poem *Mulan Ci* is the best-known work of that period. It praises the heroine Mulan who, disguised as a man, joins the army on behalf of her father and wins great merit on the battlefield. In a feudal society in which women were regarded as inferior to men, this poem had its special significance. It has maintained its great popularity and has been adapted for the screen and stage. Folk songs of the Northern Dynasty are vigorous in style, with a simple, plain language in sharp contrast to that of folk songs of the Southern Dynasty.

Folk songs of the Northern and Southern dynasties had great influence on poets of the Tang Dynasty (618-907 AD).

小注解 Footnotes

① 双关语：用词造句时，表面上是一个意思，暗中隐藏着另一个意思，常利用同音字构成，如：莲—可怜，丝—思，篱—离等。

① Pun: the use of a word in such a way as to suggest two or more of its meanings.

1. 木兰从军图
   An illustration of Mulan going to war
2. 河南商丘花木兰故里
   The hometown of Mulan, Shangqiu, Henan Province

唐诗
Poetry of the Tang Dynasty

唐代，是中国古典诗歌的全盛时期。在不到300年的时间里，唐诗的创作达到了非常高的水平，产生了许多著名的诗人和诗作。流传到今天的，有近50,000首唐诗和2,300多位诗人的名字。

唐代最著名的诗人是李白①和杜甫②，他们都是具有世界声誉的大诗人。

李白被人们称为"诗仙"，是一位热情奔放、才华横溢的诗人。他一生几乎走遍了中国大地。他的诗歌豪迈奔放，想像奇特，热情地歌颂了祖国的壮丽山河，强烈地表现了对国事的关心，对黑暗政治的不满，对美好理想的追求。李白的诗保存到现在的有990多首，其中的《将进酒》、《蜀道难》、《望庐山瀑布》等名诗，世代被人们传颂。

杜甫被后人尊为"诗圣"。他年轻时游历过许多名胜古迹，后来又有机会接触到下层人民。不平凡的经历，使他了解了人间的黑暗和人民的苦难。他在诗歌中大胆地揭露了封建王朝的腐朽，深刻地反映了人民生活的疾苦和当时社会的变化。杜甫的诗保留到今天的有1,400多首，其中著名的诗作有《春望》、《兵车行》以及"三吏"③、"三别"④等。

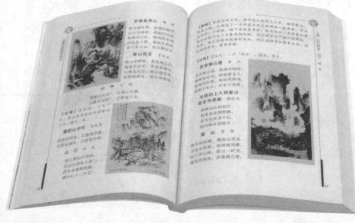

唐代的著名诗人还有王维、白居易、李贺、李商隐等。

唐诗一直受到中国人的喜爱，许多诗歌连儿童都能背诵，如：《静夜思》⑤、《春夜喜雨》⑥等。"欲穷千里目，更上一层楼"⑦、"黄河之水天上来"⑧等唐诗名句，经常被人们引用。唐诗的普及读本《唐诗三百首》，受到了中外读者的欢迎。

唐代诗歌不仅达到了中国诗歌

1

史的顶峰，而且也是世界诗歌宝库中的奇珍异宝。

附：**静夜思** 李白　　　　　**绝句** 杜甫

床前明月光，　　　　两个黄鹂鸣翠柳，

疑是地上霜。　　　　一行白鹭上青天。

举头望明月，　　　　窗含西岭千秋雪，

低头思故乡。　　　　门泊东吴万里船。

2

The Tang Dynasty witnessed the zenith of Chinese ancient poetry, with many renowned poets and famous works appearing over a period of less than 300 years. Some 50,000 poems and the names of 2,300 poets of that period remain widely known today.

The best-known poets of the Tang Dynasty are Li Bai[1] (701-762 AD) and Du Fu[2] (712-770 AD).

Being unconstrained and most talented, Li Bai traveled all over China. With lofty sentiments and powerful imagination, he created many poems in praise of its magnificent mountains and mighty rivers. He also showed deep concern for state affairs, refuting corrupt politics, or expressing his wishes for the realization of his lofty aspirations. Some 900 poems of Li Bai have been preserved, of which the most famous are *Invitation to Wine, The Sichuan Road*, and *Watching the Waterfall at Lushan*.

When Du Fu was young, he visited many scenic spots and places of historical interest. Later, he lived among the poor at the bottom of society. His turbulent experiences enabled him to know better the darkness of human society and people's sufferings. In his poems, he boldly exposed the rottenness of the feudal court, profoundly portrayed people's miserable lives and the social upheavals of the day. About 1,400 of his poems have been preserved today, of which the best-known are *Looking out on Spring, Ballad of the Army Carts, The Conscripting Officer at Shibao, The Conscripting Officer at Tongguan, The Conscripting Officer at Xin'an, Farewell to My Husband, Farewell to My Old Wife* and *Farewell of a Lonely Soul*.

Eminent poets of the Tang also include Wang Wei, Bai Juyi, Li He, Li Shangyin, to name but a few.

Chinese people are very fond of Tang poetry, and even children can recite some from memory, such as *Thoughts in the Silent Night* by Li Bai,

小注解 Footnotes

① 李白（公元701 702年）：字太白，号青莲居士。唐代著名诗人。

② 杜甫（公元712－770年）：字子美，唐代著名诗人。

③ "三吏"：杜甫所作《石壕吏》、《新安吏》、《潼关吏》三首诗的合称。

④ "三别"：杜甫所作《无家别》、《新婚别》、《垂老别》三首诗的合称。

⑤ 作者李白。诗中描写了思念家乡的心情。

⑥ 作者杜甫。诗中描写了春夜下雨的景象。

⑦ 出自王之涣的《登鹳雀楼》。

⑧ 出自李白的《将进酒》。

① Li Bai was known as the "Deity of Poetry".

② Du Fu was revered as the "Poetry Sage".

③ From *On the Stork Tower* by Wang Zhihuan

④ From *Invitation to Wine* by Li Bai

Good Rain on a Spring Night by Du Fu, etc. Verses like "If you want to widen your view three hundred miles / Go up one more flight of stairs"[3], "Do you not see the Yellow River pouring from the sky"[4] are often quoted. The book of *Three Hundred Tang Poems* is a bestseller at home and abroad, making Tang poetry also part of the world treasury of great verse.

Here are two examples:

Thoughts in the Silent Night   Li Bai

Beside my bed a pool of light

Is it hoarfrost on the ground?

I lift my eyes and see the moon,

I bend my head and think of home.

Short Impressions   Du Fu

From vivid green willows

Comes the call of two orioles;

A file of white water birds

Rises into the clear blue heavens; as if

Held in the mouth of my window

Are the mountains ranges with

Their snows of many autumns;

Anchored by our gate are

The long distance boats of Wu.

1. 春游赋诗图
   A portrait of a poets' gathering
2. 李白的《蜀道难》，写出蜀道之艰难险阻
   Li Bai's poem *The strenuous Journey to Shu* depicts the challenges of entering Sichuan Province.

宋词
Ci Poetry of the Song Dynasty

1. 苏轼像
A portrait of Su Shi

词，是古典诗歌的一种。词的名称很多，因为它可以配乐歌唱，所以也叫曲子词；因为它的句子长短不齐，也被称为长短句。词有很多种调名，叫作词牌，如西江月、满江红、如梦令等。

词作为一种新体诗歌，宋代时发展到了鼎盛时期。"宋词"与"唐诗"一样，在中国文学史上占有相当重要的地位。

宋词在发展过程中，产生了苏轼、李清照、辛弃疾、陆游等众多杰出的词人。

苏轼的词具有热情豪放，清新流畅的特点。他的词作内容十分广泛，有的抒发了报国的壮志；有的描写了农村的景象；有的写出了离愁别恨……他的创作，为宋词开辟了新天地。

李清照是宋代杰出的女词人。她的词作清新精巧，满怀真情，有的表达了她对爱情的理解和追求；有的描写了春花秋月的变化对人的影响；有的表现了国破家亡带来的人生苦难……像"知否，知否？应是绿肥红瘦"[①]、"此情无计可消除，才下眉头，却上心头"[②]等优美动人的词句，表现了李清照出众的才华。

辛弃疾是宋代词人中词作最多的作家。他的词大都洋溢着豪迈的英雄气概，如"醉里挑灯看剑，梦回吹角连营"[③]、"青山遮不住，毕竟东流去"[④]等千古流传的词句，不仅描写了豪壮的军旅生活，也抒发了他坚持抗金的决心和激昂的爱国之情。辛弃疾的词大大地拓展了宋词的思想内容和艺术风格。

直到今天，宋词仍然受到人民大众的喜爱，《宋词三百首》是许多家庭必备的读物，很多有名的词作还被重新谱曲，广为传唱。

附：**水调歌头　苏轼**

明月几时有？把酒问青天。不知天上宫阙，今夕是何年。我欲乘风归去，又恐琼楼玉宇，高处不胜寒。起舞弄清影，何似在人间！

转朱阁，低绮户，照无眠。不应有恨，何事长向别时圆？人有悲欢离合，月有阴晴圆缺，此事古难全。但愿人长久，千里共婵娟。

Ci is one of the forms of ancient poetry and can be sung to music, so it's also known as musical *ci* poetry. As the length of the lines in a *ci* poem can differ, it is also called "long and short-line verses". There are various tunes used for *ci* poems, so they can be sung in different ways.

Ci poetry reached its zenith during the Song Dynasty (960-1279 AD). Like Tang poetry, the Song *ci* poetry holds a very important position in the history of Chinese literature.

In the course of its development, many outstanding *ci* composers, such as Su Shi, Li Qingzhao, Xin Qiji and Lu You have appeared.

Su Shi's *ci* poems are unrestrained, refreshing and smooth. The contents of his *ci* poems are rich in subject matter, some expressing his patriotism, some describing country scenes, some depicting grievance when loved ones had to part.... His works blazed a new trail for the evolvement of *ci* poetry.

Li Qingzhao was an outstanding *ci* poetess. Her works are exquisite, refined and full of true feelings. She expressed her understanding and pursuit of true love, described the impact of the changing seasons on human feelings,

and reflected the misery of people suffering from the fall of their country and the disasters that befell families. Many of her verses such as *"Can't you see? / Can't you see? / The green leaves are fresh but the red flowers are fading!"*[1], *"This feeling is unable to be removed. / It was shown on my knitted eyebrows a moment ago but has now come to pain my heart"*[2] show her poetic gifts.

Xin Qiji was the most prolific among the *ci* poets of the Song Dynasty. His works are filled with heroism. His lines such as *"Half drunk I lit the lamp to look at my sword / After dreams of the bugles in our army camps"*[3], *"Green mountains are no bar / To the river flowing on to the sea"*[4] have been circulating generation after generation. They not only reflected army life in camps but also indicated his determination to resist the Jin troops and his deep love for his own country. Xin's *ci* poems greatly broadened the themes and enriched the artistic style of the Song *ci* poetry.

It remains popular even today. The book *Three Hundred Song Ci Poems* sells well, and a number of renowned *ci* poems have been set to new tunes for singing.

Here we cite Su Shi's *Prelude to Water Melody (Shui Diao Ge Tou)* as an example for your appreciation.

To the Tune of Prelude to Water Melody (*Shui Diao Ge Tou*)

Su Shi

On the Mid-Autumn Festival of the year Bingchen I drank happily till dawn and wrote this in my cups while thinking of Ziyou.

Bright moon, when was your birth?
Wine cup in hand, I ask the deep blue sky;
Not knowing what year it is tonight
In those celestial palaces on high.
I long to fly back on the wind,
Yet dread those crystal towers, those courts of jade,
Freezing to death among those icy heights!
Instead I rise to dance with my pale shadow;
Better off, after all, in the world of men.

Rounding the red pavilion,
Stooping to look through gauze windows,
She shines on the sleepless.
The moon should know no sadness;
Why, then, is she always full when dear ones are parted?
For men, the grief of parting, joy of reunion,
Just as the moon wanes and waxes, is bright or dim;
Always some flaw — and so it has been since of old.
My one wish for you, then, is long life
And a share in this loveliness far, far away!

2

小注解 Footnotes

① 出自李清照的《如梦令》，词中新颖生动地描写了春天的景物。

② 出自李清照的《一剪梅》，词中写尽了别离思念的心情。

③ 出自辛弃疾的《破阵子》，词中回忆了昔日抗击金兵、立功报国的英雄气概和战斗经历，同时也表达了壮志难酬的悲愤。

④ 出自辛弃疾的《菩萨蛮》，词中回忆了金兵入侵给人民造成的苦难，表达了自己不能去前线参加战斗的痛苦心情。

① From the tune *Like a Dream* by Li Qingzhao. The poem vividly describes spring scenery.

② From the tune *A Twig of Plum Blossoms* by Li Qingzhao. It expresses her yearning for her absent husband.

③ From *Dance of the Cavalry* by Xin Qiji

④ From *Buddhist Dancers* by Xin Qiji, which recalls how people suffered from the war and how he regretted not being able to fight at the front.

元杂剧
Zaju of the Yuan Dynasty

中国的戏曲在经历了漫长的发展过程之后，到元代（公元1271－1368年）形成了"元杂剧"。元杂剧把音乐、歌舞、表演、念白[①]融于一体，是比较成熟的戏剧形式。

元杂剧的兴盛，使元代成为中国戏曲史上的黄金时代。当时有姓名记载的杂剧作家就有200多位，有记载可查的杂剧剧本有700多种。元杂剧从多方面反映了当时的社会现实，表达了人民大众反抗压迫、追求美好生活的愿望。

关汉卿是元代成就最高、影响最大的剧作家，他一生写了60多部杂剧，现存的还有18部。关汉卿的杂剧大多表现了下层妇女的苦难和斗争，歌颂了她们的机智和勇敢。他的代表作《窦娥冤》是元杂剧中最著名的悲剧。剧中描写了善良的女子窦娥，遭到坏人陷害，被官府关进监狱，最终含冤被杀的故事。这个悲剧深刻地表现了作家对社会的不满，对弱者的同情。关汉卿的创作对后世戏曲的发展产生了巨大的影响，他不仅是中国伟大的戏剧家，也是世界文化名人。

王实甫也是元代著名的戏剧家，他一生写了14种剧本。他所创作的《西厢记》，是中国古典戏剧的杰作。剧本描写了崔莺莺和张生的爱情故事，歌颂了他们追求自由婚姻、反抗封建礼教的精神，提出了"愿普天下有情人都成眷属"的主题。剧中莺莺、张生、红娘的可爱形象，在中国几乎家喻户晓。

除此以外，元代著名的杂剧作家还有马致远、白朴、郑光祖、纪君祥等。元杂剧在中国文学史上占有很高的地位，可以与唐诗、宋词相提并论。

元杂剧中的许多剧目一直到今天仍在戏剧舞台上上演，有的还被拍成了电影和电视剧，影响十分广泛。18世纪，元杂剧《赵氏孤儿》曾流传到欧洲，被改编成《中国孤儿》，受到了世界的瞩目。

1. 《西厢记》插图
   An illustration of the drama *The West Chamber*
2. 关汉卿像
   A portrait of Guan Hanqing
3. 《窦娥冤》插图
   An illustration of the drama *The Grievance of Dou E*

It was after long years of evolvement of Chinese local opera that *zaju* came into being in the Yuan Dynasty (1271-1368 AD). It was already a relatively matured form of drama integrating music, singing, dancing, performing and speaking.

The rise of *zaju*[①] made the Yuan Dynasty the golden age of Chinese opera. As far as we know today, there were more than 200 registered playwrights and more than 700 *zaju* scripts.

Guan Hanqing was the greatest and most prolific playwright of the time. He created over 60 plays of which 18 are still extant. Most reflected the misery and struggles of women at the bottom of the society and highly praised their wisdom and courage. His representative work *The Grievance of Dou E* (also translated as *Snow in Midsummer*) is the best known of the *zaju* tragedies. It tells of a kind-hearted young woman falsely accused and thrown into prison by the local authorities and finally murdered. Through this play, the author expressed his indignation and his sympathy for the weak in society. Guan's plays had great influence on the development of drama of later generations.

Wang Shipu was another renowned playwright of the period, writing altogether 14 plays of which *The West Chamber* was considered as a masterpiece in the history of Chinese drama. This play, a love story of Cui Yingying and Zhang Sheng, acclaimed their courage in the pursuit of a free marriage in opposition to feudal ethics, declaring that, "all those in love shall be wedded". The main characters such as Cui Yingying, Zhang Sheng and Hong Niang continue to be known by most Chinese.

Other well-known playwrights include Ma Zhiyuan, Bai Pu, Zheng Guangzu and Ji Junxiang.

Like the Tang poetry and Song *ci*, *zaju* of the Yuan Dynasty also holds a very high position in the history of Chinese literature. Many items are still performed on the stage of today, and some have been made into films and TV plays. Their influence is very broad. In the 18th century, *The Orphan of the Zhao Family* was introduced to Europe and was converted into a play entitled *The Orphan of China*.

2

3

小注解 Footnotes

① 念白：戏剧中的对话和独白。

① The *zaju* of the Yuan Dynasty reflected the many facets of contemporary social reality, and expressed people's wishes to resist oppression and to seek a happy life.

明清小说

Fiction of the Ming and Qing Dynasties

1. 孙悟空三打白骨精是《西游记》的剧情之一
   A scene of *Journey to the West* : Monkey King picks a fight with the monsters
2. 《水浒传》林冲雪夜上梁山插图
   An illustration of the classic novel *Outlaws of the Marsh*: Lin Chong visiting the Liangshan Mountains at a snowy night
3. 《三国演义》主要人物的形象
   The main characters of *Romance of Three Kingdoms*

🔍 小注解 Footnotes

① 梁山：在中国山东省境内，是《水浒传》中农民起义军聚义山寨的所在地。

② 唐僧：指中国唐代著名的僧人玄奘，他曾用17年的时间去印度取佛经。

③ 文言：指1919年"五四运动"以前通用的以古汉语为基础的书面语。

① The area of Liangshan Mountains was where the rebels originally band together.

② Xuan Zang was a monk who spent 17 years in India to find the Buddhist scriptures.

③ The literary language developed through classical patterns, and it is used exclusively in writing before 1919.

明清时期，中国古典小说的创作取得了辉煌的成就，杰出的代表作品有四大文学名著《三国演义》、《水浒传》、《西游记》、《红楼梦》及鬼狐小说《聊斋志异》等。如今，这些享有世界声誉的作品，已被改编成影视剧，受到中外观众的喜爱。

《三国演义》是中国第一部完整的长篇历史小说。作者罗贯中是元末明初人。他根据历史记载和民间流传的三国故事创作了这部小说。《三国演义》主要描写了魏、蜀、吴三国之间在军事上、政治上的种种斗争，反映了当时动乱的社会现实。书中塑造了许多不同性格的人物，如神机妙算的诸葛亮、奸诈多疑的曹操、忠勇的关羽、鲁莽的张飞等，给人留下了深刻的印象。

《水浒传》是一部描写农民起义的长篇小说。作者施耐庵是元末明初人。他根据民间流传的北宋末年宋江起义的故事，写成了这部小说。全书主要描写了宋江领导的梁山①农民起义从兴起到失败的过程，揭露了"官逼民反"的社会现实。书中成功地塑造了108位梁山好汉的英雄形象，歌颂了他们的斗争精神。其中《武松打虎》、《鲁智深倒拔垂杨柳》等故事，至今令人百读不厌。

《西游记》是一部著名的神话长篇小说。明代人吴承恩根据唐僧②取经的故事和传说，创作了这部小说。小说描写了孙悟空、猪八戒、沙和尚保护唐僧去西天取经的故事。他们一路上降妖伏魔，经历了81难，终于取回了真经。书中最光辉的形象是孙悟空，他机智勇敢，本领高强，敢于反抗天神和妖魔，体现了人民反抗压迫的愿望，所以深受人们喜爱。这部小说充满了奇特的幻想，表现了丰富的艺术想像力，在中国影响极大。

《红楼梦》是中国古典小说中最优秀的作品。作者是清代文学家曹雪芹。这部小说通过贵族青年贾宝玉和林黛玉的恋爱悲剧，叙述了一个封建贵族家庭由盛到衰的历史。书中塑造了400多个栩栩如

生的人物，如王熙凤、薛宝钗、晴雯等。整部小说情节生动，语言
优美，是中国古典小说创作的最高峰，在世界文学史上也占有重要
的地位。

《聊斋志异》是一部中外闻名的文言③短篇小说集。作者是清代
人蒲松龄。《聊斋志异》中的故事生动奇特，大都与鬼怪、花仙、狐
仙有关，如：《梦狼》通过梦境告诉人们，当官的都是吃人的狼和老
虎；《香玉》描写了书生和牡丹花妖恋爱的故事……作者通过这些故
事，歌颂了美好的品德，表现了青年男女追求恋爱自由的愿望，揭
露了封建制度的黑暗、不公，控诉了贪官恶吏的罪恶，寄托了自己
的理想和希望。这部小说深受人们喜爱，是中国文言短篇小说的高
峰之作。

2

The Ming (1368-1644 AD) and Qing (1644-1911 AD) dynasties witnessed
great achievements in the creation of fiction. The representative works are
*Romance of Three Kingdoms, Outlaws of the Marsh, Journey to the West, A
Dream of Red Mansions* and *Strange Tales of Liaozhai*. Those works enjoy
a high reputation throughout the world, where audiences have been exposed
to film and TV versions as well as the books.

Romance of Three Kingdoms is the earliest complete historical novel in
China. The author Luo Guanzhong lived in the late Yuan and early Ming
dynasties. This novel was written on the basis of historical records and the
stories about the three kingdoms that circulated in public. It focuses on military
and political rivalry between the kingdoms of Wei, Shu and Wu, which reflect
the upheavals of the time. In the novel, the author successfully created a
number of impressive characters with different dispositions, such as Zhuge
Liang, a superb strategist, cunning and suspicious Cao Cao, loyal and brave
Guan Yu, rash and reckless Zhang Fei, etc.

Outlaws of the Marsh is a novel about a peasant rebellion. The author
Shi Naian lived in the late Yuan and early Ming dynasties. Based on popular
stories about a peasant rebellion led by a man called Song Jiang in the late
Song Dynasty, Shi created this novel. It describes the rise and fall of the peasant
rebellion in the area of the Liangshan Mountains① in Shandong Province,
reflecting the social reality of "rebellion of civilians driven by persecution of
officials". The novel successfully depicts 108 rebels and lauds their dauntless

曹操
Cao Cao

刘备
Liu Bei

张飞
Zhang Fei

3

acts. Episodes like "Wu Song Strikes A Tiger" and "Lu Zhishen Pulls Out a Willow Tree" remain vivid to this day.

Journey to the West is a renowned mythical novel. The author Wu Cheng'en of the Ming Dynasty wrote this book on the basis of stories about Xuan Zang[②], a monk of the Tang Dynasty who traveled to India in the face of many difficulties to learn the Buddhist scriptures. The author created a cast of capable figures like Monkey, Pig and Sandy who escort and protect the Buddhist priest on the way to the West. They subdue all kinds of demons during the journey and survive 81 calamities to eventually bring back the scriptures. Monkey is clever and brave, and possesses great power. He shows no fear in the face of heavenly gods or sinister monsters. The spirit in fighting against oppression as depicted in the book is what readers admire most. The novel is full of fantasies that indicate the author's powerful imagination. It has always had a tremendous impact on the Chinese people.

1. 《红楼梦》讲述封建贵族家庭的没落。
图中的上海大观园乃按原作描述而建
The reconstruction of the Red Mansions in Shanghai. *A Dream of Red Mansions* gives an account of the history of a feudal clan from its heyday to its final collapse.

A Dream of Red Mansions is probably the best Chinese classic novel. The author was Cao Xueqin of the Qing Dynasty. Through a tragedy of romance between Jia Baoyu of a noble clan and Lin Daiyu, the novel gives an account of the history of a feudal clan from its heyday to its final collapse. There are more than 400 vividly depicted characters in the novel, like Wang Xifeng, Xue Baochai and Qing Wen. With its fascinating stories and superb language, *A Dream of Red Mansions* has reached the zenith of the Chinese classic novels, and has an important position in the history of world literature.

Strange Tales of Liaozhai is a collection of short stories written in classical Chinese[③] in use before 1919. The author Pu Songling lived in the Qing Dynasty. Stories in this book are vivid and strange, mostly concerned with the spirit world, but have strong allegorical overtones, such as *A Dream of Wolves*, which depicts all officials as wolves and tigers that eat human beings; *Xiang Yu,* meanwhile, is an account of a love story between a scholar and the Peony Immortal. Through stories like those, the author praises fine moral ethics, expressed the wishes of young men and women to have a marriage of their own free will, exposed the dark and unfair feudal society, denounced corrupt officials and expressed his own ideals and hopes. This collection is widely read and it is the best story collection in classical Chinese.

追舟

唐伯虎和秋香的傳説家喻户曉今盡三笑中

追舟一節于戲曲博物館補壁

丙寅中秋前三日曉光畫於吳門

概述
Introduction

中华民族是一个古老的民族，也是一个有着深厚文化底蕴的民族。独领风骚的华夏艺术，动静相宜的体育运动，无不闪烁着光耀千古的智慧之光，令世人赞叹不已。

中国的传统艺术门类繁多，雅俗共存，充分地体现了中华民族对美的理解和追求。

中华民族传统的体育项目丰富多彩，其中有些已发展成为国际性的运动项目，受到世界各国人民的喜爱。

There are various types of traditional Chinese artistic works that fully manifest the understanding and pursuit of beauty of the Chinese nation.

Meanwhile, the Chinese national physical culture is rich and varied and some sports have now entered the international arena with growing popularity.

书 法
Calligraphy

书法，是中国传统的汉字书写艺术。经过千百年的创作和发展，中国书法已成为一门风格独特的艺术。

常见的书法字体有篆书、隶书、楷书、草书和行书。篆书是秦代的代表字体；隶书是汉代的通行字体；楷书由隶书发展而来；草书是隶书和楷书的快写体；行书是介于楷书、草书之间的字体，它既不像楷书那么工整，也不像草书那么难认，是一种最常用、最方便的手写体。

中国历史上出现了许多著名的书法家，如：王羲 (xī) 之[①]、欧阳询[②] (xún)、颜真卿[③] (qīng)、柳公权[④]、赵孟頫[⑤] (fǔ) 等。他们经过多年的勤学苦练，形成了不同的风格和流派，使中国的书法艺术达到了很高的水平。

书法的书写工具，是被人们称为文房四宝的笔、墨、纸、砚。学书法，首先要学会使用毛笔，初学的人应该先从楷书学起。

小注解 Footnotes

① 王羲之(公元303－361年或321－379年)：东晋著名书法家，被誉为"书圣"。

② 欧阳询(公元551－641年)：唐代著名书法家。

③ 颜真卿(公元709－785年)：唐代著名书法家。

④ 柳公权(公元778－865年)：唐代著名书法家。

⑤ 赵孟頫(公元1254－1322年)：元代著名书画家。

① Wang Xizhi (303-361 AD or 321-379 AD) of the Eastern Jin Dynasty

② Ouyang Xun (551-641 AD) of the Tang Dynasty

③ Yan Zhenqing (709-785 AD) of the Tang Dynasty

④ Liu Gongquan (778-865 AD) of the Tang Dynasty

⑤ Zhao Mengfu (1254-1322 AD) of the Yuan Dynasty

Calligraphy is a traditional art of writing Chinese characters. After centuries of creation and evolvement, calligraphy has become a unique art.

The usual styles of calligraphy include seal, official, regular, cursive and running scripts. The seal script was the representative script of the Qin Dynasty (221-207 BC). The official script was popularly used in the Han Dynasty (206 BC-220 AD). The regular script was the result of development of the official script. The cursive script is a fast way of writing the regular and official scripts. The running script is something between the regular and cursive scripts. Not as neat as the former and not as difficult to recognize as the latter, it is the most commonly used, and is the easiest way of handwriting.

There have been many famous calligraphers, such as Wang Xizhi[1], Ouyang Xun[2], Yan Zhenqing[3], Liu Gongquan[4] and Zhao Mengfu[5], to name but a few. Each, after years of hard practice, has formed a unique calligraphic style and school to raise the profile of the art.

Tools used for calligraphy are called "Four Treasures in the Study", namely, Chinese brush, ink stick, paper and ink stone. To learn calligraphy, one first has to learn how to use a Chinese brush. Beginners should start by copying the regular script.

1. "书圣"王羲之
   The script of the saint of calligraphy, Wang Xizhi
2. 颜真卿的《多宝塔》局部
   The calligraphy of Yan Zhenqing
3. 西安书法家每年都会举行书法交流会
   Xi'an's annual calligraphy meeting

篆　刻
Seal Cutting

1. 北周天元皇太后的金玺及印面
   The gold seal of Queen Tianyuan of Northern Zhou Dynasty
2. 篆刻以刀代笔，在印材上刻写书法或图像
   Seal cutting refers to carving with a knife on a seal according to a diagram or calligraphy painted on it.
3. 慈禧太后赐给云南鸡足山的王印
   The imperial seal bestowed to Jizu Mountain of Yunnan Province by Queen Cixi.
4. 篆刻的材料以石最受人喜爱
   The most popular seal material is stone.

篆刻，就是以刀代笔，在印材上按照已经写好的书法，或画好的图像，进行刻写。它是中国一门独特的传统艺术，具有实用与欣赏的双重价值。

篆刻出来的艺术品叫印章。印章的文字刻成凸 (tū) 状的称为"阳文"；刻成凹 (āo) 状的称为"阴文"。在印面左侧面上刻制作者姓名、治印年月等，叫做刻"边款"，边款多用阴文。

印章，最初仅是一种"信物"和"权力"的象征，到了唐代才由实用品转变成为一种艺术品。篆刻艺术形成于宋元年间，兴盛于明末清初。这期间，出现了许多篆刻家和篆刻流派。著名的篆刻艺术家有"篆刻之祖"文彭①及何震②、丁敬③、邓石如④、齐白石⑤等，

篆刻最常用的字体是篆字。此外，还有隶书、楷书、行书等。篆刻的材料有水晶、玉、金属、兽角、象牙、竹、木、石料等。其中，使用最广泛的是石料。最受篆刻家喜爱的石料有青田石、寿山

石、昌化石、巴林石等。

篆刻是书法、绘画、雕刻相结合的一种艺术。现在，古老的篆刻艺术也受到了广大青少年的喜爱。

Seal cutting refers to carving with a knife on a block of some substance according to a diagram or calligraphy painted on it. A unique form of traditional art in China, it is of both practical and appreciative functions.

A block thus carved is called a seal. Characters can be carved in relief or cut deep into the piece of stone or wood, which is called intaglio. On the left side, characters indicating name of the carver and the date of the carving are engraved, mostly in intaglio.

At very beginning, a seal was only used as a token of pledge or a symbol of power. It was not until the Tang Dynasty (618-907 AD) that the seal was used not only practically but also treated as an art. It turned into an art form in the Song (960-1279 AD) and Yuan (1271-1368 AD) dynasties and flourished in the late Ming Dynasty (1368-1644 AD) and early Qing Dynasty (1644-1911 AD). In this period, many carving artists and schools appeared. The renowned carving artists included Wen Peng[1], He Zhen[2], Ding Jing[3], Deng Shiru[4] and Qi Baishi[5].

The font usually adopted in a chop is the seal script. Besides, regular, official, running scripts are also used. The block for carving can be made of crystal, jade, metal, beast horn, ivory, bamboo, wood, stone, etc. Stone is most extensively used, among which, Qingtian, Changhua, Shoushan and Balin seal stones are the most valuable.

Seal cutting is a combination of calligraphy, painting and carving, and it is popular today with young people.

小注解 Footnotes

① 文彭(公元1489－1573年)：明代篆刻名家。
② 何震(公元？－1604年左右)：明代篆刻名家。
③ 丁敬(公元1695－1765年)：清代篆刻名家。
④ 邓石如(公元1743－1805年)：清代篆刻名家。
⑤ 齐白石(公元1863－1957年)：现代著名篆刻家、书画家。

① Wen Peng (1489-1573 AD) of the Ming Dynasty
② He Zhen (?-1604 AD) of the Ming Dynasty
③ Ding Jing (1695-1765 AD) of the Qing Dynasty
④ Deng Shiru (1743-1805 AD) of the Qing Dynasty
⑤ Qi Baishi (1863-1957 AD)

中国画
Traditional Chinese Painting

中国画又叫国画，它是用毛笔、墨及颜料，在宣纸或绢上画出的画。中国画与中医、京剧一起，被誉为中国的"三大国粹"。

中国画按内容分，主要有人物画、山水画、花鸟画三大类。

战国时，中国已经有了比较成熟的人物画，唐朝时达到了顶峰。著名的人物画家有顾恺 (kǎi) 之[①]、吴道子[②]等。

山水画是表现山川美景的画种。它产生于秦代，隋唐时成为独立的画种，宋代达到了很高的水平。著名的山水画家有李思训[③]、王维[④]、唐寅[⑤] (yín) 等。

花鸟画画的是自然界中的花卉、鸟兽、鱼虫。南北朝时出现了花鸟画，宋代走向成熟。著名的花鸟画家有擅长画花鸟的朱耷[⑥] (dā)、擅长画竹子的郑燮[⑦] (xiè)、擅长画鱼虾的齐白石等。

中国画按画法分，主要有工笔画和写意画。工笔画的特点是按照事物原来的样子，一笔一笔画得非常细致，尤其注重细节的描绘；写意画是一种概括、夸张的画法，要求用简单的笔墨画出事物的神韵，虽然笔墨简单，但意趣生动，表现力特别强。

一幅国画作品，除了图画以外，还有诗文和印章。因此，中国画是诗、书、画、印相结合的艺术。它的

1. 南宋画家马和之的名作"鹿鸣之什图"局部
   The famous work of artist Ma Hezhi of Southern Song Dynasty (1127 - 1279 AD)
2. 一代国画大师齐白石的"群虾图"
   The eminent artist Qi Baishi was excelled in painting shrimps.
3. 近代国画宗师张大千
   The contemporary traditional Chinese painter Zhang Daqian

艺术成就和民族风格早已受到世界人民的赞誉。中国画不仅能美化人们的生活，而且能给人们带来高雅的情趣和艺术享受。

Traditional Chinese painting refers to the execution of a picture on a piece of *Xuan* paper or silk with a Chinese brush that has absorbed black ink or colored pigments. It is regarded as one of the three quintessence of Chinese culture together with traditional Chinese medicine and Beijing opera.

If divided by content, traditional Chinese painting can be classified into three categories, namely, figurine, landscape and flower and bird.

Painting of figurines matured as early as the Warring States Period (475-221 BC) and reached its peak during the Tang Dynasty (618-907 AD). Famous artists in figurines include Gu Kaizhi[1] and Wu Daozi[2].

Painting of landscape first appeared in the Qin Dynasty (221-207 BC) and became an independent category of painting during the Sui (581-618 AD) and Tang dynasties. By the time of the Song Dynasty (960-1279 AD), it had reached a very high level. Representative artists of this category include Li Sixun[3], Wang Wei[4] and Tang Yin[5].

Painting of flowers and birds focus also includes beasts, fish, insects, etc. It came into being in the Northern and Southern dynasties (421-581 AD) and became a mature art during the Song Dynasty. Celebrated artists of this category include Zhu Da[6], who excelled in execution of flowers and birds, Zheng Xie[7], who was good at bamboo and Qi Baishi, who excelled in fish and shrimp.

If divided by styles of brushwork, traditional Chinese painting can be categorized into *gongbi*, realistic painting characterized by fine brushwork and close attention to details, and *xieyi*, freehand brushwork aimed at catching the spirit of the object and expressing the author's impression or mood. In the latter, brushstrokes may brief and simple, but they are powerful in expression.

In traditional Chinese paintings, apart from pictures, there are also inscriptions, poems and seals. Therefore, traditional Chinese painting is an art form combining poetry, calligraphy, painting and seals.

小注解 Footnotes

① 顾恺之（约公元345－406年）：东晋著名画家。
② 吴道子（约为8世纪前期人）：唐代著名画家。他画的人物衣服的带子好像在飘动，被人们称赞为"吴带当风"。
③ 李思训（公元651－716年）：唐代著名画家。
④ 王维（公元701－761年）：唐代著名诗人、画家。
⑤ 唐寅（公元1470－1523年）：字伯虎，明代著名画家。
⑥ 朱耷（公元1626－1705年）：号八大山人，清初著名画家。
⑦ 郑燮（公元1693－1765年）：号板桥，清代著名书画家、文学家。

① Gu Kaizhi (c. 345-406 AD) of the Jin Dynasty
② Wu Daozi (c. early 8th century AD) of the Tang Dynasty.
③ Li Sixun (651-716 AD) of the Tang Dynasty
④ Wang Wei (701-761 AD) of the Tang Dynasty
⑤ Tang Yin or Tang Bohu (1470-1523 AD) of the Ming Dynasty.
⑥ Zhu Da, or Badashanren (1626-1705 AD), of the early Qing Dynasty
⑦ Zheng Xie or Zheng Banqiao (1693-1765 AD) of the Qing Dynasty

民 乐
Musical Instruments

1. 女乐图
   A portrait of the ancient female musical group
2. 古筝演奏
   A *guzheng* performance
3. 十弦琴
   A 10-stringed zither
4. 战国竹排箫
   A bamboo pipe from the Warring States
5. 战国瑟
   A long, base stringed musical instrument of Warring States Period
6. 周代铜乐器
   The bronze musical instruments from Zhou Dynasty (c.1000-256 BC)

中国民乐具有浓郁的民族特色，是中华文化宝库中的瑰宝。

中国在原始社会时就已经有了乐器。中国民族乐器种类繁多，可分为吹、拉、弹、打四大类。吹的有箫（xiāo）、笛子、唢呐等；拉的有二胡、京胡、板胡等；弹的有古筝（zhēng）、古琴①、琵琶等；打的有锣、鼓等。

千百年来，中国音乐家创造了不少优秀的曲目，遗憾的是有很多曲目没能保留下来，流传至今的著名曲目有：《十面埋伏》、《阳春白雪》、《百鸟朝凤》、《广陵散》、《梅花三弄》、《春江花月夜》、《二泉映月》、《雨打芭蕉》、《步步高》、《旱天雷》等。这些名曲现已广泛流传于海内外，有的还在国际舞台演奏时获得了大奖，如：《百鸟朝凤》曾在第四届世界青年联欢会上，荣获民间音乐比赛二等奖。

中国民乐以独特的魅力受到中国人民的喜爱。在中国，几乎每个地区都有民乐团，有的还是民间音乐爱好者自发组织的。中国民乐团经常接受邀请，到世界各国访问演出。最近几年，每到春节，中国的民乐团都应邀到著名的音乐之都维也纳访问，并在举世闻名的金色大厅演奏优秀的中国民族乐曲。这些优美动听的乐曲，深深地打动了当地的听众。中国的民乐受到了世界各国人民的欢迎。

小注解 Footnotes

① 古琴：又叫七弦琴。

① Guqin - Chinese zither.

Musical instruments with strong nationalistic characteristics are treasures of Chinese culture.

As early as time of primitive society in China, musical instruments existed. There are various types, which can be divided into wind, string, plucked-string and percussion instruments. Wind instruments include *xiao* (vertical bamboo flute), *dizi* (horizontal bamboo pipe), *suona* (woodwind instrument with seven holes on top and one underneath); string instruments include *erhu* (two-stringed fiddle), *jinghu* (two-stringed bowed instrument specially used for Beijing opera), *banhu* (two-stringed bowed instrument with a thin wooden soundboard); plucked-string instruments include *guzheng* (21- or 25-stringed plucked instrument), *guqin*①, *pipa*, a plucked string instrument with a fretted fingerboard; percussion instruments include gong and drums.

For centuries, Chinese musicians have created a large number of superb melodies, but, unfortunately, many have been lost. The extant melodies include *The Ambush on All Sides*, *Spring Snow*, *A Hundred Birds Pay Homage to the Phoenix*, *Spring River Moon Night*, *The Moon Reflected on the Second Spring*, etc. Those renowned melodies are often performed at home and abroad, and some win international awards. *A Hundred Birds Pay Homage to the Phoenix*, for example, won the second prize for folk music at the Fourth World Youth Festival.

Chinese musical instruments have a unique charm much prized by the Chinese people. Musical groups at all levels throughout the country, professional and amateur, keep the ancient musical art alive. The China National Music Troupe is often invited to perform abroad. In recent years, it has been invited to Vienna to perform in the Golden Hall, and its performances have left a deep impression on audiences more used to classical Western music.

京 剧
Beijing Opera

1. 北京的古戏台上演京剧
   The stage performance of Beijing opera
2. 小生
   Xiao sheng (young male role)
3. 净
   Jing (bold and unconstrained male role)

　　京剧是中国流行最广、影响最大的一个剧种，有近200年的历史。京剧在形成过程中，吸收了许多地方戏的精华，又受到北京方言和风俗习惯的影响。京剧虽然诞生在北京，但不是北京的地方戏，中国各地都有演出京剧的剧团。

　　京剧是一种唱、念、做、打并重的艺术。唱，指按照一定的曲调演唱。念，是剧中角色的对话和独白。做，指动作和表情的表演。打，是用舞蹈化的武术表演的搏斗。

　　在长期的发展过程中，京剧形成了一套虚拟表演动作。如：一条桨可以代表一只船；一条马鞭可以代表一匹马；演员不需要任何道具，能表现出上楼、下楼、开门、关门等动作。这些动作虽经过了夸张，但是能给观众既真实又优美的感觉。

　　京剧演员分生、旦、净、丑四个行当①。"生"所扮演的是男性人物，根据角色年龄、身份的不同，又分老生②、小生③和武生④。著名演员有马连良、周信芳、叶盛兰、盖叫天、李少春等。"旦"所扮演的都是女性人物，又分青衣⑤、花旦⑥、武旦⑦、老旦⑧。最著名的旦角演员有20世纪20年代出现的四大名旦——梅兰芳、程砚(yàn)秋、尚小云、荀(xún)慧生。"净"扮演的是性格豪爽的男性，特征是要在脸上勾画花脸，所以也叫花脸，著名花脸演员有裘(qiú)盛戎、袁世海等。"丑"扮演的是幽默机智或阴险狡猾的男性，著名的丑角演员有萧长华、马富禄等。

京剧的化妆也很有特点。"生"、"旦"的化妆要"描眉"、"吊眉"、"画眼圈"；"净"、"丑"的化妆要根据京剧的脸谱⑨勾画，比如忠勇的人要画红脸，奸诈的人要画白脸。

京剧的剧目很多，据说有3,800出。目前上演的主要有传统剧、新编历史剧和现代戏三大类。

京剧作为中国民族戏曲的精华，在国内外都有很大的影响。许多外国人专门到中国来学唱京剧。许多京剧表演艺术家也曾到世界各地访问演出，受到了各国人民的喜爱。

小注解 Footnotes

① 行当：传统戏曲演员专业分工的类别。

② 老生：戏曲中生角的一种，扮演中年或老年男性。

③ 小生：戏曲中生角的一种，主要扮演青少年男子，化妆不挂胡须。

④ 武生：戏曲中生角的一种，大都扮演会武艺的青壮年男子。

⑤ 青衣：戏曲中旦角的一种，扮演庄重的青年、中年妇女。由于这个行当扮演的角色常穿青色衣服而得名，表演重唱功。

⑥ 花旦：戏曲中旦角的一种，扮演天真活泼或放荡泼辣的青年妇女，表演重做功和念白。

⑦ 武旦：戏曲中旦角的一种，扮演勇武的女性，表演重武打。

⑧ 老旦：戏曲中旦角的一种，扮演老年妇女。

⑨ 脸谱：戏曲中某些角色脸上画的各种图案，用来表现人物性格和特征。

Beijing opera is a widely circulated, most influential opera form in China with a history of almost 200 years. In the course of its formation, it has absorbed many strong points of local operas and been influenced by Beijing local dialect and customs. Though Beijing opera came into being in the capital, it is not a localized opera. There are Beijing opera troupes in most regions of China.

Beijing opera combines singing, recital, acting and acrobatic fighting. Singing refers to the singing according to set tunes. Recital refers to monologues and dialogues among performers. Acting refers to the performance of specific bodily movements and facial expressions that have a long tradition. Acrobatic fighting refers to choreographed martial art.

In the long years of its development, Beijing opera has formed a number of suppositional props. For instance, a pedal means a boat, a whip in the hand means riding on a horse. Without any physical props involved, an actor may perform going upstairs or downstairs, opening or closing a door by mere gestures. Though rather exaggerated, those actions would, with their beautiful movements, give audience a deep impression.

3

小注解 Footnotes

① *Lao sheng* - aged male role

② *Xiao sheng* - young male role

③ *Wu sheng* - young or middle-aged male role with martial art skill.

④ *Qingyi* - dignified woman usually in a black dress

⑤ *Hua dan* - lively and shrewd young woman

⑥ *Wu dan* - woman with martial art skills

⑦ *lao dan* - aged female role

Actors in Beijing opera can be basically classified into four roles: *sheng*, *dan*, *jing* and *chou*. *Sheng* refers to male roles, and this can be further divided into *lao sheng*①, *xiao sheng*② and *wu sheng*③. Famous actors playing this type of role include Ma Lianliang, Zhou Xinfang, Ye Shenglan, Gai Jiaotian and Li Shaochun. *Dan* refers to female roles and can be further divided into *qingyi*④, *hua dan*⑤, *wu dan*⑥ and *lao dan*⑦. In the 1920s, there appeared the "Great Four Dan", namely, Mei Lanfang, Cheng Yanqiu, Shang Xiaoyun and Xun Huisheng. *Jing* refers to a bold and unconstrained male. One unique characteristic of *jing* is that a performer in the role has his face painted in a certain pattern. Famous actors playing this role include Qiu Shengrong and Yuan Shihai. *Chou* refers to a witty, humorous or cunning male. Renowned actors playing this role include Xiao Changhua and Ma Fulu.

Facial makeup in Beijing opera has its own pattern. A *sheng* or a *dan* has to have his or her eyebrows painted in a way that they look slanted with the outer ends of eyebrows going upward, and their eyes circled with black color. As for *jing* and *chou*, the pattern is in accordance with the disposition of the characters. For instance, a loyal and brave man would have a red face, while a sly man would have a white face.

It is said that there are 3,800 items in Beijing opera. What are staged today are primarily three types, namely, traditional items, newly composed historical items and modern items.

Beijing opera, as national opera, enjoys a high reputation both in and outside China. Many foreigners come to China to learn Beijing opera. Many Beijing opera troupes and famous opera actors and actresses give frequent performances abroad.

1. 花旦
   Hua dan (main female role)
2. 花旦与老旦
   Hua dan (left) and *lao dan* (right — aged female role)

地方戏
Local Operas

广西著名歌剧《刘三姐》
Liusanjie is the representative item of Guangxi opera.

中国由于地域辽阔，民族众多，各地的方言不同，除了京剧以外，还形成了丰富多彩的地方戏。据统计，中国的地方戏有360多种，可以称得上世界之最。其中影响较大的有评剧、越剧、豫剧、黄梅戏、粤剧等。

评剧发源于河北唐山，流行于北京、天津和华北、东北各地。评剧具有活泼、自由、生活气息浓郁的特点，擅长表现现代生活。著名演员有小白玉霜、新凤霞等，代表剧目有《秦香莲》、《小女婿》、《刘巧儿》等。

越剧发源于浙江绍兴，流行于浙江、江苏、江西、安徽、上海等地。最初全部由男演员演出，20世纪30年代发展成全部由女演员演出。越剧唱腔委婉、表演细腻，已成为仅次于京剧的一个大剧种。著名演员有袁雪芬、王文娟、徐玉兰等，代表剧目有《梁山伯与祝英台》、《红楼梦》等。

豫剧是河南省的地方戏，也叫河南梆子、河南高调，流行于河南及邻近各省。豫剧的声腔，有的高亢活泼，有的悲凉缠绵。传统剧目有650多出。著名演员有常香玉、马金凤、牛得草等，代表剧目有《花木兰》、《穆桂英挂帅》、《七品芝麻官》等。

黄梅戏是安徽省的地方戏，旧时称黄梅调，流行于安徽及江西、湖北的部分地区。黄梅戏载歌载舞，唱腔委婉动听，表演朴实优美，生活气息浓厚。著名演员有严凤英、马兰等，代表剧目有《天仙配》、《女驸马》、《牛郎织女》等。

粤剧是广东省的地方戏，主要流行于广东、广西、福建南部一带。居住在东南亚、美洲、欧洲和大洋洲的华侨、华人及港澳同胞也十分喜爱粤剧。粤剧用广东话演唱，形成了独特的风格。著名演员有红线女、马师曾等，代表剧目有《搜书院》、《关汉卿》等。

China is a country with a large area and various ethnic groups. People in different regions speak different dialects. As a result, many local opera forms have appeared alongside Beijing opera. Statistics show that there are more than 360 types of local operas, of which the best known are *pingju* opera, Yue or Shaoxing opera, Yu or Henan opera, Huangmei opera and Yue or Guangdong opera.

Pingju opera originated in Tangshan of Hebei Province and is popular in Beijing, Tianjin, North China and the Northeast. *Pingju* opera is lively and close to life, which is suitable to reflect the life of today. The best-known performers include Xiao Bai Yushuang and Xin Fengxia. The representative items are *Qin Xianglian*, *Small Son-in-Law* and *Liu Qiao'er*, etc.

Yue or Shaoxing opera originated in Shaoxing of Zhejiang Province and is popular in Zhejiang, Jiangsu, Jiangxi, Anhui provinces and Shanghai. At first, all performers were male. But in the 1930s, all the performers became female. The tunes of this opera are mild and pleasing to the ears, and the acting is meticulous. It is next to Beijing opera in popularity. Renowned performers include Yuan Xuefen, Wang Wenjuan and Xu Yulan. The representative items are *Butterfly Lovers* (or *Liang Shanbo and Zu Yingtai*), *A Dream of Red Mansions*, etc.

Yu or Henan opera is the local opera of Henan Province and is also popular in neighboring provinces. Its tunes are sometimes high pitched and sometimes mild and sorrowful. There are about 650 traditional programs. Well-known performers include Chang Xiangyu, Ma Jinfeng and Niu Decao. The representative items are *Hua Mulan*, *Mu Guiying Takes Command*, *A Petty Official*, etc.

Huangmei opera is the local opera of Anhui and is popular in Anhui and Jiangxi provinces, and part of Hubei Province. This opera is characterized by dancing while singing. Its tunes are mild and pleasant. The acting movements are simple, but graceful. It is also very close to real life. Renowned performers include Yan Fengying and Ma Lan. The representative items are *Marrying a Fairy*, *Emperor's Female Son-in-Law*, *Cowherd and Weaving Maid*, etc.

Yue or Guangdong opera is the local opera form of Guangdong Province and is also popular in Guangxi and southern Fujian Province. Overseas Chinese living in Southeast Asia, America, Europe and Oceania, people of Hong Kong and Macao are also very fond of this type of local opera, which developed on the basis of indigenous folk music while drawing influences from other local operas. It uses Cantonese dialect and is rather unique in its singing style. The best-known performers include Hong Xiannu and Ma Shizeng. The representative items are *Searching the Study*, *Guan Hanqing*, etc.

1. 福建泰宁地方戏曲——梅村戏
   The local opera of Taining, Fujian Province
2. 川剧
   Sichuan opera
3. 昆曲已被联合国教科文组织列为"人类
   口头遗产和非物质遗产代表作"
   Kunqu (Jiangsu opera) was honored the title of
   "Masterpieces of the Oral and Intangible
   Heritage of Humanity" by UNESCO.

曲艺
Quyi

　　"曲艺"是各种说唱艺术的总称，是由古代民间的口头文学和说唱艺术发展演变形成的。它的主要艺术手段是用带有表演动作的说和唱来叙述故事、表达思想感情、反映社会生活。

　　现在流行于中国的曲艺种类有300多个，包括相声、大鼓①、快板②、二人转③、弹词④、双簧⑤等。其中最为人们所喜闻乐见的曲艺形式是相声。

　　中国的相声是一种笑的艺术，它是在古代笑话⑥和民间笑话的基础上发展起来的。现代的相声，是100多年前在北京和天津地区产生的。

　　相声表演的艺术手段是说、学、逗、唱。相声的笑料来自那些巧妙安排在相声中的"包袱"。"包袱"是相声演员的行话⑦，意思是把可笑的东西像包东西一样一件一件地包在包袱里，到了一定的时候，突然抖出里面的东西，既出乎观众的意料，又合情合理，使观众忍不住大笑起来。

　　相声说的内容，大多数是我们生活中的事情，也有的是根据民间笑话、历史人物、历史故事和语言文字游戏编写的。表演相声所用的道具非常简单，一张桌子、一把扇子或一块手绢就可以了。一个人说的叫单口相声，两个人说的叫对口相声，三个人或多人合说的叫群口相声。其中，最常见的是对口相声。它由两个演员采用问答的方式表演，一个逗，另一个捧。

　　著名的相声演员有马三立、侯宝林、马季、姜昆、牛群、冯巩等。在一代一代相声艺人的努力下，相声已成为雅俗共赏的全国性艺术形式。

　　Quyi is a general term for all kinds of talking and singing performances. It originated from oral literature, the talking and singing

1

小注解 Footnotes

① 大鼓：曲艺的一个曲种。以唱为主，说唱故事，用鼓、板、三弦伴奏。

② 快板：曲艺的一个曲种。用有韵律的语言讲故事，说时用竹板伴奏，节奏较快。

③ 二人转：曲艺的一个曲种。流行于中国的东北地区。用板胡、唢呐等乐器伴奏，一般由两人边舞蹈边说唱故事。

④ 弹词：曲艺的一个曲种。流行于中国南方各地，有说有唱，用三弦伴奏，或再加琵琶陪衬。

⑤ 双簧：曲艺的一个曲种。一个人表演动作，一个人藏在后面或说或唱，互相配合。

⑥ 笑话：指能引人发笑的谈话或故事；供人当作笑料的事情。

⑦ 行话：各行各业专门用的语言。

① *Xiangsheng* – comic dialogue

② *Dagu* – versified storytelling accompanied by beating of a drum and other instruments

③ *Kuaiban* – talking at the beat of clappers

④ *Errenzhuan* – song-and-dance duet

⑤ *Tanci* – storytelling accompanied by sanxian fiddle or pipa fiddle

⑥ *Shuanghuang* – one man acting in the front and another hidden behind him talking or singing

⑦ *Baofu* is a package that is revealed at the right moment to surprise and to make the audiences laugh.

performances of ancient people. It refers primarily to storytelling emphasized by body movements to express feelings.

There are still about 300 types of *quyi* being performed in China, including *xiangsheng*①, *dagu*②, *kuaiban*③, *errenzhuan*④, *tanci*⑤, *shuanghuang*⑥. Of these, the most popular is comic dialogue.

It evolved on the basis of ancient folk jokes. Comic dialogue of today originated in Beijing and Tianjin over a century ago.

Artistic means of the comic dialogue are talking, imitating, teasing and singing. What makes audience laugh are something called *baofu*⑦ or "packages", which is a jargon of those in the circle.

What comic dialogues ridicule are mostly the phenomena of daily life. Some are created by adapting folk jokes, tales of historical figures and events and a play on words. The stage props for a performance are very simple, namely, a table and a fan or a handkerchief. It could be performed either by one person or two, or even a group. But, normally, a comic dialogue is performed by two people. The usual pattern is that one is a straight man that asks questions and the other gives funny answers.

The best-known comic dialogue performers are Ma Sanli, Hou Baolin, Ma Ji, Jiang Kun, Niu Qun and Feng Gong. With the concerted effort of performers generation after generation, comic dialogue has become a national entertainment loved by those with both low and highbrow tastes.

1. 弹唱
   A performance of storytelling and singing
2. "双簧" 表演
   Shuanghuang performance

杂 技
Acrobatics

小注解 Footnotes

① 戏法儿：杂技的一种，也叫魔术。

① The Lion Dance is a traditional item that has existed for a thousand years.

1. 汉代杂技画像石显示中国杂技已有悠久历史
   The stone that carved with scenes of acrobatic performance during Han Dynasty show the long history of acrobatics in China.

2.-4.
   杂技表演
   Acrobatics

1

中国上古时代有一种舞蹈，人们身披兽皮，头戴牛角，做战斗表演。杂技就是由这种舞蹈发展而来的。到了汉代，中国杂技已经具有了相当高的水平。宋代，杂技从宫廷逐渐走向民间，杂技艺人们不但在城市里表演，也在农村街头表演。

现在，中国各地几乎都有杂技团。中国著名的杂技之乡河北吴桥，每年都要举办国际杂技节。杂技艺术家们创作的许多优秀节目，都表现了中国杂技演员的高超技艺。

《狮子舞》是一个有着上千年历史的传统节目。演员们身披彩衣，扮演成狮子，在锣鼓的伴奏下表演各种高难动作，表现了狮子的威武勇猛。

古彩戏法儿①也是中国杂技的传统节目，演员身穿中式长袍，肩上披着一块方布，每次掀开方布，都能托出一个盛满清水、游着金鱼的玻璃鱼缸。最后能够变出满台的玻璃鱼缸、玻璃酒瓶和一盆熊熊的烈火。

口技是中国杂技节目中一个很有特色的种类。口技演员能够用自己的口腔模仿出生活中的各种声音，如鸟的叫声、孩子的哭声、风雨声、枪炮声、各种乐器声，十分吸引观众。

中国杂技不但深受中国观众的欢迎，也得到了世界各国的好评。在国际杂技比赛中，中国杂技演员表演的节目多次获奖。"口技"、"顶碗"、"转碟"、"车技"、"高台踢碗"、"蹬技"等节目，都曾得到过金奖。中国杂技已经以它高超的技艺和独特的风格登上了国际杂技舞台。

As early as remote antiquity, there existed a kind of dance, in which dancers wearing the fur of beasts and sporting animal horns on their head gave a stylized performance of fighting. Acrobatics actually originated from this type of dance. By the time of the Han Dynasty (206 BC-220 AD), Chinese acrobatics had reached a fairly high level. During the Song Dynasty (960-1279 AD), acrobatic performance gradually came out of the imperial palace and into the public domain. It was not only performed in towns, but also in the villages.

Today, there are acrobatic troupes almost everywhere in China. Wuqiao of Hebei Province, renowned home of acrobatics, holds an annual international acrobatic festival.

2

Chinese acrobatics are not only loved by Chinese audience but also welcomed by peoples throughout the world. Many Chinese acrobatic items have won awards in the international competitions. Performances like "holding bowls on the head", "spinning plates", "bike stunts", "kicking the bowl home" and "paddling" have won gold medals. With superb skill and unique style, Chinese acrobatics is a well-known item on the international stage.

The Lion Dance[①] is another popular show. Performers dressed like lions prance about and make all kinds of difficult movements to demonstrate majesty and the dauntless spirit of the king of beasts to the sound of gongs and drums.

Ancient juggling is also a traditional item, which has evolved over the centuries through the desire of seasoned jugglers to enhance the difficulty and complexity of their performances to please audiences.

Vocal mimicry is another unique performing item, in which the mimics reproduce all sorts of sounds in life such as bird's chirrup, child's wailing, wind and rain, gunfire, all kinds of musical instruments, that are considered most appealing to the audience.

3

4

中国象棋
Chinese Chess

1. 象棋是中国国粹之一
   Chinese chess is one of the national cultural heritages.
2. 象棋棋局千变万化
   There are endless possibilities in the game of Chinese chess.
3. 江南水乡周庄的一盘"大棋"
   A "giant chess game" at the water village Zhouzhuang, south of Yangtze River

　　中国象棋，古代叫"象戏"。大约起源于战国时代，是根据春秋战国时两军对垒的战阵创造的战斗游戏。唐朝时，象棋已很普及。到了宋代，中国象棋基本定型，并且在全国流行。

　　中国象棋的棋盘是正方形的，棋盘的中间有一条"界河"，把对垒的双方隔在两边。两边画有交叉线的地方共有90个交叉点，棋子就摆在这些交叉点上。中国象棋共有32枚棋子，分为黑红两组，下棋的双方各用一组，每组各有一帅(将)、两士、两相(象)、两马、两车、两炮、五兵(卒)。两人对局时，按照规定的位置将各自的棋子摆好，红方先走，然后轮流下棋子。各种棋子走法不同，如：马走日字，相走田字，车可以"横冲直撞"，兵只可前行……最后以把对方将[①](jiāng)死为胜，不分胜负为和棋。

　　1949年以后，中国象棋被列入全国正式体育比赛项目。20世纪

70年代后，中国象棋开始走出亚洲，走向世界。现在，世界上已经有40多个国家和地区建立了中国象棋组织。

Chinese chess is a game created on the basis of two confronting military formations of that period. By the time of the Tang Dynasty (618-907 AD), it had already become very popular, with its style of play basically fixed by the Song Dynasty (960-1279 AD).

The chessboard is shaped in square, in the middle of which there is a border called the Chuhe River that separates the two sides. On both sides, there are parallel vertical and horizontal lines. Chessmen are placed at the points where the lines cross. There are 90 such intersections. There are altogether 32 chessmen, which are divided into two groups. Characters carved on chessmen are painted red or black respectively to represent the two sides. Each side has a "marshal" or a "general", two "guards", two "elephants", two "horses", two "chariots", two "cannons" and five "soldiers", each with its designated move. At the start of play, all the chessmen must be placed in fixed positions, and the red side moves first. When the "marshal" is checked and there is no way to save him, that side has lost, but sometimes there can be a stalemate.

Since 1949, Chinese chess has been included as an event in the national sport games. In the 1970s, Chinese chess players began to promote the game abroad. Today, more than 40 countries and regions have established their own Chinese chess clubs.

围 棋
Go

围棋起源于中国。它比象棋出现得更早，至少已有2,500多年的历史，是世界上最古老的棋类。在古代，帝王将相、文人学士、才人淑女①都喜爱这种棋艺。

围棋的棋盘面由纵横的19条交叉线组成，构成361个交叉点，棋子就下在这些交叉点上。围棋棋子分黑白两色，各有180枚。围棋对弈（yì），千变万化，紧张激烈。双方动用各种技术、战术攻击对方，非常富有战斗性。由于围棋奥妙无穷，古人曾经夸张地说，只有神仙才能发明它。

围棋是一种智力型运动，学围棋既可锻炼提高人们的逻辑思维能力，又能陶冶性情，培养人们顽强、冷静、沉着的性格。因此，它越来越受到现代人的欢迎。

隋唐时期，围棋传到日本，19世纪时又传到欧洲。现在，世

小注解 Footnotes

① 才人淑女：才人：有才华的人。
淑女：美好的、有才学的女子。

① China is the birthplace of go chess; however, the exact date for the appearance of the game is still unclear at present.

1. 高士对弈图
A portrait depicting a game of go
2. 新疆吐鲁番一座古墓内出土的唐代"弈棋图"屏风画
A screen made in Tang Dynasty (618 - 907 AD) was unearthed in an ancient tomb in Turpan, Xinjiang. The portrait on the screen depicted a go tournament at that time.
3. 南京莫愁湖公园内的胜棋楼，有明太祖朱元璋和大臣徐达的下棋腊像
The wax statues of the Ming Emperor, Zhuyuanzhang, and his minister, Xuda, playing go at the Shengqilou Mansion, Mochouhu Garden, Nanjing
4. 围棋
Go

界上已有40多个国家和地区开展了围棋运动。其中，以中国、日本、韩国的围棋运动水平最高。中国的围棋选手聂卫平、马晓春等，都是国际著名的选手。围棋已发展成为一种重要的国际体育竞赛项目。

Go①, or *wei qi*, originated in China. It appeared earlier than Chinese chess, and could date back at least 2,500 years. Go is the earliest form of chess in the world. In ancient days, it was a favorite game of rulers, literati, scholars and even young ladies.

The board is marked with 19 parallel horizontal lines and 19 parallel vertical lines, which form 361 intersections. Stones are placed on the intersections in such a way as to gradually command more territory by surrounding and eliminating the opposition. Each of the two sides, one with black stones and the other with white stones, possesses 180 of them. It is a tense game and the situation on the board keeps changing. Players have to resort to all sorts of tactics in order to defeat the opponent. As tactics used in the go are so variable and profound, ancient Chinese said in an exaggerate manner that the inventors of go must have been deities.

Playing go exercises the brain and enhances one's sense of logic. At the same time, it can also cultivate temperament through the development of willpower and calmness.

Go was introduced into Japan during the Sui (581-618 AD) and Tang (618-907 AD) dynasties and into Europe in the 19th century. Players from China, Japan and South Korea are of the highest skill in the world, and competitors like Nie Weiping and Ma Xiaochun enjoy international renown.

武　术
Martial Arts

武术是中国传统的体育项目，有着悠久的历史和丰富多彩的内容。

远古时候，人们通过与野兽搏斗和参加战争，获得了格斗和搏杀的技能。他们使用的各种工具和兵器，经过发展演变，逐渐形成了武术中"十八般武艺"①的器械，如：刀、枪、剑、戟、棍等。传统武术中，还有许多健身运动是人们根据动物的形态和动作编排的。

随着练武活动在民间的盛行，中国出现了许多武术名家，形成了河南少林寺、河北沧州等著名的武术基地。1956年，中国国家体育运动委员会把武术正式列为竞赛项目。一些体育学校设有武术教学、研究部门，许多业余体育学校也设立了武术培训班。群众性的武术活动在中国更加活跃。

武术是指用武的技术。内容大体可以分为拳术、器械、对练、

1. 少林功夫
   Shaolin martial arts
2. 有谓"天下功夫出少林"。这是少林武僧练功的情况
   Popular saying has it that all kinds of martial arts are originated from Shaolin.
3. 不少青少年醉心习武，跑到少林寺一带的武术学校学武
   Many passionate young people are training at the martial arts schools near the area of Shaolin Temple.

对抗性项目、集体项目等五大类。拳术是武术的基础,包括长拳、太极拳、形意拳等。器械类包括刀术、剑术、棍术、枪术等。对练类包括徒手对练、器械对练、徒手与器械对练等。对抗项目包括散手等。集体项目指的是许多人集体表演的武术。

武术要求动作连贯,快速多变,节奏鲜明,以及身法、手、眼、步和精神、气、力、功内外相合,高度协调。练武术可以起到锻炼身体,培养意志的作用。

武术运动不仅适合青壮年练习,许多项目也适合老年、少年、妇女和体弱多病的人锻炼。武术既是防身之术,又是健身之法,因此深受中国各族人民的喜爱,也逐渐被推广到了世界各地。古老的中国武术,正以崭新的面貌受到世人的瞩目。

🔍 小注解 Footnotes

① 十八般武艺:指使用刀、枪、剑、戟等18种古式兵器的武艺,一般用来比喻各种技能。

① 18 standard traditional weapons are eventually developed here.

Martial arts, a traditional sports item in China, have a long history and rich variety.

In ancient times, people learned how to fight and kill through hunting or tribal clashes. Through long years of evolvement, tools used for hunting or fighting gradually developed into weaponry[①] like the knife, spear, sword, cudgel, etc. Many bodily movements of practitioners of martial arts are, in fact, developed from animal postures and their movements.

Martial arts have long been popular among Chinese, and many famous martial arts masters and martial arts bases, such as the world-renowned Shaolin Temple in Henan Province, Cangzhou of Hebei Province, have emerged. The National Physical Culture and Sport Commission formally listed martial arts as a sport in 1956. Some physical cultural institutions formally established departments specialized in the education of and research into martial arts. Many spare-time sport schools began to run

martial arts training classes.

Martial arts can be classified roughly into five types, namely, boxing, fighting with weaponry, pair-up exercise, confrontational fighting and collective practice. Boxing is the basis of martial arts and can be divided into long boxing, *Taiji* boxing and *xingyi* boxing. Fighting with weaponry can be divided into fighting with a knife, sword, cudgel, spear, etc. Pair-up exercise includes fighting with fists, with weapons and fists-to-weapon fights, etc. Confrontational fighting refers to a fight between two practitioners. Collective practice refers to exercise of martial arts by a group of people.

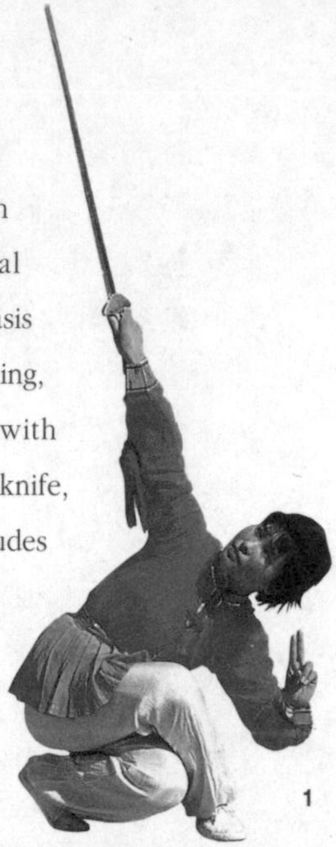

Martial arts require continuous movements, speed, quickness and dexterity, clear-cut rhythm, harmonious coordination of the body, hands, eyes, steps, mood, breathing, power, etc. Practicing martial arts can help one keep fit and train the willpower.

Martial arts are physical exercises suitable for the young, but many are also fitted to the needs and abilities of the aged, women, the weak and the sick. Martial arts not only can be used to protect oneself, but also to keep one in good health, which is why they enjoy perhaps even more popularity today than ever before.

1. 舞剑
   Sword practice
2. 武当功夫
   Wudang martial arts
3. 长枪
   Spear

概述
Introduction

建筑，是人类文明的一个重要标志。在这方面，中国人具有非凡的创造力和智慧。

从金碧辉煌的宫殿，到多姿多采的民居；从诗情画意的亭台楼阁，到奇巧别致的宝塔古桥，千百年来，中国人民继往开来，博采众长，用勤劳和智慧，创造着一个又一个奇迹。

Architecture is an important symbol of human civilization. From resplendent imperial palaces to all kinds of civilian residences, from picturesque pavilions and kiosks to unique pagodas and bridges, Chinese people have for centuries created one architectural wonder after another.

宫廷建筑
The Imperial Palace

　　宫廷，是封建帝王居住的地方。为了显示皇家至高无上的地位和统领天下的威严，中国古代宫廷的设计、建筑都特别追求雄伟壮观和富丽华贵。

　　古代宫廷的设计，一般分为前后两部分：前面是皇帝处理朝政的地方，后面是帝王、后妃们居住的地方。皇宫中的主要宫殿都建在一条南北中轴线上，两侧的建筑整齐而对称。重重院落，层层殿堂，展示了皇宫的齐整、庄严和浩大。

　　宫廷中的建筑，大都由金碧辉煌的大屋顶、朱红的木制廊柱、门窗和宽阔洁白的汉白玉台基组成。

宫廷建筑大都采用大屋顶。这种大屋顶不但华美壮丽，而且对建筑物起到了很好的保护作用。大屋顶层层飞翘的屋檐和屋角，使屋面形成了巧妙的曲线，这样，雨水从屋顶流下，会被排得更远，从而保护了木造的宫殿不受雨淋。大屋顶上装饰的鸟兽，不但给庄严的宫殿罩上了一层神秘的色彩，也对古建筑起到了固定和防止雨水腐蚀的作用。宫廷建筑的屋顶上，一般都铺设金黄色的琉璃瓦，因为金黄色象征皇权，所以只有王室才能使用这种颜色。

用木材建造房屋，是中国古代建筑的基本特点。宫廷建筑的梁柱、门窗等，都是用木材建造的，而且被漆成了象征喜庆、富贵的朱红色。有的地方，还描绘着龙凤、云海、花草等彩画。鲜艳的颜色，不但体现了帝王殿宇的华贵，也对木制的建筑起到了防潮、防蛀的保护作用。北京故宫的太和殿，就是中国最大的木结构大殿。

洁净宽阔的汉白玉台基，是雄伟宫殿的基座。北京故宫的太和殿就建在三层汉白玉台基上。台基四周的石柱和台阶上，雕刻着精美的石龙和各种花纹。殿后用整块巨石铺就的石阶御道，雕刻着海浪、流

1. 北京故宫
   The Imperial Palace, Beijing
2. 故宫内慈禧太后"垂帘听政"的地方
   ——养心殿东暖阁
   The Hall of Mental Cultivation in the Imperial Palace was where Empress Cixi governed the country.
3. 故宫中的云龙石阶御道
   Reserved for the emperor only, the huge one-piece rock at the Imperial Hall is carved with floating clouds and surging dragons.
4. 故宫角楼
   The watch tower of Imperial Palace

云和翻腾的巨龙，十分壮观。

几千年来，中国历代帝王都不惜人力、物力和财力，建造规模巨大的宫廷。可惜的是，这些辉煌的建筑大都在战火中毁坏了。目前保存最完整的古代宫廷建筑，就是位于北京市中心的故宫博物院。这座明清两朝的皇宫，是目前世界上最大的木结构建筑群。

The imperial palace was the residence of the emperor and his family. In order to show supremacy of the imperial house and its authority to rule the country, palace architects in ancient China pursued grandeur and magnificence in their design and construction.

The complex of the imperial palace in ancient China was usually divided into two parts. The Emperor used the front part to meet his ministers to handle state affairs, while the rear was used for residential purposes. The main buildings were all built along a central south-north axis, while auxiliary buildings stood symmetrically on each side. Row upon row of halls and one compound after another demonstrated imperial solemnity and dignity.

Buildings in an imperial palace mostly have large sloping roofs with golden-colored tiles, huge red-painted wooden eave-supporting pillars, windows and gates and a large white marble base.

The roof was not only decorative, but also protective, as the overhang with upturned corners ensured that rain water would flow along the roof grooves and fall into places far from the wooden structures of the building. Zoomorphic ornaments on the upturned roof corners were not only intended to add to the mysterious air of the place, but also had a practical purpose in fastening the roof and keeping water out. The roofs were made of golden-colored glazed tiles (the color was a symbol of imperial power and could only be used by the imperial house).

Wooden buildings were a basic feature of ancient Chinese architecture. Beams, pillars, windows, gates were all made of wood and were painted red to symbolize happiness and good fortune. Pictures of dragons, phoenixes, clouds, flowers and grass were sometimes painted on the surface, which not only made the buildings look more magnificent but had the practical purpose of protecting the wood from damp and infestation by insects. The Hall of Great Harmony in the Palace Museum in Beijing is the largest extant structure built of wood.

The base for the huge structures was always white marble. The base on which the Hall of Great Harmony stands, for example, is a huge piece of three-tier white marble. The posts around this base are carved with dragons and all kinds of floral patterns. The huge one-piece rock at the back of the hall, which served as a path solely for the emperor, is carved with sea waves, floating clouds and surging dragons.

For several thousand years, emperors in Chinese history spared no manpower, materials and money in building many huge imperial palaces. Unfortunately, most were destroyed in war. The best-preserved imperial palace today is the Palace Museum, also known as the Forbidden City, in Beijing, used by emperors of both the Ming (1368-1644 AD) and Qing (1644-1911 AD) dynasties, which is the largest wooden structural complex in the world today.

1. 故宫雨花阁屋顶精巧华丽
   The exquisite carving on the roof of Yuhua Tower of Imperial Palace
2. 华表
   Memorial Column
3. 太和殿是故宫最宏伟的大殿
   The Hall of Supreme Harmony is the grandest hall in the Imperial Palace.
4. 慈禧太后的起居之所储秀宫，装修豪华精美
   Empress Cixi lived in the refined courtyard of Chuxiugong.

寺庙建筑
Temples

中国是个多宗教的国家。既有土生土长的道教，又有从外国传入的佛教、伊斯兰教和基督教等。这些宗教的建筑各有各的名称。道教的建筑称"宫"或"观"（guàn），佛教的建筑有寺、塔和石窟（kū），伊斯兰教有清真寺，基督教有教堂。世界上不同宗教的建筑有不同的风格，但建筑在中国大地上的宗教建筑，在融合了外国宗教建筑的特点后，都明显地"中国化"了。

1. 河南洛阳白马寺，是佛教传入中国后兴建的第一座寺庙
   Baima Temple, Luoyang, Henan Province, is the first Buddhist temple in China.
2. 建于清代的北京西黄寺灵塔
   The Xihuang Temple in Beijing was built during the Qing Dynasty (1616-1911 AD).
3. 山西五台山显通寺大雄宝殿
   Hall of Mahavira, Xiantong Temple, Wutai Mountain, Shanxi Province

下面主要介绍遍布中国大地的佛教寺庙的建筑。

佛教的寺庙大都建在远离闹市的山中。在许多景色秀美的山上，都建有寺庙，尤其是四大佛教名山五台山、峨眉山、九华山、普陀山，更是集中了中国历代著名的寺庙建筑，如五台山的佛光寺、南禅寺。

佛教是从印度传入中国的，但中国的佛教建筑与印度的寺院大不相同。印度的寺院以塔为中心。中国的寺庙受古代建筑的影响，以佛殿为中心，整个寺庙的布局、殿堂的结构、屋顶的建造等，都仿照皇帝的宫殿，创造出了中国佛教建筑的特色。

中国寺庙的主要建筑都建在寺院南北的中轴线上，左右的建筑整齐对称。一般来说，中轴线从南往北的建筑有供奉着佛像的山门殿、天王殿、大雄宝殿、法堂以及藏经楼。建在这些大殿两侧的，有钟鼓楼和一些配殿、配屋及僧人们的生活区。整个寺院的建筑金碧辉煌，气势庄严。

佛教在中国流传很广，不计其数的佛教寺庙遍布中国各地。它们庄严雄伟，精美华丽，和自然的风景融为一体，不但是佛教徒朝拜的圣地，也是中外游客参观游览的好地方。

China is a country with various religions. Apart from the indigenous Daoism, there are Buddhism, Islam and Christianity introduced into China from foreign lands. The structures built by the different religions have their own Chinese names. Daoist structures are called *gong* (palace) and *guan* (temple), Buddhist structures are called *si* (temple), *ta* (pagoda) and *shiku* (grotto); *qingzhenci* is the term for a mosque and *jiaotang* for a Christian church. Religious structures around the world have their own architectural styles. However, the religious structures built in China have integrated more or less the Chinese style.

Now let's focus on architectural characteristics of Buddhist structures which can be seen all over China.

Most of Buddhist temples are built in picturesque mountains, far from bustling towns and cities. In China, there are four famous mountains affiliated with Buddhism, namely, Wutai, Emei, Jiuhua and Putuo. Many renowned temples are located in those four mountains, such as Foguang Temple and Nanchan Temple in Wutai Mountains.

1. 五台山显通寺成所作智塔
   Chengsuozuozhi Pagoda, Xiantong Temple,
   Wutai Mountain
2. 五台山龙泉寺汉白玉石牌坊
   White marble memorial arch, Longquan Temple,
   Wutai Mountain
3. 北京戒台寺的汉白玉石戒坛号称"天下
   第一坛"
   Made of white marble, the altar in Jietai Temple
   of Beijing is named the "Best Altar in the World".

Buddhism was first introduced into China from ancient India. However, the Buddhist structures in China are different from those of India. In India, the center of a temple is a stupa. In China it is the central hall. This may be the result of the influence of ancient Chinese architecture. The layout of the buildings, the structure of the hall and construction of the roofs in a temple are all imitations of the imperial palace. This has become one of the features of Chinese Buddhist temples.

Main buildings in a temple are normally built along the central axis with auxiliary buildings placed symmetrically on both sides. Generally speaking, along the south-north axis, there are the entrance hall, Hall of Heavenly Kings, Hall of the Mahavira, scripture-chanting hall and scripture storage building. Beside those halls, there are the Drum and Bell Towers and some other buildings and living quarters of monks.

Buddhism has been practiced extensively in China and there are numerous temples throughout the country. Integrated into nature, these grand structures become part of the scenery. They are not only sacred places for Buddhist pilgrims, but also beauty spots for tourists.

民居
Residences

1. 安徽西递村古民居
The ancient residences in Xidi Village, Anhui Province

　　由于中国疆域辽阔，民族众多，各地的气候条件和生活方式不同，因此，各地人们居住的房屋的样式和风格也不相同。

　　在中国的民居中，最有特点的是北京四合院、西北黄土高原的窑洞、安徽的古民居和福建、广东等地的客家土楼。

　　北京四合院　在北京城大大小小的胡同中，坐落着许多由东、南、西、北四面房屋围合起来的院落式住宅，这就是四合院。

　　四合院的大门一般开在东南角或西北角，院中的北房是正房，正房建在砖石砌成的台基上，比其他房屋的规模大，是院主人的住室。院子的两边建有东西厢房，是晚辈们居住的地方。在正房和厢房之间建有走廊，可以供人行走和休息。四合院的围墙和临街的房屋一般不对外开窗，院中的环境封闭而幽静。

　　北京有各种不同规模的四合院，但不论大小，都是由一个个四面房屋围合的庭院组成的。最简单的四合院只有一个院子，比较复杂的有两三个院子，富贵人家居住的深宅大院，通常是由好几座四合院并列组成的。

窑洞 中国黄河中上游一带，是世界闻名的黄土高原。生活在黄土高原上的人们，利用那里又深又厚、立体性能极好的黄土层，建造了一种独特的住宅——窑洞。窑洞又分为土窑、石窑、砖窑等几种。土窑是靠着山坡挖成的黄土窑洞，这种窑洞冬暖夏凉，保温隔音效果最好。石窑和砖窑是先用石块或砖砌成拱形洞，然后在上面盖上厚厚的黄土，又坚固又美观。由于建造窑洞不需要钢材、水泥，所以造价比较低。随着社会的发展，人们对窑洞的建造不断改进，黄土高原上冬暖夏凉的窑洞越来越舒适美观了。

安徽古民居 安徽省的南部，保留着许多古代的民居。这些古民宅大都用砖木作建筑材料，周围建有高大的围墙。围墙内的房屋，一般是三开间或五开间的两层小楼。比较大的住宅有两个、三个或更多个庭院；院中有水池，堂前屋后种植着花草盆景，各处的梁柱和栏板上雕刻着精美的图案。座座小楼，深深庭院，就像一个个艺术的世界。建筑学家们都称赞那里是"古民居建筑艺术的宝库"。

客家土楼 土楼是广东、福建等地的客家人的住宅。客家人的祖先是1,900多年前从黄河中下游地区迁移到南方的汉族人。为了防范骚扰，保护家族的安全，客家人创造了这种庞大的民居——土楼。一座土楼里可以住下整个家族的几十户人家，几百口人。土楼有圆形的，也有方形的，其中，最有特色的是圆形土楼。圆楼由两三圈组成，外圈十多米高，有一二百个房间，一层是厨房和餐厅，二层是仓库，三层、四层是卧室；第二圈两层，有30到50个房间，一般是客房；中间是祖堂，能容下几百人进行公共活动。土楼里还有水井、浴室、厕所等，就像一座小城市。客家土楼的高大、奇特，受到了世界各国建筑大师的称赞。

Due to the country's vast size, the presence of many ethnic groups, different climatic conditions and ways of life, the residences of people in different parts of the country differ in terms of design and style.

The most representative residences of the Chinese people are the *siheyuan* of Beijing, cave-dwellings of the Loess Plateau in northwest China, ancient houses of Anhui Province and the earthen tower of Kejia (or Hakka) people in Guangdong Province.

Siheyuan: There are a large number of quadrangles called *siheyuan*, a compound enclosed by inward-facing houses on four sides, in the alleyways of Beijing.

The entrance gate of a *siheyuan* is usually set at the southeast or northwest corner of the compound. The main south-facing house, the center of a *siheyuan*, stands on a terrace built with bricks and rocks. Larger than other houses in the compound, it is used by the master of the family. On both sides of the compound are houses for the younger generations. Corridors connect all the houses. The enclosure walls and the houses on the side of the alley usually do not have windows. Therefore, the inside of the compound is tranquil and peaceful.

Beijing has *siheyuan* of all sizes, but, no matter what the size, there will be an enclosure wall with houses built on four sides. The simplest *siheyuan* has only one courtyard in the middle, but there are ones with three or four courtyards surrounded by houses. A large *siheyuan* formerly occupied by a wealthy family actually comprises several *siheyuan*.

Cave-dwellings: The middle and upper reaches of the Yellow River comprise the Loess Plateau. People living on the plateau make use of the solid and thick loess to build unique residences called cave-dwellings. These can be further divided into earthen, rock-walled and brick-walled types. Earthen cave-dwellings are hollowed out of mountain slopes; they are warm in winter and cool in summer, and are also soundproof. Rock or brick-walled cave-dwellings are usually built with rocks or bricks first into an arch shaped house and then covered with a thick layer of earth. Since there is no need for steel and cement, the building costs are low. As society progresses, construction of cave-dwellings keeps improving and today such homes are

1. 客家土楼
   The earthen tower of Kejia people
2. 客家楼屋
   The mansion of Kejia people
3. 北京四合院
   The *siheyuan* of Beijing

1. 陕北窑洞
   Cave-dwellings of northern Shaanxi Province
2. 窑洞的小居民
   The inhabitants of the cave-dwellings

more comfortable inside and more pleasant in appearance.

Ancient houses of Anhui : In the south of Anhui Province, many ancient houses have been preserved. Those houses are mostly built with bricks and wood with high enclosure walls. Within the wall, there is a two-storey, three- or five-bay house. In large compounds, there might be two, three, or more such houses, each having a courtyard. There is a pool in the compound. Flowers and bonsai grow in front of and at the back of the house. Beams, pillars and partition panels are all carved with refined patterns. A little house in a deep compound looks like a small world of art. Architects call them "treasures of ancient architectural art".

Earthen tower of Kejia people: Earthen towers, or *tulou*, are residences of the Kejia (Hakka) people in Guangdong and Fujian provinces. The forefathers of Kejia people were Han Chinese who migrated to the south from the middle and lower reaches of the Yellow River over 1,900 years ago. For both privacy and security, they built large residences known as earthen towers. One such tower is able to hold a score of families of a whole clan with a total of several hundred people. The towers are round or square in shape, but the round-shaped tower is the most impressive. It is made up of two or three circles of houses. The outer circle could be as high as a dozen meters, with one hundred to two hundred rooms. The ground floor is used as kitchens and dining rooms. The second floor is used for storage. The third and fourth floors are the living quarters and bedrooms. The second circle has two stories with 30 to 50 rooms. They are mostly used as rooms for guests. In the middle there is an ancestral hall with a holding capacity of several hundred people where public activities are carried out. Within an earthen tower, there are bathrooms, toilets and a well. It is like a small town indeed. The huge size and the unique design of the earthen tower are highly acclaimed in international architectural circles.

园林
Classical Garden

中国古代的园林艺术是中国文化的一朵奇葩，现存于中国各地的古典园林，风景优美，建筑奇特，是中外游人向往的游览胜地。

中国古典园林的最大特点是讲究自然天成。古代的园林设计家在建园时，巧妙地把大自然的美景融合在人造的园林中，使人能从中欣赏到大自然的奇峰、异石、流水、湖面、名花、芳草，感觉就像在画中游览。

中国古典园林在布局上还有含蓄、变化、曲折的特点，比如园路要"曲径通幽"，讲究景中有景，步移景；园中的建筑要与自然景物交融在一起，形状式样变化多样；花草树木要高低相间，四季争艳……

中国古典园林的另一个特点，是巧妙地将诗画艺术和园林融于一体。如园林建筑上的匾额、楹联、画栋、雕梁等，形成了中国古典园林艺术的独特风格。

中国的古典园林大致可以分为北方皇家园林和南方私家园林两类。北方的皇家园林往往利用真山真水，并且集中了各地建筑中的

1. 承德避暑山庄
   Summer Resort in Chengde

精华。黄色的琉璃瓦，朱红的廊柱，洁白的玉石雕栏，精美的雕梁画栋，色彩华美，富丽堂皇。保存到现在的著名皇家园林有北京颐和园、北海公园、承德避暑山庄等。南方的私家园林大多建在苏州、南京、杭州和扬州一带，如苏州的拙政园、留园，无锡的寄畅园，扬州的个园等。私家园林一般面积不大，但经过建筑家的巧妙安排，园中有山有水，景物多变，自然而宁静。

The classical Chinese garden art is another treasure of Chinese culture. The extant classical gardens throughout China, with their beautiful scenery and unique structures, attract many tourists.

The most prominent feature of classical Chinese gardens is the emphasis on creating a natural feeling. Ancient garden architects successfully integrated man-made scenes into the natural landscape, creating the impression of traveling in a picturesque environment of grotesque peaks, strange rock groupings, flowing water, calm lakes, flowers and plants.

Classical Chinese gardens are often full of surprises in terms of scenes, and being variable in composition and complicated in design. Serpentine walkways, for instance, lead to places of tranquility. Much attention is given to creation of varied scenery; with each step, one can see a different scene. Buildings of different forms and different architectural styles are well integrated with the garden scenery. Flowers, plants and trees are elaborately

1. 北京北海公园
   Beihai Park, Beijing
2. 苏州拙政园
   Zhuozheng Garden in Suzhou
3. 苏州留园
   Liuyuan Garden in Suzhou
4. 无锡寄畅园
   Jichang Garden in Wuxi

cultivated and planned with a definite eye on their heights and flowering seasons.

Another feature of classical Chinese gardens is that decorative art is ingeniously merged with the garden scenery. On buildings there are horizontal boards carved with calligraphy, antithetical couplets, and painted beams with carvings.

Classical Chinese gardens can be roughly divided into two types, namely, royal gardens of the north and private gardens of the south. Royal gardens tend to make use of natural mountains and waters and have clusters of stylish architectural structures in imitation of such structures of the whole country. With golden glazed titles, vermilion colonnades, white marble balustrades, refined ornamented beams, they are filled with a sense of magnificence and grandeur. The best-preserved royal gardens are the Summer Palace, Beihai Park in Beijing and the Summer Resort in Chengde. Private gardens of the south are mostly seen in Suzhou, Nanjing, Hangzhou and Yangzhou, such as Zhuozheng Garden and Liuyuan Garden in Suzhou, Jichang Garden in Wuxi, Geyuan Garden in Yangzhou, etc. Small in size, those gardens are characteristic of ingenious designs; with miniature mountains and rivers and variable sceneries, they are natural and tranquil.

亭台楼阁
Kiosk, Tower and Pavilion

在中国旅游和观赏名胜古迹，常常会遇到亭台楼阁等建筑物，这些建筑物坐落在奇山秀水间，点缀出一处处富有诗情画意的美景。

亭 是一种有顶无墙的小型建筑物。有圆形、方形、六角形、八角形、梅花形和扇形等多种形状。亭子常常建在山上、水旁、花间、桥上，可以供人们遮阳避雨、休息观景，也使园中的风景更加美丽。中国的亭子大多是用木、竹、砖、石建造的，如北京北海公园的五龙亭、苏州的沧浪亭等。

廊 是园林中联系建筑之间的通道。它不但可以遮阳避雨，还像一条风景导游线，可以供游人透过柱子之间的空间观赏风景。北京颐和园中的长廊，是中国园林中最长的廊，长廊的一边是平静的昆明湖，另一边是苍翠的万寿山和一组组古典建筑。游人漫步在长廊中，可以观赏到一处处美丽的湖光山色。

榭 是建在高台上的房子。榭一般建在水中、水边或花畔。建在水边的又叫"水榭"，是为游人观赏水景而建的，如北海公园的水榭、承德避暑山庄的水心榭等。

楼阁 是两层以上金碧辉煌的高大建筑。可以供游人登高远望，休息观景；还可以用来藏书供佛，悬挂钟鼓。在中国，著名的楼阁很多，如临近大海的山东蓬莱阁、北京颐和园的佛香阁、江西的滕王阁、湖南的岳阳楼、湖北的黄鹤楼等。

Traveling in China, you may often see kiosks, towers and pavilions in scenic spots. Sitting by the waters or standing on mountains, they give much charm to the landscape.

Kiosk refers to small-sized structure with a roof, but without walls. There are various shapes, such as circular, square, hexagonal, octagonal, etc. Some are even in the shape of a plum blossom or a fan. Usually built on mountains, by water, amidst flowers, or on bridges, kiosks not only provide a resting place and shelter from rain, but also beautify the place. Most kiosks in China are built with wood, bamboo, bricks, rocks, etc. Such examples are the Five Dragon Kiosk in Beihai Park in Beijing and Canglang Kiosk in Suzhou.

Corridor refers to passageways linking buildings in a garden. This not only provides a shelter from the weather but also functions as a guiding line for visitors. It is also a good place to rest and enjoy scenery. The Long Corridor in the Summer Palace in Beijing is the longest of its kind in Chinese gardens, linking tranquil Kunming Lake on one end to the verdant Longevity Hill and clusters of buildings in ancient architectural style at the other. Sauntering along this corridor, one can contemplate the beautiful scenery of the lake and the hills around it.

Xie refers to a pavilion built on a high terrace, over or by an expanse of water or flowers. A pavilion built by water is called a "waterside *xie*", which is used by people to enjoy the surrounding scenery. For instance, in Beihai Park, there is the Waterside *Xie*; in Chengde Summer Resort, there is the Lake Center *Xie*.

Pavilion refers to a magnificent building of two or more stories. It provides people with a high point to observe the surrounding landscape. It may also be used to store books, to worship Buddha and to hang a drum and bell. There are many famous pavilions in China, such as Penglai Pavilion overlooking the sea in Shangdong Province, the Buddhist Incense Pavilion in Beijing's Summer Palace, Tengwang Pavilion in Jiangxi Province, and Yueyang Pavilion in Hunan Province and the Crane Pavilion in Hubei Province.

1. 北京故宫万春亭
   Wanchun Kiosk of Imperial Palace, Beijing
2. 北京颐和园长廊
   The corridor of Summer Palace, Beijing
3. 江西滕王阁
   Tengwang Pavilion, Jiangxi Province
4. 湖北黄鹤楼
   Huang He (Yellow Crane) Pavilion in Hubei Province

古塔
Ancient Pagoda

塔是中国传统的建筑物。在中国辽阔的大地上，随处都能见到保留到今天的古塔。

其实，塔并不是中国的"原产"，而是起源于印度。汉代，随着佛教从印度传入中国，塔也"进口"到了中国。"塔"是印度梵语的译音，本义是坟墓，是古代印度高僧圆寂①后，用来埋放骨灰的地方。

现在我们所见到的中国古塔，是中印建筑艺术相结合的产物。中国的古塔建筑多种多样，从外形上看，由最早的方形发展成了六角形、八角形、圆形等多种形状。从建塔的材料分，有木塔、砖塔、石塔、铁塔、铜塔、琉璃塔，甚至还有金塔、银塔、珍珠塔。中国古塔的层数一般是单数，通常有五层到十三层。

中国古代的小说中，常常描写到塔具有的神奇力量。如托塔李天王手中的宝塔能够降妖伏魔；神话故事《白蛇传》中的白娘子被和尚法海镇在雷峰塔下等等，这是因为佛教认为塔具有驱逐妖魔、护佑百姓的作用。

在中国城乡的高山上、江河边，屹立着数以千计的古塔。现存的著名古塔有：西安的大雁塔、山西应县木塔、河南开封铁塔、河北定县开元寺砖塔、杭州的六和塔、北京香山的琉璃塔等等。这些古塔反映了中国悠久的历史和高超的建筑艺术，也把中国的山河点缀得更加美丽。

1. 山西应县木塔
   Yingxian County Wooden Pagoda, Shanxi Province
2. 北京香山琉璃塔
   Liuli Pagoda, Xiangshan Mountain, Beijing
3. 西安大雁塔
   Greater Geese Pagoda, Xi'an Province
4. 云南大理三塔
   The Three Pagodas of Dali, Yunnan Province

Pagoda or *ta*[①] is a traditional Chinese structure. Extant ancient pagodas can be found everywhere in China.

In fact, the pagoda is not an indigenous building of China. It originated in ancient India. As Buddhism was introduced into China during the Han Dynasty (206 BC-220 AD), the pagoda came with it.

The ancient pagodas we see today are a product of a combination of both Indian and Chinese architecture, and they come in various types. As far as appearance is concerned, there are circular, hexagonal and octagonal pagodas. If classified by building materials, there are pagodas built with wood, bricks, rocks, iron, bronze, glazed tiles or even gold, silver or pearls. Normally, the number of stories varies from five to 13, but it is always an odd number.

In ancient Chinese fiction, pagodas were often described as possessing magical powers. For instance, the pagoda on the palm of Heavenly King Li can subdue any demons. The White Snake Lady in the mythical story *Romance of the White Snake* is interred beneath Leifeng Pagoda by Monk Fa Hai as a punishment. This is because Buddhists believe that a pagoda is able to expel evil spirits and protect people.

On mountains and by rivers, there tower several thousand pagodas in China. The existing ancient pagodas include the Greater Geese Pagoda in Xi'an, the Wooden Pagoda in Yingxian County of Shanxi Province, the Iron Pagoda in Kaifeng of Henan Province, the Kaiyuansi Brick Pagoda in Dingxian County of Hebei Province, the Liuhe Pagoda in Hangzhou, the Liuli Pagoda at the Fragrant Hills in Beijing. Those ancient pagodas reflect the long history of China as well as the high level of architectural craftsmanship, and add much charm to the landscape of China.

古桥
Ancient Bridge

在中国古代建筑中，桥梁是一个重要的组成部分。

几千年来，勤劳智慧的中国人修建了数以万计奇巧壮丽的桥梁，这些桥梁横跨在山水之间，便利了交通，装点了河山，成为中国古代文明的标志之一。

西安灞桥是中国最古老的石柱墩桥，建于汉代。灞桥全长386米，有64个桥洞，自古就是连接古都长安以东广大地区的交通要道。古时候，长安人送别亲友，一般都要送到灞桥，并折下桥头柳枝相赠。久而久之，"灞桥折柳赠别"便成了一种特有的习俗。如今，经过整修的古灞桥已焕然一新，周围的风景也更加动人。

位于河北省赵县的赵州桥，建于1,400多年前的隋代，是世界上第一座用石头建造的单孔拱桥，它的设计者李春是一位著名的工匠。赵州桥的设计有许多独到之处：50多米长的赵州桥，桥面坡度非常平缓，十分便于车马、行人上下；桥拱两肩上的四个小拱洞，不但节省了石材，减轻了桥的重量，还加大了洪水的流量。这些精心的设计和高超的技术，使古老的赵州桥至今十分坚固。赵州桥不但是中国古代建筑工程中的杰作，也是世界古代桥梁的奇迹。

北京城外永定河上的卢沟桥，已经有900多年的历史，是一座中外闻名的桥梁。卢沟桥全长260多米，桥两侧200多根护栏石柱上，雕刻着形态各异的石狮子，那些很难数清的石狮，是卢沟桥上最有趣的景致。卢沟桥还是中国人民反抗侵略者的历史见证。1937年7月7日，中国军队就是在卢沟桥上英勇抗击了入侵的日本侵略军，揭开了抗日战争历史新的一页。

中国古代著名的桥梁还有很多，如福建晋江的五里长桥平安桥、泉州洛阳桥、杭州西湖九曲桥、苏州宝带桥及北京颐和园的工带桥等。

The bridge is one of the most important components of ancient Chinese architecture.

For several thousand years, Chinese have built tens of thousands of ingeniously designed and magnificent bridges. Crossing over mountains, spanning rivers, they have facilitated smooth communications, helped to beautify landscape and become one of the marks of ancient Chinese civilization.

Baqiao Bridge in Xi'an, built in the Han Dynasty (206 BC-220 AD), is the earliest bridge with stone piers in China. It is 386 m long with 64 arches. It served as the key passage linking the capital Chang'an and the extensive areas to the east. In ancient days, when local residents of Chang'an bade farewell to a relative or a friend, they would usually see him off at Baqiao Bridge. Besides, they would break a twig of a nearby willow tree and give it to the traveler as a token of good wishes. Gradually, this practice became a local custom. Today, the bridge has been renovated and its surroundings have become more picturesque.

Zhaozhou Bridge in Zhaoxian County of

1. 甘肃渭源灞陵桥已有600多年历史
   Baling Bridge, Weiyuan, Gansu Province, is more than six hundred years old.
2. 浙江泰顺县泗溪廊桥，建筑极为精美
   The sophisticated corridor bridge in Sixi, Taishun County, Zhejiang Province

1. 见证"七七事变"的北京卢沟桥
   Lugou Bridge was where the key event in the anti-Japanese war took place on July 7, 1937.

2. 建于隋代的河北赵州桥，是世界上第一座单孔石拱桥
   Zhaozhou Bridge, Hebei Province, was built in Sui Dynasty (581-618 AD), and it is the world's first single arch stone bridge.

Hebei Province dates back 1,400 years ago to the Sui Dynasty. It is the first single arch stone bridge in the world. Its designer Li Chun was a famous mason. There are many unique features about this bridge. Some 50 m long, it has mild slopes that make it easy for horse-pulled carts and pedestrians to cross. On its shoulders there are four arch-shaped holes, which not only saved building materials and lessened the weight of the bridge but also helped ease the flow of water in time of flood. The elaborate design and superb building technique have ensured the solidness of the bridge.

Lugou Bridge over the Yongding River in the suburbs of Beijing has a history of more than 900 years. It is 260 m long with more than 200 stone posts on balustrades on both sides of the bridge. Each post is carved with lions of different sizes and postures. Lugou Bridge has its place in Chinese history, as it was the place where, on July 7, 1937, the Chinese army heroically resisted the invading Japanese troops, a key event in the anti-Japanese war.

There are many more ancient bridges in China. The famous ones include Ping'an Bridge in Jinjiang and Luoyang Bridge in Quanzhou of Fujian Province, Jiuqu Bridge in the West Lake of Hangzhou, Baodai Bridge in Suzhou and the Yudai Bridge in the Summer Palace of Beijing.

概述
Introduction

中国的工艺美术有着悠久的历史。原始社会新石器时期的陶器，可以说是最早的工艺美术品。此后，商周的青铜器，战国的漆器，汉唐的丝织品，宋朝的刺绣，明清的景泰蓝和瓷器等，都是以其精美、名贵闻名于世。

中国传统的工艺美术，制作精美，技艺高超，不但具有鲜明的民族风格和地方特色，而且种类繁多。很早以前它们就已走向世界，向世人展示了自己的风采。

Chinese arts and crafts have a long history. Earthenware of the primitive society of the Neolithic Age are the earliest artistic works. The bronze ware of the Shang (17th-11th century BC) and Zhou (11th century-221 BC) dynasties, lacquer ware of the Warring States Period (475-221 BC), silk fabrics of the Han (206 BC-220 AD) and Tang (618-907 AD) dynasties, embroidery of the Song Dynasty (960-1279 AD), cloisonné and porcelain of the Ming (1368-1644 AD) and Qing (1644-1911 AD) dynasties are all known for their exquisiteness and refinement.

Made with high craftsmanship, traditional Chinese arts and crafts are of striking nationalistic features and rich varieties. They have long been shipped around the world.

陶瓷
Pottery and Porcelain

英语中的"china"一词有两个意义，一个是中国，一个是瓷器。西方人很早就把中国与瓷器联系在一起，这是因为制瓷技术是中国人发明的。

早在六七千年以前，中国就出现了陶器。瓷器是从陶器发展来的，如果从生产原始瓷器的商代算起，中国的瓷器大约有3,000多年的历史了。

中国的制瓷技术从东汉以后发展很快，各个历史时期都出现了别具特色的制作瓷器的名窑和陶瓷新品种。唐代浙江越窑的青瓷和河北邢窑的白瓷是非常名贵的瓷器。宋代河北定窑的白瓷，河南钧窑的钧瓷，以及浙江龙泉窑的青瓷，都是瓷器中的无价珍宝。从宋代起，龙泉窑的青瓷开始远销到世界上许多国家。现在土耳其伊斯坦布尔博物馆里就收藏有宋、元、明初的龙泉青瓷1,000多件。

元代以后，制瓷业迅速发展起来的江西景德镇，被称为中国的"瓷都"。景德镇瓷器轻巧精美，其中的青花瓷①、粉彩瓷②、青花玲珑瓷③、薄胎瓷④被视为珍宝。中国明代著名的航海家郑和，七次率船队远涉重洋，到达东南亚各国和非洲等地，随船带去的物品中，就有大批青花瓷器。

中国陶器的品种也很多，其中江苏宜兴的陶器历史悠久，品种繁多，特别是制作精巧的紫砂茶壶更是举世闻名。

后来发展起来的湖南醴陵 (lǐlíng)、河北唐山、广东石湾、山东淄博 (zìbó) 等地的陶瓷，也都以它们各自的特色闻名于世界。

中国瓷器不仅是精美的日用品，也是珍贵的艺术品。自汉唐以

1

2

来，中国瓷器就大量销往国外，中国的制瓷技术也逐渐传遍了世界各地。中国，这个古老的瓷国，现在仍然在不断地创造、生产着名贵的陶瓷新品种，为世界文明增添着光彩。

China in English has two meanings, China as a country and china as porcelain. Long ago, Westerners linked the country and porcelain together because the technique of manufacturing porcelain was invented there.

Pottery appeared in China as early as six or seven thousand years ago. Porcelain, developed on the basis of pottery, and, if calculated from the appearance of primitive porcelain in the Shang Dynasty, has a history of about 3,000 years.

Porcelain manufacturing techniques developed rapidly after the Eastern Han Dynasty (25-220 AD). Famous kilns producing porcelain products with unique features and new pottery and porcelain varieties kept appearing in subsequent dynasties. Celadon manufactured in the Yue Kiln of Zhejiang Province and white porcelain produced in the Xing Kiln of Hebei Province in the Tang Dynasty are very precious. Products made of white porcelain of the Ding Kiln in Hebei Province, Jun porcelain of the Jun Kiln in Henan Province, and celadon of the Longquan Kiln in Zhejiang Province in the Song Dynasty are all priceless treasures. After the Song Dynasty, celadon wares produced by the Longguan Kiln in Zhejiang began to be exported. Istanbul Museum in Turkey alone has a collection of more than 1,000 pieces of celadon wares made in the Longquan Kiln in the Song, Yuan (1271-1368 AD) and the early Ming dynasties.

小注解 Footnotes

① 青花瓷：景德镇瓷器的名贵品种。是一种白底蓝花的瓷器。

② 粉彩瓷：景德镇瓷器的名贵品种。是在吸收中国绘画技法后发展起来的。先在烧成的白瓷上画出图案，再填上颜色，经过高温烧成，瓷面颜色绚丽多彩。

③ 青花玲珑瓷：景德镇瓷器的名贵品种。先在瓷胎的主要部位一刀一刀雕出米粒形状的洞，再在其他部位画上青花图案，然后上釉烧成。

④ 薄胎瓷：景德镇瓷器的名贵品种。这种瓷器薄得像蛋壳，在薄而透明的瓷胎上画有各种花纹。

1. 元朝的青花瓷
   The blue and white porcelain of the Yuan Dynasty
2. 清代瓷瓶
   A pottery jar of Qing Dynasty
3. 明朝瓷炉
   The porcelain burner
4. 仿古陶器
   imitation of antique clay potteries

1. 彩瓷瓶
   The colorful porcelain jar
2. 景德镇薄胎瓷灯罩
   Jingdezhen's eggshell porcelain lampshades

After the Yuan Dynasty, the porcelain industry rose swiftly in Jingdezhen of Jiangxi, which became known as the "Capital of Porcelain". The porcelain ware of Jingdezhen is light in weight, refined and exquisite, the most precious including blue and white porcelain, colored porcelain[1], linglong (exquisite) blue and white porcelain[2] and eggshell porcelain[3]. A famous navigator named Zheng He in the Ming Dynasty sailed seven times across seas to many countries in Southeast Asia and Africa. Most of the commodities he took with him were blue and white porcelain wares.

There are many types of pottery in China, of which pottery of Yixing of Jiangsu Province has a long history. Of various types, boccaro teapots made of purple clay in Yixing are known all over the world.

Later on, there appeared the ceramics of Liling of Hunan Province, Tangshan of Hebei Province, Shiwan of Guangdong Province, Zibo of Shandong Province, which are also well known for their respective features.

Chinese porcelain wares are not only handy daily necessities, but also precious arts and crafts. From the Han and Tang dynasties, Chinese porcelain wares and their manufacturing technique gradually spread all over the world. Today, China continues to create new varieties of precious porcelain wares.

 小注解 Footnotes

① Colored porcelain was developed by absorbing traditional Chinese painting techniques. It is done by first making a design on a piece of white porcelain, and then filling in the colors before firing. It has splendid colors.

② It is produced firstly by carving small holes in the main part of the base, then drawing the blue pattern on the other parts of the base, before glazing and firing.

③ It is as thin as an egg shell, with patterns painted on its transparent walls.

扇 子
Fan

1. 苏扇
Fan of Jiangsu Province

扇子是人们消暑纳凉的工具。在炎热的夏季，它能给人带来阵阵清凉。但是自古以来，中国的扇子就带着艺术品的风韵，具有独特的民族风格。

大约在3,000多年前的商周时期，中国就有扇子了。中国扇子的种类非常多，有纸扇、绢扇、葵扇、羽毛扇、竹编扇、麦秸扇等。扇子的形状也有方有圆，还有梅花、海棠、葵花形的。

在扇面上题诗作画，是中国扇子的一大特色。从古到今，中国许多著名的书法家、画家都喜欢"题扇"、"画扇"，留下了不少精美的佳作。

在中国最常见的是折扇，拿在手里既方便又潇洒。中国生产折扇最有名的地方是杭州。杭州折扇往往采用名贵的材料做扇骨。著名的黑纸扇、檀香扇、象牙扇，不但是中国扇子中的佳品，在世界上也很有名。

The fan is very useful in summer, providing cooling wafts of air in the crushing heat. Since ancient days, the Chinese fan has been closely connected with art.

Fan came into being in the period of the Shang and Zhou dynasties about 3,000 years ago. There are many types such as fans made of paper, thin and tough silk, palm, feather, bamboo, straw, etc. There are square, round-shaped fans and some are made to look like a plum blossom, crab apple, sunflower, etc.

One feature of Chinese fans is that they are painted with pictures or carry calligraphic works. This is because many artists, ancient and present, are fond of writing or painting on fans. Many excellent artistic works have been handed down in this way.

A fan that can be folded up is the most popular. It is easy to hold and looks smart. The best-known place for fans is Hangzhou, which often uses precious material to make fan strips. Black paper fan, sandalwood fan and ivory fan are not only the best in China, but are well known in the world.

灯彩
Lantern

灯彩，民间也叫"花灯"。每逢春节、元宵节等喜庆的日子，中国的城市和乡村，家家户户都要挂灯笼。

中国的灯彩是用竹、木或金属做框架，再裱糊上纸或绫绢做成的。有的灯笼上还画着彩色的古今故事，或者贴上剪纸。

中国花灯的品种非常多，比如逢年过节时悬挂的大红宫灯；能够转动的走马灯；孩子们喜爱的公鸡灯、狮子灯、金鱼灯、莲花灯、白菜灯、花篮灯等动物花卉灯……据说，广东佛山还有一种奇特的芝麻灯，灯上的图案是用一粒粒的芝麻粘贴成的，人们说它是"能吃的灯"。近年来，四川等地制作的巨型灯、电动灯等，更是多姿多采，美不胜收。

现在，每逢年节，中国各地仍然举行各种大型的灯会，灯会上除了展览各种传统的灯彩，还展出许多运用现代科学技术制作的科

技灯。此外，在北京、哈尔滨等北方城市，每年冬季还要举行冰
灯灯会。人们用冰块雕刻成高大的建筑、可爱的动物和神话传说
中的仙女，在灯光的照耀下，晶莹剔透的冰灯，仿佛把人带到了
神仙的世界。

On the occasion of the Chinese Lunar New Year in the past, all households in both rural and urban areas would hang up colorful lanterns.

The frames of Chinese lanterns are made of bamboo, wood or metal and the outer covering of paper or durable silk. Some lanterns are painted with characters in ancient or current stories, or pasted with paper cuts.

There are many varieties of Chinese lanterns, namely, large palace lanterns, revolving lanterns, lanterns in the shape of animals or plants such as a rooster, lion, goldfish, lotus, Chinese cabbage, flower basket, etc. It is said that there is a kind of lantern whose pictures are made of sesames in Guangdong, which people call an "edible lantern". In recent years, Sichuan Province and other places have developed new products such as huge lanterns, electronic-controlled lanterns, etc.

Large lantern fairs are held everywhere in China on festivals. Apart from traditional lanterns, there are many made with state-of-the-art technology. In winter, cities in north China such as Beijing and Harbin hold ice lantern fairs. Huge sculptures of buildings, animals and fairies are illuminated by colorful lights to give the transparent look of a magical wonderland.

1. 南京夫子庙灯饰
   The lanterns at the Confucius Temple, Nanjing
2. 龙船灯
   Dragon boat lantern
3. 灯笼
   Lantern
4. 寿星灯
   Lantern of the God of Longevity

刺绣
Embroidery

刺绣，是中国著名的传统手工艺品，已经有3,000多年的历史。人们用丝、绒或棉线，在绸缎和布帛上穿针引线，绣出各式各样美丽的花纹和图案。中国刺绣的品种很多，江苏的苏绣、湖南的湘绣、广东的粤绣和四川的蜀绣，被人们称为中国的"四大名绣"。

苏州出产的苏绣，已经有2,000多年的历史。苏绣艺人能用40多种针法，1,000多种花线绣出各种花鸟、动物和幽雅的苏州园林。苏绣绣工精细，图案秀丽，特别是苏绣小猫，明亮的眼睛，蓬松的毛丝，就像真的一样，称得上是苏绣的精品。

湖南省的别称是湘，湖南出产的刺绣被称为湘绣。湘绣至少也有2,000多年的历史了。由于一些画家参加了湘绣的设计工作，所以湘绣作品带有中国画的特色和意境。俗话说："苏绣猫，湘绣虎"，湘绣狮虎，生动地表现出了狮、虎的凶猛，是湘绣的传统产品。

广东省的别称是粤，出产在广东的刺绣就被称为粤绣。粤绣至少有1,000多年的历史。粤绣色彩艳丽，图案整齐，其中最多的是龙、凤。"百鸟朝凤"、"九龙屏风"是粤绣中的优秀作品。

四川省的别称是蜀，出产在四川的蜀绣，早在1,000多年前就已经十分有名了。蜀绣的针法有1,000多种，既能刺绣花鸟鱼虫，又能创作山水人物。蜀绣的传统作品有"芙蓉鲤鱼"和"公鸡鸡冠花"等。

除了"四大名绣"之外，北京的京绣、温州的瓯 (ōu) 绣、上海的顾绣、苗族的苗绣也都很有特色。

刺绣的用处很多，可以做服装、被面、枕套、床罩等生活用品，也可以成为华贵的艺术品和陈设品。千百年来，中国的刺绣产品一直受到人们的喜爱。

Embroidery is a renowned traditional Chinese handicraft dating back more than 3,000 years. On a piece of silk or cloth, people embroider all kinds of beautiful pictures and patterns with threads of silk, wool or cotton. There are various kinds of embroidery, the best-known coming from Jiangsu, Hunan, Guangdong and Sichuan provinces.

Suzhou embroidery, or *su xiu*, has a history of 2,000 years. Suzhou artists are able to use more than 40 needlework and 1,000 different types of threads to make flowers, birds, animals and even gardens on a piece of cloth. The Suzhou embroidery is refined and exquisite, the best-known work being an embroidered cat with bright eyes and fluffy hair looking vivid and lifelike.

Hunan embroidery, or *xiang xiu*, has a history of at least 2,000 years as well. Since artists of traditional Chinese painting are involved in designing pictures and patterns, the embroidery of Hunan has an air of traditional Chinese painting. Typical embroidery shows images of lions and tigers that are so vivid that one can feel their elegance and ferocity.

2

Guangdong embroidery, or *yue xiu*, dates back at least 1,000 years. It is usually colorful and bright with neat patterns, with a dragon and phoenix predominating among the images. Prominent works are "A Hundred Birds Pay Homage to the Phoenix" and "Screen of Nine Dragons".

Sichuan embroidery, or *shu xiu*, became known as early as 1,000 years ago. With over a thousand needlework, artists are able to create flowers, birds, fish and insects, as well as landscapes and human figurines. Its exemplary works are "Hibiscus and Carps" and "Roosters and Coxcombs".

3

Apart from the above four types, fine embroidery is also made in Beijing, Wenzhou, Shanghai and by the Miao ethnic communities.

Embroidery can be used in many ways. It is often adopted in clothing, quilt covers, pillowcases and bed sheets. It can also be displayed as a work of art or used for decorative purpose.

1. 刺绣在中国已有3,000多年历史
   The art of Chinese embroidery has a long history of three thousand years.
2. 蜀绣
   The embroidery of Sichuan
3. 粤绣
   The embroidery of Guangdong

景泰蓝
Cloisonné

在中国的北京，有一种驰名中外的特种工艺品——景泰蓝。

景泰蓝也叫珐琅（fàláng），是在明朝景泰①年间发展起来的，因为当时使用的釉色多是宝石一样的蓝色，所以，人们把这种工艺品称为"景泰蓝"。

制作一件精美的景泰蓝产品，一般需要经过30多道工序。工人们首先要把铜料打成瓶、罐、盒、盘等器物，然后用头发那么细的铜丝，在铜胎上镶出美丽的花纹图案，再填上各种颜色的釉料，放在炉子里烧四五次，最后还要打磨光亮，镀上黄金，一件美丽多彩的艺术品才算最后完成。

独具民族特色的北京景泰蓝，从它问世以后，一直是明清两代皇宫中贵重的陈设品。
在1904年美国芝加哥世界
博览会上，北京景泰蓝还
获得过一等奖。目前，中
国保留下来最早的景泰蓝
制品，是明朝宣德②年间
的产品。

2

　　景泰蓝可以制成瓶、
罐、盒等珍贵的陈设装饰品，也可以制成很多种实用工艺品，如花
瓶、台灯、烟具、酒具、茶具等。目前，中国的景泰蓝产品已经远
销到世界各地。

4

Cloisonné, or *Jingtai Lan*[1], also known as inlaid enamel, is one of the
renowned arts and crafts made in Beijing. As the enamel used was navy blue
in color, people called it *Jingtai Lan* (blue).

It requires about 30 processing methods
to complete the cloisonné. Copper is first used
to make the base, after which the pattern is stuck
on the bronze body by oblate and brass wires as
thin as hairs; the inlay pattern is then filled in by
enamel glaze material in different colors,
followed by firing four to five times. Finally,
it is polished until it is glossy, and coated
in certain places with gold. Since cloisonné
was invented[2], it was used as exhibit in the
imperial palaces of the Ming and Qing
dynasties. At the World Expo of 1904 held in
Chicago, Beijing cloisonné won a first prize.

Cloisonné can also be made into many
tools for daily use, such as vases, lamps,
cigarette cases, wine jars, tea services, etc.

3

小注解 Footnotes

① 景泰：明朝皇帝代宗朱祁钰用过
　的年号。
② 宣德：明朝皇帝宣宗朱瞻基用过
　的年号。

① *Jingtai Lan* was invented in the reign of
　Jingtai (1450-1455 AD), Emperor Zhu
　Qiyu, of the Ming Dynasty.
② The earliest cloisonné still existing in
　China was made in the reign of Xuan De
　(1426-1435 AD), Emperor Zhu Zhanji, of the
　Ming Dynasty.

1. 北京的商店展出景泰蓝产品
　A Beijing antique shop displaying the cloisonné
　enamel art products
2. 景泰蓝龙形摆件
　Cloisonné dragon
3. 景泰蓝花瓶
　Cloisonné vase
4. 景泰蓝壶
　Cloisonné wine pot

风筝
Kite

风筝，古时候也叫纸鸢[①]（yuān）、鹞（yào）子[②]，是中国人发明的。相传2,000多年前，中国著名的能工巧匠鲁班用竹木削制成了会飞的木鹊。五代时，李邺（yè）用纸扎糊成纸鸢，用线放飞到天空。后来，古人又在纸鸢头上安了丝弦，风吹丝弦，发出了好像古筝一样的声音，从此，人们把纸鸢称为风筝。风筝出现以后，曾经被用来为军事和通信服务。

1

北京、天津、山东潍坊、江苏南通和广东阳江等地，是中国风筝的著名产地。制作风筝，要先用竹条捆扎风筝的骨架，再把纸或绢糊在骨架上，然后画上色彩均匀的图案。制作风筝需要十分精巧的技艺，放飞风筝也要有独到的技术，这样，才能使风筝在空中自由平稳地飞翔。

中国的风筝品种式样很多，有禽、兽、虫、鱼等动物形风筝，最常见的是燕子、蝴蝶和鹰形风筝；也有以"孙悟空"等神话人物为题材的风筝；还有一种蜈蚣或龙形的长串风筝，最长的有30多米，升上天空后，就像巨龙凌空飞舞，十分壮观。

放风筝是一项有益于身体健康的体育活动。所以，世界上许多国家十分流行放风筝的活动。中国人不仅把放风筝当作有趣的游戏和有益于身体健康的体育活动，也常常把精美艳丽的风筝挂在墙壁上欣赏。目前，中国的风筝已经远销到日本以及东南亚和欧美的许多国家，受到了世界各国人民的欢迎。

近年来，中国山东的潍坊每年都要举行盛大的国际风筝大会，因为，中国是风筝的故乡。

It is said that Lu Ban, a well-known ingenious carpenter, made a wooden magpie that would fly. During the Five Dynasty Period (907-979 AD), a man named Li Ye invented a paper kite[1] in the shape of an eagle and flew it in the sky. Later on, people put some strings on the head of the eagle. When the kite was flown, the wind passing through the strings made a sound as though from a *guzheng*[2]. So, people began to call it *feng zheng* (wind zither). It was once used for reconnaissance for military purposes as well as for delivering letters.

2

The renowned places producing kites in China today are Beijing, Tianjin, Weifang of Shandong Province, Nantong of Jiangsu Province and Yangjiang of Guangdong Province. To make a kite, one has to make a frame first and then cover it with paper or thin tough silk, which can then be painted with pictures. It needs high craftsmanship to make a good one. To fly a kite steadily in the sky, one also needs to have some skill.

There are various types of kites in China. There are ones in the shape of birds, beasts, insects and fish, but the most popular are the swallow, butterfly and eagle. There are also kites made in the shape of characters of mythical stories such as the Monkey King. Kites in the shape of a caterpillar or dragon can be as long as 30 m.

To fly a kite is beneficial to human health, so it is popular in many countries. Chinese regard it as a game as well as a sport. Some people hang kites on the wall for decoration. Chinese kites are now available for sale in Japan, Southeast Asia and many countries in Europe and America.

3

In recent years, an international kite festival has been held annually in Weifang of Shandong Province and participants come from all over the world.

小注解 Footnotes

① 鸢：老鹰。
② 鹞子：雀鹰的通称。

① Kite, *feng zheng* in Chinese, used to be called "paper bird" in ancient China.
② *Guzheng* is the Chinese zither.

1. 风筝是精致的民间艺术
   Kite-making is an exquisite folk art.
2. 以神仙为图案的风筝
   Kites made in the shape of mythical characters
3. 老虎风筝
   A tiger-shaped kite

唐三彩
Tri-colored Glazed Pottery of the Tang Dynasty

1

在中国的陶瓷制品中，有一种色彩斑斓的陶器制品，叫唐三彩。

唐三彩，是盛于唐代的一种带有多种釉色的彩色陶器的通称。它的釉色有绿、蓝、黄、白、赭（zhě）、褐（hè）等多种，而一般以黄、绿、赭为主，所以称为唐三彩。

唐三彩种类很多，主要分为人物、动物和器物三种。人物有文臣、武将、贵妇、男僮、女仆、艺人、胡人等。动物有马、骆驼、牛、羊、狮、虎等。器物有盛器、文房用具、室内用具等。古时，唐三彩很少用作日用品和陈设品，大部分用作随葬品，主要出产、流行于中国的中原地区，供这一带的大小官僚们使用。

唐三彩经过艺人们的精心制作，呈现出了各种深浅不同的黄、赭、绿、翠蓝、茄皮紫等色彩，产生了一种斑斓富丽的艺术效果。由于在制作过程中釉质的自然下流，烧制好的唐三彩会产生许多复杂奇妙的变化，因此，没有任何两件唐三彩作品是完全一样的。

唐三彩的艺术造型，反映了当时社会的风貌和时代特征。强壮有力、神态潇洒的武士俑、天王俑和肥壮丰满的马、骆驼等，充分表现了唐初国力的强盛，从脸部稍胖、体态丰满的女俑，可以看出唐朝人是以胖为美的……

千姿百态、色彩绚丽的唐三彩制品，是中国独特的艺术瑰宝。

Of Chinese ceramics, a type of colorful, glossy pottery known as *tangsancai,* or tri-colored glazed pottery, flourished in the Tang Dynasty (618-907 AD). Glazes used are green, blue, yellow, white, ochre, brown, etc. But the basic pigments are yellow, green and ochre.

There are various types of *tangsancai,* and could be classified as types of human figurine, animal and objects. Human figurines include images of ministers, generals, ladies, boy servants, maids, artists and Hun people, etc. Animals include models of horses, camels, cattle, sheep, lions and tigers, etc. Objects include containers, stationery and tools for daily use. In ancient days, *tangsancai* was rarely used for display or as tools, but mostly as burial objects. It was produced in Central Plain of China and popularly used by local officials.

When making a *tangsancai,* deliberate care is taken in making different shades of yellow, ochre, green, blue and dark purple so that they can produce a gorgeous colorful effect. In the process of firing, glazes would drip down the surface of a piece of *tangsancai* and get mingled so as to cause a myriad of changes, so that two pieces never looked exactly alike.

The artistic modeling of *tangsancai* well reflects the life of the society at that time. Robust and elegant warriors, Heavenly King, strong and rampant horses, and camels all indicate the prosperity of the early Tang Dynasty. Female figurines of the Tang Dynasty all look plump, so, obviously, plumpness was regarded as a kind of beauty.

Tri-colored glazed pottery of the Tang Dynasty are of such great variety in terms of shapes, postures and colors that it is regarded as uniquely Chinese.

1. 女坐俑
   A lady figurine
2. 马俑
   A horse figurine
3. 骆驼载乐俑
   A figurine of camel and musical band

丝绸
Silk

中国是最早生产丝绸的国家。传说是黄帝的妻子嫘祖发明了养蚕、缫 (sāo) 丝和织绸的技术。考古学家们认为，中国的桑蚕丝织技术，至少有4,000多年的历史。丝绸很早就成了古代宫廷贵族的主要衣料和对外贸易的重要商品。

中国古代丝绸品种丰富多彩。有的轻软细薄，有的织有花纹和图案，有的是多彩的精美艺术品，分为绫 (líng)、罗、绸、缎、纱、绮 (qǐ)、纨 (wán) 等许多品种。

自从2,000多年以前，汉代著名的外交家张骞 (qiān) 打通了通往欧洲、西亚许多地区的"丝绸之路"，华美的中国丝绸就开始源源不断地输往欧洲和西亚各国。西方人十分喜爱中国丝绸，据说，公元1世纪，一位古罗马皇帝曾穿着中国的丝绸袍去看戏，顿时轰动了整个剧场。从此，人们都希望能穿上中国的丝绸衣服，中国也因此被称为"丝国"。

千百年来，丝绸美化了人们的生活，也促进了中国和世界各国的友好往来。

China is the earliest country to have produced silk. Legend has it that Lei Zu, wife of Emperor Huangdi, invented sericulture, silk reeling and weaving. Chinese archaeologists believe the technology of silk weaving has at least a history of 4,000 years. Silk fabrics were the main material for making the clothes of noblemen and their families as well as an important commodity for export.

There were various kinds of ancient Chinese silk, such as thin and light ones, and colorful ones woven with patterns and pictures. They can be classified into *ling* (silk fabric resembling satin, but thinner), organza, woven silk, satin, gauze, damask, fine silk fabric, etc.

As early as the Han Dynasty of some 2,000 years ago, Zhang Qian, a famous diplomat of the time, opened up a Silk Road leading to Western Asia and Europe. It was along this road that silk was continuously transported to those countries. Westerners were very fond of Chinese silk. It is said that during the first century AD, a Roman emperor went to a theater wearing silk, which made a great stir in the audience. Since then, people wished to wear clothes made of Chinese silk. China, therefore, was called a "silk country".

For centuries, silk has beautified people's life and promoted friendly exchanges between China and other countries.

4

5

1. 收购春茧
   The trading of silk worms
2. 养蚕
   Raising silk worms
3. 织成精美丝绸
   Wonderful silk products
4. 清代丝质女外套
   Silk lady coat of the Qing Dynasty
5. 通过"丝绸之路"，中国丝绸输往欧洲
   Silk products found their way to Europe through the Silk Road as early as 2,000 years ago.

3

231

蜡染和蓝印花布
Batik and Blue Print

蜡染和蓝印花布是中国民间的传统印染工艺品。

蜡染的主要方法是：先在白布上画好几何图案或花、鸟、鱼、虫的轮廓，然后用蜡刀把溶化了的蜡液填在画好的花纹上，再把布浸入靛（diàn）蓝液中浸染。颜色达到一定的深度后，把布取出晾干，再用水煮脱蜡，就印成了蓝底白花的蜡染布。由于蜡性较脆，容易产生裂纹，染料渗入裂缝后，印成的花纹中往往产生一丝丝很细的冰裂纹，产生了一种意想不到的装饰效果。蜡染有单色染和复色染两种，有的民族还用四五种颜色套色印染，色彩自然而丰富。许多民族喜欢用蜡染布做衣裙、被面、头巾、背带等。

蓝印花布也是一种蓝白两色的花布，在中国的南北各省都有生产。蓝印花布的制作方法是：先把纸刻成花板，蒙在白布上，然后用石灰、豆粉和水调成防染粉浆进行刮印，再放入靛蓝染液中浸染，晾干以后，刮去防染浆，就成了蓝白两色的花布。蓝印花布有白底蓝花的，也有蓝底白花的，花样一般有花卉、人物及传说故事，大多用来做衣料、被面、门帘、帐子、围腰等。

在现代的都市生活中，别具民族风格的蜡染和蓝印花布，赢得了越来越多人的喜爱。

Both batik and blue print are traditional printing and dyeing arts and crafts popular among Chinese.

The principal method of making a piece of batik is first to draw some designs or contours of images of a flower, bird, fish or insect on a piece of white cloth, use a small scraper to scoop melted wax to fill in those designs or contours and then dip the cloth into an indigo dye bath. When the shade reaches a satisfactory degree, the cloth is removed and dried in the shade. Finally, it is put into boiling water to melt away the wax. What you have then is a piece of batik with a blue background and

white designs or pictures. Since wax is easy to crack and when a piece of such cloth is dyed, indigo liquid tends to seep through the fine cracks, it leaves something like a fishnet effect on the cloth. This has resulted in an unexpected decorative effect. Batik can be dyed with a single or multiple

colors. Some ethnic peoples like to adopt four or five colors. Of course, they look even more gorgeous. Batik is used by local residents to make clothes, quilt covers, headscarves and belts for

carrying bags, etc.

Blue print is basically white-and-blue cloth, which is produced in many provinces of China. The method of making blue print is to cover a piece of white cloth with a paper cut, then spread a layer of a mixture of lime, bean powder and water over it and dip it in an indigo dye bath. After being dried in the shade, the layer of the mixture is scraped off and there is a finished blue print with two colors, either white background with blue designs or blue background with white designs. Pictures on such cloth are usually flowers, human figurines or legends. Blue print is used for making clothes, quilt covers, door curtains, canopies and belts.

Batik and blue print with strong nationalistic features become more and more popular with city dwellers.

1. 浙江温州村民在晾晒蓝印花布
   The villager of Wenzhou, Zhejiang Province, is sun drying the batik clothes
2. 贵州苗族腊染布
   Miao's batik cloth of Guizhou Province
3. 贵州腊染孔雀
   The batik peacock print of Guizhou Province
4. 云南腊染布
   The batik print of Yunnan Province

剪纸
Paper Cuts

　　很多西方人都喜欢中国的剪纸，因为它美丽精巧，带着独特的东方神韵，能使人感到浓浓的生活气息和欢乐喜庆的气氛。

　　剪纸，就是用剪子、刻刀在大红纸或其他有色纸上剪刻出各种装饰性的花样和图案。中国的剪纸艺术大约有2,000多年的历史，是中国民间十分常见的工艺品。

　　中国的剪纸大多出自农村妇女之手，她们剪刻出的各种花样，大都是农民最关心、最向往的事物，有家禽、家畜、农作物、花鸟、娃娃、戏曲故事、吉祥图案等，常常在过年过节和喜庆吉日时使用。贴在窗子上的叫窗花，贴在门楣上的叫挂签，还有墙花、顶棚花、喜花、灯花和刺绣的花样，品种特别多。鲜艳美丽的剪纸给中国普通百姓的生活带来了欢乐和喜气。

　　中国剪纸分单色和彩色两种，单色的朴素大方，彩色的绚丽多彩。由于各地人民的生活习惯不同，各地民间剪纸的风格也不同。中国比较有名的剪纸有陕西的窗花、河北蔚县的戏曲人物以及南方少数民族的绣花底样等。内容丰富，花样繁多的民间剪纸，已经成为美化人们生活的艺术品。

　　目前，中国剪纸已被列入世界文化遗产。

Many Westerners are fond of Chinese paper cuts, because they are pretty and exquisite with a unique oriental style. Indeed Chinese paper cuts help viewers to feel the real daily life and a festive air.

As the name indicates, paper cuts refer to decorative patterns or pictures

2

cut out of a piece of red paper or other colorful paper by a pair of scissors or cutters. Artistic paper cuts have existed in China for more than 2,000 years. They are common arts and crafts of Chinese folks.

Chinese paper cuts are mostly created by women in rural areas. The designs are familiar ones, such as fowls, domestic animals, crops, flowers, birds, baby, episodes from local operas, auspicious symbols, etc. They are used on the Chinese Lunar New Year or other festivals. They are usually pasted on windowpanes, door lintels, walls, ceilings, lamps, etc. Some are used as copies for embroidery. Those simple and bright-looking paper cuts add delight and festivity to the life of ordinary Chinese people.

There are mono-colored and multi-colored paper cuts. Mono-colored paper cuts are simple and natural, while multi-colored paper cuts are gorgeous and colorful. As custom varies from place to place, paper cuts of different regions are different in style. Well-known paper cuts in China are those for windowpanes from Shaanxi Province, figurines of local operas from Weixian County of Hebei Province and paper cuts used as copies for embroidery from areas of some ethnic groups in southern China. Rich in content, great in variety, paper cuts serve to beautify people's life.

Today, the Chinese paper cut has been listed as one of the world cultural heritages.

1. 吉祥物的剪纸
   Paper cuts of auspicious symbols
2. 陕西剪纸
   Paper cuts of Shaanxi Province
3. 陕西庆阳地区剪纸老艺人
   Paper cuts artist from Qingyang, Shaanxi Province

3

玉　雕
Jade Carving

玉雕是中国最古老的雕刻品种之一。早在新石器时代晚期，中华民族就有了玉制工具。商周时期，制玉成为一种专业，玉器成了礼仪用具和装饰佩件。玉石历来被人们当作珍宝，在中国古代，玉被当作为美好品物的标志和君子风范的象征。

1

玉，实际是优质的石。玉石的种类非常多，有白玉、黄玉、碧玉、翡翠及玛瑙、绿松石、芙蓉石等。

玉石加工雕琢成为精美的工艺品，称为玉雕。工艺师在制作过程中，根据不同玉料的天然颜色和自然形状，经过精心设计、反复琢磨，才能把玉石雕制成精美的工艺品。

玉雕的品种很多，主要有人物、器具、鸟兽、花卉等大件作品，也有别针、戒指、印章、饰物等小件作品。北京的故宫博物院中收藏的大型玉雕"大禹治水"，高224厘米，宽96厘米，重约5,300多千克，充分显示了中国玉雕的高超技艺。

中国玉器的主要产地有北京、上海、广州、辽宁、江苏、新疆等地。中国的玉雕作品在世界上享有很高的声誉。

Jade carving is one of the oldest carving arts in China. Tools made of jade appeared in China as early as the late Neolithic Age. Jade carving

2

became an industry in the Shang (17th century-11th century BC) and Zhou (11th century-221 BC) dynasties, and jade wares were used in rituals or as decorative pendants. In ancient China, jade was also regarded as a symbol of refinement and moral ethics.

Jade is a high-quality stone and has a good many variants. There are white jade, yellow jade, jasper, jadeite, agate, turquoise, etc.

Jade carving refers to a piece of jade that has been carved and processed. A carving artist has to

thoroughly examine a piece of jade, cudgel his brains to make a design according to its natural colors and shape, and turn it into an artistic work.

Jade can be carved into human figurines, containers, images of birds, animals, flowers as well as small things like a brooch, ring, seal or decorative object. What is worth mentioning is the huge jade carving in the Palace Museum in Beijing. It is called *Da Yu Harnesses Flood*, which is 224 cm in height, 96 cm in width, and weighing about 5,300 kg. It demonstrates the high skill of Chinese carving artists.

Jade wares are mainly produced in Beijing, Shanghai, Guangzhou, Liaoning, Jiangsu, Xinjiang, etc.

1. 经过反复琢磨，玉石被雕制成精美的玉雕
   Delicate jade carving has to undergo a rigorous polishing process.
2. 白玉洗象
   White jade carving of elephant washing
3. 玉观音
   Jade carving of bodhisattva
4. 玉瓶
   A pair of jade vase
5. 翡翠仙桃
   Peach jadeite

石 狮
Stone Lion

狮子是中国人心目中的"灵兽",被誉为"百兽之王"。在中国,随处都可以见到石雕的狮子。

由于中国人把狮子视为吉祥、勇敢、威武的象征,所以人们在修建宫殿、府第、房屋及陵墓时,总喜欢用石头雕成各种各样的狮子,安放在门口,用来"驱魔避邪",把守大门。在古代,设置石狮子是有一定规矩的,一般门左边的是雄狮,雄狮的右脚踩着一个绣球,象征威力。门右边的是雌狮,雌狮用左脚抚慰着小狮子,象征子孙昌盛。

在中国历史上,北京曾是五个封建王朝的都城。因此,在北京城内外,遗存下许许多多各式各样的石狮。其中,天安门前的那对最大,中山公园社稷坛门外的那对最古老。人们都说"卢沟桥的石狮子——数不清",可见卢沟桥的石狮之多。现在,人们在北京看到的石狮,大多是明清时代的工匠们雕刻的,显得比较温顺。如果要看汉唐时期强健威猛的石狮,只能到中国的另一个古都西安去观赏了。

如今,石狮子作为威武和健美的象征,又出现在很多繁华的街头和银行、商厦、公园的门前。据说,狮子爱玩"夜明珠",所以,至今石狮的口中多半都含着一颗能活动的圆球。

In the minds of Chinese, the lion is a "magical beast", "king of all animals". Wherever you go, you can see lions made of stone.

As Chinese regard lion as a symbol of auspiciousness, bravery and power, stone lions of all kinds are often placed in front of palaces, mansions, houses and tombs to guard against evil. But there were rules about it in ancient days. Normally, a male lion was placed on the left side of the gate with its right paw on a ball, a symbol of power. A female lion was placed on the right side of the gate with its left paw fondling a small cub, a symbol of a prosperous lineage.

In Chinese history, Beijing served as the capital for five dynasties. So, in and outside the city, there exist numerous stone lions of various types. The largest pair stand in front of the Tiananmen Gate, while the oldest pair guard the entrance to the Altar of Land and Grain in Zhongshan Park. The balustrades of Lugou Bridge in the western suburbs of Beijing are carved with numerous lions, hence the saying, "as many as the lions of Lugou Bridge, too numerous to count." The stone lions we see today in Beijing were mostly carved during the Ming (1368-1644 AD) and Qing (1644-1911 AD) dynasties. They look rather mild. Powerful and fierce-looking stone lions carved in the heyday of the Han (206 BC-220 AD) and Tang dynasties (618-907 AD) can be found only in Xi'an, another ancient capital.

Today, stone lions also appear at the entrance of banks, office towers, parks or even in the street. The lion is said to be fond of the legendary luminous pearl. So, most stone lions have a movable stone pearl held in the mouth.

1. 天安门前的石狮
   The stone lion at the Tiananmen Square
2. 北京卢沟桥桥身两侧共雕有大小石狮485只
   A total of 485 stone lions flank both sides of the Lugou Bridge of Beijing.
3. 神态各异的卢沟桥石狮
   Each stone lion of Lugou Bridge has a different expression.

文房四宝
Four Treasures of the Study

自古以来，人们写字作画离不开纸、墨、笔、砚。这四种文具被称为"文房①四宝"。

中国文房四宝的品种十分丰富。其中最著名的是宣纸、徽墨、湖笔和端砚。

纸 宣纸是一种名贵的纸张，早在唐代，就已经成为献给皇帝的贡品了。由于这种纸的产地在安徽省的宣城附近，所以被人们称为"宣纸"。宣纸洁白、细密、均匀、柔软，拉力大，吸水力强，墨色一落到纸上，就能很快渗透，最能表现出中国书法和绘画的特点。由于宣纸存放很长时间都不会破碎、变色，也不易被虫蛀，所以，很多中国古代的宣纸字画保存了几百年、上千年，仍然完好无损。

墨 历代的中国书画家对用墨都十分讲究。安徽徽州生产的徽墨是中国最好的墨。徽墨从唐朝开始生产，到现在已经有1,000多年的历史了。由于制作徽墨的原料中加入了名贵的中药和香料，有的还加入了黄金，所以，这种墨不但色泽黑润，而且香气浓郁，保存几十年后仍然可以使用。

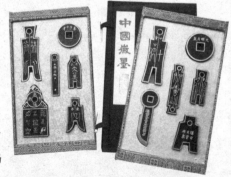

笔 文房四宝中的笔指毛笔。毛笔的生产和使用可以追溯(sù)到几千年以前。毛笔的原料主要是兽毛和竹管。制作一支好的毛笔要经过70多道工序，制笔工人们要从千千万万根羊毛、兔毛、黄鼠狼毛中一根一根地挑选，然后进行搭配组合，才能制成优质的毛笔。中国最有名的毛笔是浙江湖州生产的湖笔。湖笔有200多种，是中国文房四宝中的珍品。

　　砚　砚是研墨的工具，在中国已有3,000多年的历史。端砚、歙(shè)砚②、澄泥砚③和洮(táo)砚④被称为中国的四大名砚。其中最著名的是端砚，由广东省肇(zhào)庆市端溪出产的端石制成。端砚出墨快，墨汁不易干燥结冰。端砚不但是名贵的工艺品，还是献给皇帝的贡品。

　　纸、墨、笔、砚对中国文化和传统书画艺术的发展起到了非常重要的作用，一直到今天，人们仍称它们为"文房四宝"。

In the old days, one needs paper, ink stick, Chinese brush and ink stone to write or to paint. They are called "four treasures of the study". There are a great number of varieties of them, and the best-known ones are paper of Xuancheng, ink stick of Anhui, Chinese brush of Huzhou and ink stone of Duanxi.

Paper The best paper used for writing or painting with a Chinese brush is called *Xuan* paper since it was produced in a place near Xuancheng of Anhui Province. Being a high quality paper, it was used as a tribute to the emperor as early as the Tang Dynasty (618-907 AD). *Xuan* paper is white, smooth, refined, even, soft, resilient and absorbent. As soon as the ink touches the paper it quickly seeps in, which can best present the characteristics of Chinese calligraphy and painting. As *Xuan* paper can be preserved for a long time without decay or change of color, and is insect proof, many ancient calligraphic works and traditional Chinese paintings have been preserved intact for several hundred years or even a thousand years.

Ink stick Chinese calligraphers and artists paid particular attention to the quality of the ink stick. The best ink stick is produced in Huizhou of Anhui Province. It was first produced in the Tang Dynasty more than a thousand years ago. Some Chinese medicine and perfume or even gold flakes are mixed into the materials for making the ink stick. Ink made by such a stick is particular black with some fragrance. Ink sticks made in Huizhou can still be used after scores of years.

Chinese Brush Production and use of the Chinese brush can be dated back several thousand years. A Chinese brush is made primarily of some hairs from a beast and a small bamboo pipe. It takes 70 processing methods

1. 宣纸制作
   The process of making Xuan paper
2. 安徽徽州出产的墨，墨色浓润，称徽墨
   Ink produced in Huizhou, Anhui Province, is among the top quality brands.
3. 浙江湖州毛笔生产车间
   Workshop of Chinese brush of Huzhou, Zhejiang Province
4. 毛笔制作手工精细
   The brush is delicately made from sheep's wool.
5. 浙江湖州毛笔全国闻名，称湖笔
   Chinese brush of Huzhou is the number one seller of China.

小注解 Footnotes

① 文房：书房。

② 歙砚：安徽省歙县生产的砚台，是中国名砚。

③ 澄泥砚：河南、河北、山西等地出产的名砚。据说，这种砚是用绢袋漂洗淘澄出的细泥制成的。

④ 洮砚：用甘肃省临潭县洮河内的洮河石制成的石砚。

① Duanxi of Zhaoqing in Guangdong Province

② Shexian County in Anhui Province

③ Taohe River of Lintan County in Gansu Province

④ Chengni ink stone is produced in Henan, Hebei and Shanxi provinces

1. 广东肇庆出产的端砚是中国四大名砚之一
   One of the four finest ink stones in China, Duanxi inkstone of Zhaoqing, is known for its sophisticated carvings and superior texture.

2. 徽砚
   The ink stones of Anhui

to make a good Chinese brush. Tens of thousands of hairs of a sheep, rabbit or weasel have to be chosen one by one and bound together to make the brush. The best-known Chinese brush is manufactured in Huzhou of Zhejiang Province, which produces more than 200 types.

Ink stone Ink stone is used for grinding the ink stick in order to produce ink. Ink stone has a history of 3,000 years in China. Ink stones produced in Duanxi[②], Shexian County[②], Taohe River[③] and Henan, Hebei and Shanxi provinces[④] are the best-known types. Ink produced on a ink stone of Duanxi takes less time to prepare and will not easily dry up. In ancient times, the ink stone of Duanxi was not only a precious artistic object but also a tribute to the emperor.

Paper, ink stick, Chinese brush and ink stone have played very important roles in the development of traditional Chinese calligraphy and painting.

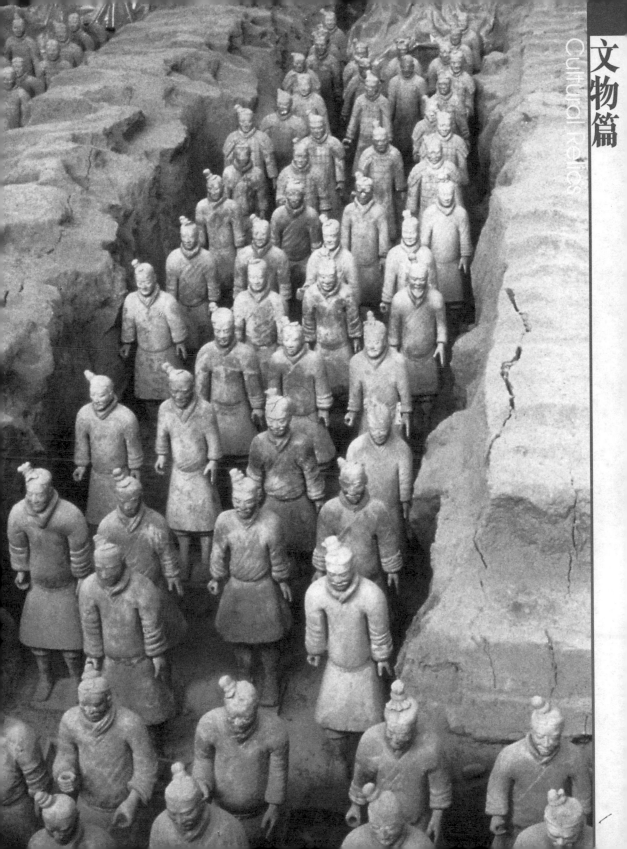

概述
Introduction

中国古代文物多如繁星。它们包含着丰富的时代和文化信息，形象地展示了中国文化发展的历程。它们在艺术和技术上所达到的高度，常常令世人惊叹不已。

这一件件文物，都是中国古代人民血汗和智慧的结晶，也是中华民族宝贵的文化财富。

There are myriads of ancient cultural relics in China. They embody rich information about history and culture and materially display the process of Chinese cultural development. The high artistic and technological levels shown in those relics continue to impress people today.

Each cultural relic is the crystallization of the hard work and wisdom of the ancient Chinese people as well as being part of the cultural wealth of the Chinese nation.

司母戊方鼎
Simuwu *Ding*

司母戊（wù）方鼎，是1937年在河南安阳发现的一件珍贵文物，它是中国商代晚期的遗物，距今已有3,000多年的历史。这个大方鼎是世界上已发现的最大的青铜器，现收藏在北京中国历史博物馆。

鼎，在原始社会是煮食物用的炊具。那时的鼎是用陶土制成的。到了商周时代，中国的青铜铸造技术达到了很高的水平，人们就用青铜浇铸制鼎。这时的鼎，已不再是寻常百姓使用的东西，它成为一种祭祀用的礼器，是王权的象征。

司母戊大方鼎是商王文丁为祭祀他的母亲而铸造的。"司母戊"原是这只方鼎内壁上的铭文。据考古学家解释，"司"是祭祀的意思，"母戊"就是商王文丁的母亲，后来，"司母戊"就成了这只大方鼎的名称。

司母戊方鼎高1.33米，长1.10米，宽0.78米，重832.84千克。在当时，需要1,000多千克的金属材料，二三百名工匠同时操作，才能铸成。它造型生动，气魄雄伟，制作工艺十分精巧。鼎下面有四根柱足支撑，显得粗壮有力。鼎身上的各种纹样，精美清晰，表现了丰收、吉祥的内容。司母戊方鼎集中代表了商周青铜铸造技术的最高成就。

由于鼎是王权的象征，所以汉语里有些与鼎有关系的词语，也表达了这样的意思，比如："问鼎"指图谋夺取政权；"一言九鼎"指起决定作用的言论。

Simuwu *Ding* was a most precious cultural relic, unearthed in 1937 in Anyang of Henan Province. It was produced in the late Shang Dynasty more than 3,000 years ago. This square-shaped *ding* is the largest extant bronze ware in the world. It is now housed in the Chinese Historical Museum in Beijing.

Ding is a cooking vessel probably used to boil or cook food in the primitive society. At that time, *ding* was made of clay. During the Shang and Zhou (11th century-771 BC) dynasties, bronze cast technology reached a very high level in China. So, people used bronze to cast *ding*. But by that time, *ding* was no longer a piece of cooking utensil in ordinary people's life but an object for important ceremonies to offer sacrifices. It was a symbol of imperial power.

Simuwu *Ding* was cast by Emperor Wen Ding of the Shang Dynasty as a ritual object for a ceremony to offer sacrifices to his mother. The three characters "si mu wu" form an inscription on the inside of the sidewall. According to archeologists, "si" means sacrificial ceremony and "mu wu" is the name of the Emperor's mother. Later on, Simuwu became the name of this huge *ding*.

Simuwu *Ding* is 1.33 m high, 1.10 m long and 0.78 m wide, weighing 832.84 kg. At that time, it needed 1,000 kg of metal and two to three hundred workers to produce it. This *ding* is solid in build, magnificent in appearance and was made with fine craftsmanship. The four pillar legs are thick and powerful. The motifs on its body are exquisite and clear, symbolic of harvest and auspiciousness. Simuwu *Ding* represents the highest level of bronze cast technology in the Shang and Zhou dynasties.

As *ding* is a symbol of imperial power, *ding* is often used in phrases and expressions in the Chinese language to imply authority. *Wen ding* (literally "inquiring about ding"), for instance, means plotting to usurp political power; *yi yan jiu ding* means a decisive comment.

1. 司母戊方鼎
Simuwu *Ding*

1

越王勾践剑
Sword of King Gou Jian of Yue

1965年，在中国湖北江陵的一座古墓中，出土了一把青铜剑，剑身上刻着"越王勾践自作用剑"八个字，原来，它竟是2,000多年前越王勾践使用过的宝剑。

勾践是2,000多年前春秋末期越国的国王。传说，越国被吴国打败后，越王勾践受到了吴王的羞辱。从此，他发愤图强，立志报仇雪耻。后来，日益强盛的越国，终于打败了吴国，成为当时的强国。

越王勾践剑是一件稀世珍宝。铜剑全长55.70厘米，剑身上刻满了菱形的暗纹，剑柄上缠着丝线，还镶嵌着蓝色琉璃和绿色的宝石，铸造得非常精细。这把铜剑虽然深埋地下2,000多年，但出土时没有一点生锈的痕迹，依然寒光闪闪，锋利异常，保持着耀眼的光泽。

专家研究认为，约3,000多年前，中国的工匠就已经掌握了高超的铸剑技术，这在科学技术史上具有重要的意义。

In 1965, a bronze sword carved with eight characters meaning "the sword of King Gou Jian of Yue, made for himself and for his own use" was discovered in an ancient tomb in Jiangling, Hubei Province.

King Gou Jian lived some 2,000 years ago, and ruled the State of Yue in the late Spring and Autumn Period. It is said that, when Gou Jian was defeated by the State of Wu, he was disgraced and insulted by the King of that state. Gou Jian determined to take revenge. Later, the State of Yue grew stronger and finally defeated the State of Wu and became a superpower of the time.

The bronze sword, 55.70 cm in length, is decorated with veiled rhombus patterns. The hilt of the sword is wrapped with silk thread, and inlaid on the one side with a blue glaze and on the other a turquoise glaze. It is most exquisitely cast. Though buried for more than 2,000 years, the sword showed no rust at all, and the sharp blade gleamed with cold light as ever.

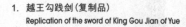

1. 越王勾践剑 (复制品)
   Replication of the sword of King Gou Jian of Yue

长信宫灯
Changxin Palace Lamp

中国古代的灯具品种繁多,其中最精美的是专门为宫廷皇室制作的宫灯。汉代的长信宫灯,就是一件精美的灯中珍品。

长信宫灯,是1968年从河北满城汉墓——刘胜夫妇墓中出土的。因灯上刻有"长信家"等字,所以被称为长信宫灯。人们推测,这盏灯原本是放在汉代长信宫中的。现在,长信宫灯收藏在中国河北省博物馆。

长信宫灯是铜制的灯具,表面通体鎏 (liú) 金[1],金光灿灿。灯的外形是一个汉代宫女[2],宫女的表情非常文静,衣服的造型也相当生动。她左手拿着灯,右手和衣袖笼在灯上,形成了灯罩。点灯时,蜡烛燃烧产生的烟尘可以通过右臂到达中空的体内,这样,就避免了烟尘污染室内的空气。宫女的头部和手臂可以拆卸,便于清洗。这盏灯的灯盘可以转动,灯罩可以开合,能够随意调节灯的亮度和照射的角度。

1. 长信宫灯
Changxin Palace Lamp

小注解 Footnotes

① 鎏金:把溶解在水银里的金子用刷子涂在器物表面,用来装饰器物。

② 宫女:在宫廷里服务的女子。

① Liu Sheng's tomb contains over 2,000 burial objects. Among them, bronze and iron items predominate.

② Today, it is housed in the Hebei Provincial Museum.

There were a great many varieties of lamps in ancient China, the best of all was the palace lamp for the imperial household. The Changxin Palace Lamp of the Han Dynasty (206 BC-220 AD) is a veritable treasure.

It was excavated from the tomb of Liu Sheng[1] and his wife in Mancheng of Hebei, and received its name from the fact that the characters "Changxin Jia" were carved on it. This lamp is believed to have been used in the Changxin Palace, residence of Liu Sheng's grandmother, of the Han Dynasty[2].

Changxin Palace Lamp is made of bronze and is gold plated. The shape of the lamp is that of a palace maid. The maid wears a calm and gentle expression, and her dress is rather impressive. She holds a lamp in her left hand, while the wide sleeve of her right arm covers the top of the lamp so as to create a shade. When the lamp is lit, candle smoke would go through the sleeve into the hollow body so as to prevent smoke from polluting the air of the room. The part of the head and the right arm of the maid can be removed for cleaning. The lamp plate can be turned and the lampshade can be opened and closed to adjust the amount and direction of light.

秦始皇陵兵马俑
Terracotta Figurines of Soldiers and Horses

秦始皇陵兵马俑，被称为世界第八奇迹。

秦始皇是中国历史上一位很有作为的帝王，他生前用了大量人力、物力为自己修造陵墓。秦陵兵马俑就是为陪葬这位皇帝而制作的陶兵和陶马。

秦始皇陵兵马俑是1974年被发现的。考古队经过探测，发现了8,000多个与真人真马一般大小的陶俑陶马。那些威风凛凛的兵马俑，排列着整齐的方阵，再现了秦始皇统一中国时兵强马壮的雄伟军阵。

秦始皇陵中的陶俑武士，个个身材魁梧，体态匀称，身高一般在1.80米左右。这些陶俑按照不同的兵种，又分为步兵俑、骑兵俑、车兵俑、弓弩手和将军俑等。他们身穿战袍，手执兵器。有的牵着战马；有的驾着战车；有的单膝跪地，张弓搭箭；有的挺立阵前，凝视前方……军阵中的陶马，高1.50米，长2米，体型健美，表情机警，仿佛正嘶啸着要奔向战场。

在秦始皇陵墓的附近，还出土了两套青铜车马，每辆车上都坐着一个驾车的铜人，赶着四匹拉车的铜马。铜车马的大小是真车真马的一半。这样大的青铜器，在世界上也很少见。

秦始皇陵兵马俑和其他珍贵文物的出土，为研究秦代的历史、军事和文化艺术，提供了重要的实物资料。现在，在兵马俑坑原址，已建起了一座大型博物馆，供中外游人参观。

The terracotta figurines of soldiers and horses in the Mausoleum of Qinshihuang are regarded as the eighth wonder of the world.

The first emperor of the Qin Dynasty, known as Qinshihuang, made great achievements in Chinese history. When still alive, he mobilized huge manpower and used a great deal of materials to build his mausoleum. The

1

terracotta figurines of soldiers and horses were used as burial objects to accompany the emperor in the next world.

The terracotta figurines were first discovered by a farmer in 1974, and archeologists have since unearthed some 8,000 lifelike soldiers and horses. Standing in formation, they indicate the powerful military might of the Qin when it unified China.

All the soldiers look robust and are physically well proportioned. Normally, each one is about 1.80 m high. They are further divided into infantry, cavalry, archers, generals, etc. Dressed in armor, holding weapons, some lead horses, some ride in carriages, some have one knee on the ground pulling back their bow to release an arrow, while some stand aloof, gazing to the front. Each clay horse is 1.50 m in height and 2 m in length. They all look robust, beautiful and alert as if they are ready to charge onto the battlefield at any moment.

Not very far from the Mausoleum of Qinshihuang, two sets of bronze horse-pulled chariots were found. On each chariot there sits a man driving four horses. The size of the bronze chariot is about half size of a true machine. Such big bronze ware is rarely seen in the world.

1. 跪射俑
   A kneeling Terracotta Soldier
2. 兵马俑坑
   The terracotta figurines of soldiers and horses in the Mausoleum of Qinshihuang
3. 铜车马
   A bronze chariot

曾侯乙编钟
Chime Bells of Yi,
the Marquis of Zeng

编钟,是中国古代一种打击乐器,由青铜制成。

人们按钟的大小、音律、音高,把钟编成组,悬挂在钟架上,制成编钟。演奏时用小槌或木棒敲打,钟声清脆响亮,幽雅柔美。

曾侯乙[①]编钟,是中国现存最大、保存最完整的一套大型编钟。1978年从湖北的一座战国古墓——曾侯乙墓中出土。出土时,整套编钟仍完好地挂在钟架上。

曾侯乙编钟共64件,分8组悬挂在铜、木制成的钟架上。钟架全长10.79米,高2.67米,分上、中、下3层,由6个佩剑的青铜武士和几根圆柱承托着重量。64件编钟的总重量是2,500多千克,最大的一口钟高度超过1.5米,重量超过200千克。这套编钟的数量、重量和体积,在编钟中是很少见的。

曾侯乙编钟的制作非常精致美观。为便于人们敲击、演奏,每口钟上还刻有铭文,记载了关于编钟的佩挂和音乐乐理方面的内容。这套编钟虽然已经在地下深埋了2,000多年,但仍然音色优美,音质纯正,可以演奏动听的中外乐曲。

曾侯乙编钟的出土充分说明,远在战国时期,中国就已经拥有了非常丰富多彩的音乐文化。

曾侯乙编钟出土后，中国音乐家创作的《编钟乐舞》，再现了中国古老音乐的迷人魅力。

The chime bells, or *bianzhong*, are a kind of percussion musical instrument made of bronze.

Chime bells were divided into groups according to size, temperament, pitch and were hung on a rack. A small hammer or wooden club is used to hit the bell to make a resonant and agreeable sound.

The chime bells of Yi, the Marquis of Zeng, are the largest and the most complete ancient chimes existing today in China. They were unearthed from the tomb of Yi, the Marquis of Zeng, a small state of the Warring States Period (475-221 BC), in 1978. When they were found, all bells were still hanging on their rack.

There are altogether 64 bells, hung in eight groups on wooden or bronze bars. The rack, 10.79 m long, 2.67 m high, is made of three bars, namely, the

upper, middle and lower bars, held up by six bronze warriors and a few round, wooden posts. The 64 bells weigh 2,500 kg. The largest bell exceeds 1.50 m in height and weighs more than 200 kg. It is extremely rare to see a set with so many bells of such weight and size.

The chime bells of Yi are exquisitely cast and look very elegant. To help artists best perform music, there are instructions on each bell as the proper way of hanging. There are also words about their musical temperament. The chime bells had been underground for more than 2,000 years, but still produce a pure and accurate note, and can even play Chinese and foreign music.

Discovery of the chime bells of Yi shows that, as early as the Warring States Period, China already had a very rich musical culture.

After excavation of the chime, Chinese musicians created a melody entitled *Bianzhong Yue Wu* (music and dance accompanied by chime bells), to once again demonstrate the charm of ancient Chinese music.

1. 编钟是2,000多年前的乐器
   The chime bell is a 2000-year-old musical instrument.
2. 击奏编钟表演
   The chime bells performance
3. 曾侯乙编钟出土现场
   The site where the chime bells of Yi were unearthed.

小注解 Footnotes

① 曾侯乙：战国时期一个小国——曾国的国君，名字叫乙。

① Yi is the emperor of Zeng (one of the small countries during the Warring States Period).

金缕玉衣
Jade Suit Sewn with Gold Thread

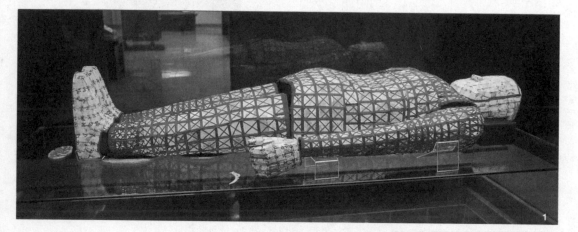

　　玉衣，是古代皇帝、贵族死后穿的衣服。由于编制玉衣时，按等级分别用金丝、银丝、铜丝编结玉片，所以有金缕（lǚ）玉衣、银缕玉衣、铜缕玉衣之分。

　　1968年，从中国河北满城的一座汉墓中出土的两套金缕玉衣，向世人展示了古代玉衣的真面目。这两套玉衣的主人，是西汉中山靖王刘胜和他的妻子窦绾（dòuwǎn）。刘胜是西汉第三个皇帝汉文帝的孙子。

　　从外观上看，玉衣的形状几乎与人体一模一样，分为头部、上衣、裤管、手套和鞋五个部分。玉衣的各部分由玉片组成，玉片的大小、形状，是根据人体的不同部位设计的，绝大多数玉片是长方形和方形，少数是梯形、三角形和多边形。制作时，先在玉片的角上穿孔，再用黄金制成的丝缕把它们编结起来。刘胜的玉衣比较肥大，全长1.88米，由2,498块玉片组成，用了大约1,100克金丝。窦绾的玉衣稍小，全长1.72米，由2,160块玉片和700克金丝组成。在2,000多年前的汉代，能制作出这样精美的玉衣，可见当时的工匠已具有了相当高的设计水平和精湛的制作工艺。

汉代帝王、贵族用玉衣作葬服，是因为他们错误地认为玉衣能保护尸体不朽，实际上所有被玉衣包裹的尸体都避免不了腐烂。这种以玉衣作葬服的制度，到三国时才被下令制止。

A jade suit was a special shroud for deceased emperors or noblemen of ancient times. Gold thread, silver thread or copper thread was used to link each piece of jade according to the rank of the deceased.

The two sets of jade suits unearthed in a Han Dynasty tomb in Mancheng of Hebei Province in 1968 revealed to the world the true nature of such garments. Their owners were Liu Sheng, Prince Jing of Zhongshan, and his wife, Dou Wan, of the Western Han Dynasty (206 BC-25 AD). Liu Sheng was a grandson of the third emperor Wendi of the Western Han.

In appearance, a jade suit follows the shape of a human body. It consists of five parts, i.e., head mask, coat, trousers, gloves and shoes. Each part is made of pieces of jade. The size and shape of each jade piece was designed according to its position. Most jade pieces are shaped in square or rectangular form, but there are a few in trapezoid, triangle or multisided shapes. Each jade piece is perforated at its corners, through which a gold thread goes through to sew the pieces together. Liu Sheng's jade suit is rather large, 1.88 m long and made up of 2,498 pieces. The gold thread used for this suit is about 1,100 g in weight. Dou Wan's jade suit is smaller, 1.72 m long and made up of 2,160 pieces. The gold thread used for this suit is about 700 g in weight. Such refined suits made some 2,000 years ago in the Han Dynasty indicate the high design level and excellent craftsmanship of that time.

The reason the Han Dynasty rulers chose jade suits for a shroud is because they believed it would prevent body from decaying. This is, of course, not true. The practice of wearing jade suits was banned during the Three Kingdoms Period (220-280 AD).

1. 广州南越王墓出土的丝镂玉衣
   A jade suit sewn with silk-thread (Nanyue Mausoleum, Guangzhou, Guangdong Province)
2. 银镂玉衣 (江苏，徐州博物馆)
   A jade suit sewn with silver-thread (Xuzhou Museum, Jiangsu Province)

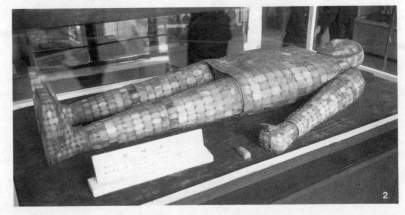

铜奔马
Galloping Horse in Bronze

1. 铜奔马
   Galloping Horse in Bronze

1969年，在中国西部甘肃省武威的一座东汉古墓中，出土了一件珍贵的文物——铜奔马。

这匹青铜骏马，浑身布满了斑驳的铜绿，虽然身高只有34.50厘米，但它强健饱满的身躯，显得十分雄浑矫健。那奔腾的四蹄、飞扬的长尾、微微张开的口鼻，逼真地表现了骏马疾驰的形象。更巧妙的是，它的右后蹄下踏着一只展翅疾飞的龙雀，形象地表现出骏马奔驰的速度超过了飞鸟，展现了快马飞奔蹄不沾土的雄姿，并反映了古代人民对骏马的喜爱。

无论从艺术构思、工艺技术，还是从结构力学的角度来说，铜奔马都达到了极高的水平，是一件珍贵的古代艺术作品。铜奔马的出土和展示，在国内外都引起了强烈的反响。

In 1969, a galloping horse in bronze was unearthed in a Eastern Han Dynasty (206 BC-220 AD) tomb in Wuwei, Gansu Province in Western China.

The 34.50 cm high bronze horse, covered with spots of verdigris, has a full and robust body. The prancing legs, flying tail, slightly dilated nostrils portrays a galloping horse. What is ingenious about it is that one of its hind feet is stepping on a flying swallow. That means the galloping horse is faster than a flying swallow. This also shows ancient people's love for horses.

Whether from the point of view of artistic design, technology or structural mechanics, it is a superb piece of art. Discovery and display of this galloping horse in bronze made a great stir both at home and abroad.

1

永乐大钟
Great Bell of Yongle

北京的大钟寺，是一座专门收藏、研究、鉴定、展览各种钟铃的古钟博物馆。在这座著名的寺院里，珍藏着一口堪称世界古钟之王的巨大铜钟——永乐大钟。这座大钟铸于明代永乐十八年（公元1420年）前后，距今已有500多年的历史。

永乐大钟高6.75米，钟口直径3.30米，重46,500千克，悬挂在寺内一座高约20米的钟楼里。悬钟的柱子上绘有五彩金龙，显示着大钟的皇家身份。

永乐大钟最为绝妙的地方，是钟身内外都铸有佛经、咒语，总计23万多字。这些经咒字迹清晰、端正，没有一个错字、漏字；铭文布局合理，字距相等，不留一处空白。可见，当时造钟的工匠在布局计算上是多么的精细严密。

大钟的铜质极好，历经500多年，依然完好无损。大钟的声音非常洪亮，撞击一下，悠扬的钟声能持续3分钟，传到四五十千米以外。大钟的音色也十分优美，一位日本声学专家听了钟声后说："这是我听到的世界上最美的钟声。"

永乐大钟的钟声平时是不容易听到的。过去，只有皇宫举行重大庆典或寺里做法事时才能敲响。现在，也只有在新年之际和春节除夕的夜晚，大钟才会以它悠扬的钟声，向普天下的人们恭贺新禧，祝福平安。

永乐大钟在铸成后的300年间，一直是世界上最大的钟。后来，俄国皇帝用了大量人力、物力，铸造了一口约193,000千克重的钟。那口钟虽然在重量上超过了永乐大钟，但由于技术方面的原因，从来没有敲响过。

要铸造像永乐大钟这样巨大而精美的铜器，即使在现代技术条件下也是很不容易的。它的铸造成功，体现了中国古代杰出的冶铸技术。

1. 永乐大钟
   Great Bell of Yongle

The Great Bell Temple in Beijing is a museum specialized in the collection, study, appraisal and display of ancient bells. This famous temple houses a huge bronze bell named the Great Bell of Yongle. It was cast in the 18th year of the reign of Emperor Yongle (1420) and has a history of more than 500 years.

The Great Bell of Yongle, 6.75 m high with a diameter at its bottom edge of 3.30 m and weighing 46,500 kg, hangs in a 20 m high bell tower. The beam on which the bell is hung is covered with a golden dragon, indicating its royal status.

What is unique about this bell is that it is covered with Buddhist scriptures and incantations, totaling more than 230,000 Chinese characters. They are clear, neat with not a single wrong character or omission. The whole inscription is well arranged. The distance between the characters is identical and there are no blank spaces. This shows the meticulous and careful calculation of the bell makers.

The bronze of the bell is of high quality and remains perfect after 500 years. Its sound is loud and resonant, lasting three minutes and carrying a distance of 40 to 50 km. The sound is so melodious that a Japanese acoustics expert commented, "This is the most beautiful sound I have ever heard in the world."

This bell was not struck on normal days, but only when the imperial house held important ceremonies or the temple held Buddhist ceremonies. Today, only on the New Year or on the eve of the lunar Chinese New Year, is it struck to express good wishes to people and usher in a new cycle.

For 300 years since it was cast, it has been the largest bell in the world. Later, a Russian emperor built a bell weighing 193,000 kg. It exceeded the Great Bell of Yongle as far as weight is concerned. But due to technical problems, it has never made any sound.

It is not easy to cast such a large bell even today with modern techniques. It marked the outstanding metallurgic level of ancient China.

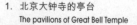
1. 北京大钟寺的亭台
The pavilions of Great Bell Temple

古代钱币
Ancient Coins

中国古代货币是世界上起源最早的货币之一，它不仅历史悠久，而且还影响了中国邻近的国家和地区，从而形成了具有东方特色的货币体系。

在钱币出现之前，人们只能用实物交换东西，比如，用一只羊换一袋米。三四千年前，中国人的祖先开始把珍贵的贝壳当作钱，叫贝币。随着商品交换的发展，天然的贝壳不够用了，于是人们又用铜来制造钱币。

2,000多年前，在中国的春秋战国时期，出现了刀形、铲形和圆形的铜钱。

公元前221年，秦始皇统一中国后，把秦国使用过的圆形有方孔的铜钱作为全国统一的货币，这种钱可以用绳子穿起来带在身上。钱上面的文字，具有很高的考古价值。

到了公元前118年，汉武帝改用"五铢（zhū）"钱币作为全国统一的货币。这种五铢币一直沿用了700年，是中国历史上使用时间较长的古货币。西汉末年，王莽（mǎng）也铸造了几种货币，多是仿刀形、铲形的钱币，看起来也古朴美观，但使用寿命很短。

公元621年，唐高祖废除了五铢币，改用通宝、元宝等名称，铸造了"开元通宝"钱币。从这以后，钱币多用国号[①]、年号[②]命名，并在背面铸上文字，说明铸造的时间、地点或铜钱的价值。这种通宝形的钱币，唐以后各个朝代都沿用，到清朝末年、民国初年为止，经历了1,000多年的时间。

中国还是世界上最早使用纸币的国家。北宋末期，四川成都有16家富商共同印制发行了一种纸币——交子，上面印有房屋、树木、人物等图案。这是中国最早的纸币。

现在中国古代钱币成了收藏家珍贵的收藏品。

1. 春秋时期钱币
   Ancient coins of Spring and Autumn Period

China is one of the earliest countries to adopt coins. This also had influence on neighboring countries and regions, which led to a monetary

1. 泰和重宝（金）
   Taihe zhong bao (Jin)
2. 天庆元宝（辽）
   Tianqing yuan bao (Liao)
3. 大康通宝（辽）
   Dakang tong bao (Liao)

🔍 小注解 Footnotes

① 国号：国家的称号，如汉、唐、宋、元、明等。
② 年号：一般指古代帝王用来纪年的名称。

---

① *"Kaiyuan tong bao"* — the current coins of the reign of Kaiyuan.
② The paper currency was known as *jiaozi*, printed with patterns of houses, trees and human figures.

system with oriental characteristics.

Before the appearance of coins, people resorted to barter trade. For instance, a sheep was traded for a bag of rice. About 3,000 to 4,000 years ago, ancient Chinese used precious shells as money. As commerce developed, people began to use copper to mint coins.

During the Spring and Autumn Period more than 2,000 years ago, there appeared copper coins in the shape of a knife, spade and circle.

In the year of 221 BC, Emperor Qinshihuang unified the whole country and adopted a round coin with a square hole in the middle as a unified currency. Such coins could be held together by a string and carried about. Characters cast on the sides of the coin are of high value for archeology today.

In 118 BC, Emperor Wu of the Han Dynasty used *wuzhu* as a national currency. *Wuzhu* lasted for 700 years. In the late Western Han Dynasty (206 BC-25 AD), Wang Mang also minted some coins, mostly in the shape of a knife or spade. They looked rather antique and pretty, but their life was short.

In 621, Emperor Gaozu of the Tang Dynasty abolished *wuzhu* and adopted coins with such characters as *"Kaiyuan tong bao"*[①]. Since then, coins were named after the name of the reign or the dynasty, and the time, location of mint and the value were indicated on them. This system continued until the late Qing Dynasty (1644-1911 AD) and the early Republic of China (1911-1949 AD), namely, more than 1,000 years.

China is also the earliest country to use paper currency. In the late Northern Song Dynasty (960-1127 AD), 16 wealthy merchants of Chengdu of Sichuan jointly issued, the earliest paper currency[②] in China.

Today, ancient Chinese currency has become a precious item for collection.

再版后记
Postscript for New Edition

《中国历史常识》、《中国地理常识》和《中国文化常识》于2002年1月与海外广大华裔青少年读者见面，及时缓解了海外华文教学辅助读物短缺的局面，并以其通俗易懂、生动活泼的编写风格受到了社会各界的热烈欢迎和好评。

由于初版时间比较仓促，三本书中尚存在一些不尽完善之处，诸位作者与编辑本着精益求精、认真负责的态度，对书中的某些内容和数据进行了全新的修订，以求进一步完善；全书并以中、英文对照再版。在修订再版工作中，潘兆明、杨伯震两位教授在百忙之中审读书稿并提出了许多宝贵意见，对我们的再版工作给予了大力支持和热情帮助，对此，我们谨表诚挚的谢意。

书中考虑不周或疏漏之处，期盼广大读者不吝赐正，以供今后再修订时参考。

编者

2004年9月

Common Knowledge about Chinese History, Common Knowledge about Chinese Geography, Common Knowledge about Chinese Culture were published in January 2002 and are now available to overseas young readers of Chinese origin. This has helped meet the demand for reference material for Chinese teaching abroad. The plain language and lively way of writing are both acclaimed by the general reading public.

There are places in the first edition of the three books for improvement. The authors and editors have carefully revised the books and updated some data and content. This editon is printed in bilingual format. Professor Pan Zhaoming and Yang Bozhen have, despite their own busy schedule, read the books and gave very valuable comments. We are most grateful to them for their time and support.

In case of any error or omission, please let us know. They will be used as reference for the next edition.

Compilers

September 2004

主编　任启亮

副主编　时序

编写人员　任启亮　时序　李晨　李嘉郁　赵菁华　彭俊

责任编辑　金红

英文编辑　林美琪

美术编辑　阮永贤　刘玉瑜

Chief Compiler : Ren Qiliang

Deputy Chief Compiler : Shi Xu

Writers : Ren Qiliang, Shi Xu, Li Chen, Li Jiayu, Zhao Qinghua, Peng Jun

Executive Editor : Jin Hong

English Editor : Maggie Lam

Designer : Yuen Wing Yin, Lau Yuk Yu

中国文化常识

图书在版编目 (CIP) 数据

中国文化常识/任启亮主编.—香港：香港中国旅游出版社，2004.9

ISBN 962-8746-49-9

Ⅰ.中… 　Ⅱ.任… 　Ⅲ.文化—中国—儿童读物 　Ⅳ. K203-49

中国版本图书馆CIP数据核字 (2001) 第081772号

出版：香港中国旅游出版社 (中国·香港)

电话：(852) 2561 8001

2004年9月第3版/2004年9月第1次印刷

印制：香港美雅印刷制本有限公司